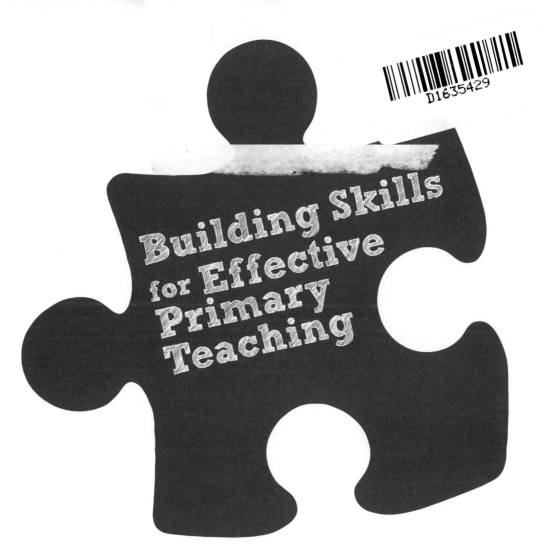

Building Skills
for Effective
Primary
Teaching

Sara Miller McCune founded SAGE Publishing in 1965 to support the dissemination of usable knowledge and educate a global community. SAGE publishes more than 1000 journals and over 800 new books each year, spanning a wide range of subject areas. Our growing selection of library products includes archives, data, case studies and video. SAGE remains majority owned by our founder and after her lifetime will become owned by a charitable trust that secures the company's continued independence.

Los Angeles | London | New Delhi | Singapore | Washington DC | Melbourne

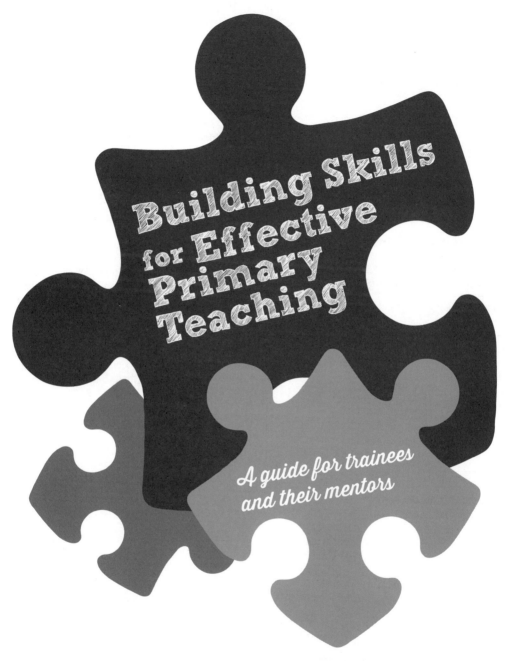

Building Skills for Effective Primary Teaching

A guide for trainees and their mentors

RACHAEL PAIGE
SUE LAMBERT
REBECCA GEESON

Learning Matters
An imprint of SAGE Publications Ltd
1 Oliver's Yard
55 City Road
London EC1Y 1SP

SAGE Publications Inc.
2455 Teller Road
Thousand Oaks, California 91320

SAGE Publications India Pvt Ltd
B 1/I 1 Mohan Cooperative Industrial Area
Mathura Road
New Delhi 110 044

SAGE Publications Asia-Pacific Pte Ltd
3 Church Street
#10-04 Samsung Hub
Singapore 049483

Editor: Amy Thornton
Production editor: Chris Marke
Marketing manager: Lorna Patkai
Cover design: Wendy Scott
Typeset by: C&M Digitals (P) Ltd, Chennai, India
Printed by: CPI Group (UK) Ltd, Croydon, CR0 4YY

Library of Congress Number: 2017931592

British Library Cataloguing in Publication Data

A catalogue record for this book is available from the British Library

ISBN 978-1-4739-9403-4 (pbk)
ISBN 978-1-4739-9402-7

At SAGE we take sustainability seriously. Most of our products are printed in the UK using FSC papers and boards. When we print overseas we ensure sustainable papers are used as measured by the PREPS grading system. We undertake an annual audit to monitor our sustainability.

Contents

The editors

Rachael Paige is Head of Programmes: Primary and Early Years at Bishop Grosseteste University, Lincoln. She started her career as a primary school teacher, leading in areas such as special needs, English and music. Moving into a Headship of a primary school, she completed her Masters's in Leadership and Management, focusing upon improving behaviour systems through distributed leadership. Her work in initial teacher education has focused upon professional teaching skills, with a particular emphasis upon behaviour. Rachael's research interests are linked to social communication within the classroom and her doctorate is an exploration of the phenomenon of teacher presence.

Sue Lambert is Course Leader for the PGCE Primary and Early Years' programmes at Bishop Grosseteste University, Lincoln. She taught for 19 years in primary schools, teaching all ages in the primary phase. She was a SENCo for many years, an advisory teacher for history and a deputy head teacher. While in school, she mentored trainees, NQTs and supported staff in developing their mentoring role. Her MA in Education focuses on the role of questioning and whole-school curriculum development. Sue is a Fellow of the HEA and has furthered her research in exploring trainees' reflective practice. Her work in initial teacher education has included all aspects of the professional role (particularly safeguarding), assessment, leading learning, the creative curriculum, behaviour and PE.

Rebecca Geeson is Course Leader for the Undergraduate Primary ITT programmes at Bishop Grosseteste University, Lincoln. She taught for 12 years in primary schools, focusing in the main in KS2. She was a phase leader and an Advanced Skills Teacher in mathematics and art. Much of her AST outreach work was spent supporting NQTs and more experienced teachers in developing their classroom practice. Rebecca completed her MA in Education, focusing on the role of mentoring, and effective teaching approaches in teacher education. Her doctoral research considers the role of the teacher, reflection for professional development, and changes in professional identity during teacher training.

The contributors

Emma Clarke taught in primary schools for 18 years, and has experience in nurture groups and pupil referral units. She completed her Masters's degree in managing challenging behaviour and her Ph.D. focuses on Teaching Assistants managing behaviour.

Dr Ashley Compton is a former primary school teacher and mathematics advisory teacher. Currently a Senior Lecturer in Primary Education at Bishop Grosseteste University, she has co-authored several education books on mathematics, music and creativity. She teaches on both undergraduate and postgraduate degree programmes, as well as supervising research students on the Master's and Doctorate programmes. Ashley has also led teacher professional development for mathematics, including MaST (Mathematics Specialist Teachers). She has a range of research interests, including mathematics, assessment and creativity.

Andrew Dickenson is currently a Senior Lecturer in teacher development at Bishop Grosseteste University. He teaches on both undergraduate and postgraduate degree programmes. He also contributes to teacher professional development programmes throughout the Midlands, often teaching in settings to cement the application of his sessions. He also works for Lego Education (Denmark), writing materials for the Far East. Andrew's current research is centred around serious play and the mental health issues surrounding social media.

Elizabeth Farrar is a former primary school teacher and headteacher with a wide experience, particularly in small school and mixed year group teaching. Currently a Senior Lecturer at Bishop Grosseteste University and a Fellow of the HEA, she teaches on the postgraduate degree programme. She also contributes to undergraduate programmes, and to the mentoring and coaching skills professional development courses. Elizabeth's current doctoral research is centred on the educational issues surrounding poverty of language in KS2 pupils, and in particular ITT students' perceptions of the teacher's role in addressing these issues.

Dr Adam Hounslow-Eyre is a former primary school teacher and headteacher with a wide experience in small school and mixed-year group teaching. Currently Senior Lecturer in Education Studies in the School of Social Sciences at Bishop Grosseteste University, Adam teaches on both undergraduate and postgraduate degree programmes. Adam also contributes to teacher professional development programmes that develop mentoring and coaching in schools. His current research interests centre around complexity theory and the call for evidence-based teaching approaches.

Steve McNichol is currently a Senior Lecturer in Primary Education at Bishop Grosseteste University, where he leads the provision for developing the behaviour management skills of trainee teachers. Prior to this, he taught across the primary age range and held roles as a specialist behaviour teacher, Special Educational Needs Co-ordinator (SENCO) and deputy head teacher. Steve's current research interests centre around the behaviour of pupils during school lunchtimes and how this impacts on teaching and learning during afternoon lessons. He is also involved in research about how trainee teachers can develop effective behaviour management skills.

Ami Montgomery is a former primary school teacher with a wide experience of teaching in multicultural classrooms, where she held a variety of roles which included EAL provision and support. During this time she developed a comprehensive understanding of the professional competence and theoretical implications of the practice of English Language Teaching, spending a substantial amount of time teaching English to newly-arrived children. Ami leads the MA in Education with TESOL at Bishop Grosseteste University and is a senior lecturer within the teacher development team for both the undergraduate and postgraduate degree programmes. With an emphasis on the integration of practice and theory, she has acquired expertise in approaches and techniques to teaching language to speakers of other languages and developed a range of practical skills. Ami's current research interests include the development of EAL training within teacher development.

John Paramore taught in primary schools for 18 years before moving into initial teacher education in 2006. He currently works at Bishop Grosseteste University where he teaches on the PGCE Primary Education course. His writing and research interests focus on geography, assessment and critical pedagogy.

Jane Sharp is a lecturer on the post graduate certificate of education in SEN Coordination at Leeds Beckett University. Her current research centres on the academic writing experiences and practices of post graduate students. Jane was formerly a learning development tutor at Bishop Grosseteste University, a senior lecturer in primary education and ICT at the University of Winchester and a researcher at the University of Exeter.

Shaun Thompson has worked as a teacher in a variety of mainstream and special education settings. He has also been a head teacher of a primary school prior to working in initial teacher education. His current research focuses upon pupils with autism, with a particular focus on the teaching and learning of mathematics.

Introduction

About this book

Who is this book for?

Trainees and mentors, this book is for both of you! We have designed the book so that the chapters help to develop skills for trainees and new teachers in key areas of professional practice, and also to support the mentor in reflecting upon their own practice, with prompts for mentoring and coaching discussion. This should support you both in gaining the most from the time you have in your mentor discussions – and also to create opportunity for deeper understanding and reflection.

About the contributors

In each chapter you will gain a sense of enthusiasm and commitment to education from the authors. All the contributors work within the primary age phase and within teacher education, and so you will sense the specialness we all feel for this important age phase. Each of the chapter authors are specialists within the topic presented in their chapter, and will offer practical ideas which are informed by research.

This book offers initial topics that will help you in beginning to build the skills to support you in becoming an excellent teacher. We have used the pictorial representation of jigsaw pieces to represent how different aspects of pedagogy and subject interlink. As you start to make the connections between the different pieces, the picture becomes clearer and has a greater sense of coherence. Take, for example, assessment and planning. While initially you may see assessment as one type of activity undertaken by the teacher (one piece of the jigsaw), and planning for a lesson as a separate activity (another piece of the jigsaw), as you become more proficient you will see how these two pieces of the jigsaw interlock and create a greater sense of the whole picture. You may already realise the important connection between planning and assessment, but other aspects of the professional role also interlink with each other: your pedagogic decisions about how you will engage the pupils in learning and behaviour management and how you work with your Teaching Assistant, for example. All these things (and many more) interdepend and enhance each other. Trainee, at the moment it may feel like there are so many tasks, but as you develop your proficiency as a teacher you will see that aspects all contribute to the most important thing: the learners in your class. Mentor, we encourage you to use the activities in this book as part of the trainee and mentor discussions to enable connections to be made and a deeper understanding of why teachers do what they do.

Key features of this book

Reflection and discussion

In each chapter, you will see reflection and discussion activities. These are an extremely important part of the book as they encapsulate our intention to support deeper reflection and quality dialogue between trainee and mentor. The intention is that you can use these suggestions in your meetings together and you can specifically select activities based upon your own personal targets. As an introduction, let us use the following to begin your journey of reflection and discussion together:

 Reflection and discussion activity

Reflection

Trainee and mentor, reflect upon what motivated you to decide to become a teacher. Identify two or three key influences upon that decision. Consider this aspect of motivation even further by considering how these influences relate to your own values. For example, an influence upon your decision could be, like Rachael, that education creates choices and possibilities which she has seen in her own family. This would link to the value of opportunity for all and a strong belief in inclusion. For Sue, it was about passion for learning, and this links to her value of all having opportunity to achieve and to be the best they can be. Rebecca was influenced by her parents and grandparents, all inspirational teachers who valued creativity in teaching and learning, and who really cared about the children whom they taught.

Discussion

Now, discuss your personal reflection with each other. Has anything changed in your understanding of the purpose of education and schooling in the time between when you decided to become a teacher and your stage of teaching now?

In the activity above it is the intention to support you in thinking about what it is that motivates you to pursue a career in teaching. Certainly, your awareness of the political, social and economic situation will also impact your view of the work you do as a teacher and may change or influence your motivation at different times. As experienced educators, we encourage each of you to keep returning to your own values and motivations to support you in understanding the important work you do with pupils.

This reflection and discussion leads us to an important point that we trust is communicated throughout this book. You are part of an excellent profession that has the well-being of pupils always at the forefront of their practice. In our own institution, our values statement says: *learners and learning at its heart*. This means that our whole team commits to ensuring that our time and energies are directed towards activities that fulfil this statement. It helps us decide what is important, and what is less so. In education, the 'to do' list never appears to come to an end. A key skill is to prioritise and to think about the importance of the task. Sadly, sometimes opportunity to reflect and discuss with other professionals are seen as luxuries we do not have time to undertake, and sometimes the trainee and mentor meeting is full of operational tasks rather than a truly developmental discussion. However, we know that the impact of reflecting specifically and carefully is very powerful and will enable you to become a much more effective teacher and mentor. Take time to read Rebecca Geeson's exploration of the impact of reflection in Chapter 1 and also Adam Hounslow-Eyre's chapter on mentoring and coaching (Chapter 15).

Find out more from . . .

Each author presents information about the chapter in a way that should enable you to easily contemplate key ideas. However, behind these ideas will be research and evidence-based approaches which have informed the author. If you want to find out more, then we have provided a feature which allows you to choose your level of engagement. Sometimes we have provided links to practical ideas or video clips to further illustrate or give you more information. Sometimes we have provided links to more academic writing, such as journal articles. This will require you to engage in a deeper way, considering the critical aspects of the topic.

Case studies . . .

Another way we have enhanced the key points is to provide case studies, which place the topic of the chapter in to a real life scenario. In some chapters, such as Rachael Paige's *Teacher presence* (Chapter 2), you will follow the progress of a case through several short extracts about the same participants to support you in building up your own understanding of a topic. In other chapters, such as in Ashley Compton's chapter *Mastery* (Chapter 7), several case studies are presented to illustrate how different schools have implemented an approach. This feature should support you in understanding how aspects are translated to practice in the classroom. The example from Ashley Compton's chapter also supports you in understanding that there are a variety of ways that different schools approach the organisation and application of learning and teaching activity. For trainees, it is understanding that key principles motivate the decisions made about these approaches, and you need to develop as an evaluative and critical thinker, who is not just mimicking the practice they see, but has really thought about the reasons for a particular approach. These case studies should support you in doing just that.

Gratitude

It has been a team effort to create this book and, as the editors, there are a few people to whom we owe gratitude and appreciation. First, the chapter authors who have worked hard to communicate clear ideas that will support you in developing as practitioners. The photographs in Chapter 2 have been taken by Emily Bennett, and Julie Tinnion kindly agreed to be photographed to help illustrate the points in the chapter. This support and contribution is much appreciated. Rebecca Geeson has provided the cartoons at the beginning of each chapter, again enhancing the messages in the book. Helen Fairlie has supported the editing and has advised us well along the way. Finally, to Amy and the team at Learning Matters: we appreciate the opportunity to share our ideas and contribute to the development of teachers.

We hope you will gain a great deal from the book. Remember, you can select the chapters that are most appropriate to you at particular times and use the reflection and discussion activity as part of your professional discussions together.

The Editors

1
Reflection for professional development
Rebecca Geeson

This chapter will

- develop your understanding of reflection and reflexivity;
- consider how developing your ability to reflect will impact upon your practice;
- consider what to reflect upon, and what strategies you can use in order to reflect effectively;
- think about different approaches to reflection.

Introduction

We have deliberately positioned the chapter on reflection at the start of this book, not because it is more important than aspects which are discussed in other chapters later on, but because the theme of reflection underpins everything in this book. Through the activities and discussions in each chapter, we encourage you both (trainee and mentor) to engage in reflective practice, and consequently, develop your own effective practice as teachers and in your mentoring role.

Seminal authors

Donald Schön, one of the seminal writers on reflective practice, presents a very useful metaphor which helps us think about what reflection is. In an ideal world, we would be able to position ourselves high on a hillside from which we could see a view before us of everything we need to know, and use this to create a map or plan of our professional lives. However, the reality is that we are down in the 'swampy lowlands' (Schön, 1987) where we cannot see everything, and sometimes become stuck in the mud; we do not know everything, and we have to learn from the situations we encounter and the mistakes that we make as we go along. The way that Schön proposed we develop a workable map of our professional worlds – one that we can use to navigate the unexpected road blocks or diversions that appear – is through reflection.

Schön's work (1983) centred on his distinction between *reflection-in-action* and *reflection-on-action*. Reflection-in-action is the process that you undertake with very little time and fairly immediately as and when you need to act in any situation. You will make use of your own previous knowledge and your understanding of theory as you decide how to act. Reflection-on-action is the reflective process that occurs after the event, usually once you have a little time and space to think through things.

Understanding these two ideas is central to the argument for developing reflective practice in teachers. Beaty (1997) guards us against becoming the teacher who has 20 years of experience which is actually only one year of experience repeated 20 times over. If you simply respond to situations without engaging in reflection, you may apply the same action in a future situation. This may be the most appropriate action, and will not necessarily be a negative response to a situation, but how would you know that the situation could not have been resolved in a different, and possibly better, way if you have not considered it in more depth? If you *reflect-on-action*, you will have opportunity to consider alternatives, relate your actions to theory, and crucially, in doing so, develop a greater 'bank' of knowledge and theory upon which to draw next time you are *reflecting-in-action*.

It is important to point out here the mentor's key role in encouraging and developing reflective practice. Often, the mentor may be the one who initially points out aspects of practice which deserve further reflection, and can support and encourage the trainee in making links to theory and applying their learning to their future professional development (Argyris and Schön, 1974). Discussion with somebody else can be a beneficial part of reflection; trainees value the opportunity to talk about their experiences so that they can consider others' perspectives and appreciate having someone to encourage them to interpret and justify their ideas in order to make sense of them (Bain *et al.*, 1999).

Schön's work built on that of John Dewey, and this work can also help us to understand benefits of reflective practice. Dewey (1933, 1938) believed that the learner should be an active participant in learning, making their own sense of the world with encouragement from teachers who should foster an experimental approach to learning in their classrooms.

 Reflection and discussion activity

Reflection

Trainee, having considered Schön's ideas (1987) about reflection-in-action and reflection-on-action, think back to an event or situation that has occurred in the classroom recently. It could be how you responded to low-level disruption in the classroom, the resources you found to support a particular child during an English lesson or how you arranged groups in PE. It does not necessarily have to be something that you thought went badly. However, it should be a situation which your mentor was present for and also witnessed.

i.   Briefly, letting your mentor know what you are planning to write about, note down what happened and what you did.

ii.   Write down what knowledge and theory you think you had about this beforehand. What do you think made you make your decisions?

Mentor, think about the situation or event that your trainee has identified to you.

i.   Briefly note down your perception of the event. What happened? What did your trainee do?

ii.   Think about how you would have dealt with the situation. Write down other events that you have experienced that would have contributed to your own actions in the same situation.

Before you discuss this with your trainee, think back to Dewey's (1933, 1938) suggestion that the learner (or in this case, your trainee) should be encouraged by the teacher (or you, the mentor) to be experimental and to develop their own understanding of the world.

Discussion

Trainee and mentor, compare notes. First, consider whether you both saw things in the same way, and whether you relied upon the same prior knowledge and theory to inform your actions.

Now think back to Schön's (1987) 'swampy lowlands'. You are *reflecting-in-action* to make your *reflection-on-action* more effective next time. How can you both use what you have learned to add to the trainee's 'map'?

Reflection, reflexivity and reflective practice

The terms reflection, reflexivity and reflective practice are sometimes erroneously used interchangeably. Effective *reflective practice* is made up of both *reflection* and *reflexivity*.

Reflection is the detailed consideration of events or situations, with careful thought about what happened, who was involved and the perception of the event. Considering why and how it happened and what theory can be applied can illuminate the situation further. There might be aspects that initially seemed inconsequential but, on further reflection, can be seen to have had a bigger impact on the situation than expected.

Reflexivity takes this in-depth consideration further and involves greater criticality. Argyris and Schön (1974) considered reflexivity to be the consideration of and possible tension between the values that a trainee or teacher claims to have (known as *espoused theory*) and what they actually do in practice (known as *theories-in-use*). To be *reflexive*, you should be asking questions about the event or situation relating to your own values and beliefs, your place within the school/classroom, your own background etc.

Bolton suggests that the type of questions that might be as follows asked by a *reflexive* practitioner might be as follows:

Why did this pass me by?

- What were my assumptions which made me not notice?

- What are the organisational etc. pressures or ideologies which obstructed my perception?

- How and in what way were my actions perceived by others?

(Bolton, 2014, pp.7–8)

The case study below is one that Matthews and Jessel (1998) used in their article, and the commentary that follows it illustrates ideas we have considered above.

 **Case study**

Trainees' written reflection	Commentary
	The process of thinking and writing about this situation is **reflection-on-action**.
'I just do not get on with my classes. They do not respect me and I cannot seem to establish my authority.	The trainee **reflected-in-action** during the lesson. Although we cannot tell, perhaps her own understanding of social interactions and what she expected in the pupils' responses to her based on her experience of working with other classes or seeing other teachers teach supported her **reflection** and informed this view.
The school-based tutor has suggested that I sit and work with a group of pupils during some lessons and talk to them to see how they are feeling . . .	The school-based mentor suggested an activity (Argyris and Schön, 1974) that might allow the trainee to construct her own understanding of the situation (Dewey, 1933, 1938).
When I worked with the pupils I realised how boring they found much of the work, and that they did not respect teachers who were not interested in them. I realised that they did respect, and responded to, some of the teachers, but that the teacher has to earn respect.	The trainee again **reflects-in-action**, but (again, making a guess) perhaps in a situation which involves less pressure (leading the whole class, thinking about all aspects of the lesson, rather than just the one issue), she is able to look at the situation differently.
I have begun to realise that I had been brought up to believe that the young should automatically respect their elders, and that pupils should therefore obey teachers.	The trainee becomes **reflexive**. She questions her previously held beliefs (or *espoused theory*) . . .

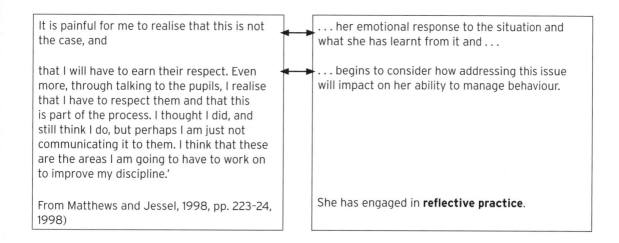

It is painful for me to realise that this is not the case, and

that I will have to earn their respect. Even more, through talking to the pupils, I realise that I have to respect them and that this is part of the process. I thought I did, and still think I do, but perhaps I am just not communicating it to them. I think that these are the areas I am going to have to work on to improve my discipline.'

From Matthews and Jessel, 1998, pp. 223-24, 1998)

... her emotional response to the situation and what she has learnt from it and ...

... begins to consider how addressing this issue will impact on her ability to manage behaviour.

She has engaged in **reflective practice**.

 **Discussion activity**

Trainee and mentor, in thinking about the case study above, and questions that Bolton (2014) suggests, consider further questions that you could have also asked yourself to develop reflexivity further.

We are not made aware in the excerpt above whether the school-based mentor knew that their suggested activity would provide the answers that the trainee needed. This is an important point to consider as both a teacher and as a mentor; experienced teachers and mentors are also wading through Schön's 'swampy lowlands' (1987), albeit with hopefully a clearer map, and do not always have all the answers.

Choosing your focus for reflection

Before we consider *how* to reflect, we need to think about *what to reflect upon*.

It is important when you come to reflect that you choose a relevant focus for each reflection. As in your academic writing (*see* Chapter 14), it is better to analyse one or two experiences in depth, rather than attempt to consider everything. For example, do not use 'Today's maths lesson' as your theme; instead perhaps focus on 'The progress made by the high attaining children in the weighing activity' or 'When Max suggested an alternative method for division, I felt . . .'. It might be that you make the decision with the support of your mentor.

Over time, do make sure that you consider a range of experiences, rather than just those that your mentor suggested were areas for development. Think about both positive and negative experiences, and keep in mind that you need to choose something very specific on which to focus. Different types of experience will support your professional development in different ways. Here are some ideas to get you started:

- **An experience that went really well**

    Trainee teachers often focus on the negative and ignore the things that went well. As well as pointing out the things that did not go well, it is just as important to be able to identify positive aspects of your own practice (and this sometimes needs some practise). Think about a time when you had planned for something to happen in a particular way and it did. While you are reflecting on this experience, think about why it went well and how you can use what you have learned in another context.

- **An experience that went much better than you expected it to**

    At all stages in your career, you will surprise yourself; sometimes things work better than you had hoped or expected. These are particularly useful learning experiences. How can you make sure this happens again?

- **Something that didn't go as well as you had hoped**

    You had perhaps planned something for a lesson, and thought it would work and it did not. These situations can be quite demoralising and knock your confidence. However, again, these experiences are very valuable. They often become targets for development, so it is particularly important that you confront them and decide how you can plan for a more positive outcome next time.

- **A situation where your mentor pointed out something (either a positive point or an area for development) that you had not noticed**

    This often occurs when your mentor sees something going on in the classroom that you had not picked up on. As well as thinking about what they saw, also consider why you did not see it.

 Reflection and discussion activity

Reflection

Trainee, look back over a lesson and see if you can identify situations that would fit in each of the categories above.

Discussion

Trainee and mentor, thinking about too much at once will not enable in-depth reflective thinking. Of the four aspects you have chosen, discuss which will be the most valuable to reflect upon in more depth.

In the following chapters of the book, you will be encouraged to reflect on a wide range of aspects relating to your teaching. As you do this always aim to consider:

- *Other perspectives*: What might different people's views be?

  Think about those involved in the situation or experience (for example, you, the children, your mentor, other adults in the classroom).

  Those others who know about the situation (other teachers in school, other trainees, parents, your university-based tutors).

  Those in literature (who has written something about this?). Also consider why they may think in a particular way about the situation.

- *Causality*: What made this or that happen? Think about the people involved, timings, the context (would things have been different in a different lesson or with different groupings?).

How to reflect: using models of reflection

Many writers have proposed models to support reflection, and most are based on describing an experience, interpreting and analysing the experience, and then adapting one's approach in subsequent similar situations. Models for reflection are useful frameworks to support trainees in developing their reflective practice. Over time and with experience, you may find that you have adopted your own approach to reflection, but initially becoming familiar with, and making use of an approach, will support you.

Two particularly well-used cyclical models for reflection were presented by Kolb (1984) and Gibbs (1988).

Kolb's Learning Cycle

Kolb's Learning Cycle (1984) shows how you can learn from experiences through reflection and analysis in order to support you in future experiences.

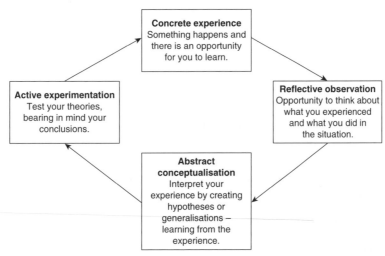

Figure 1.1 Kolb's Learning Cycle

Adapted from Kolb (1984)

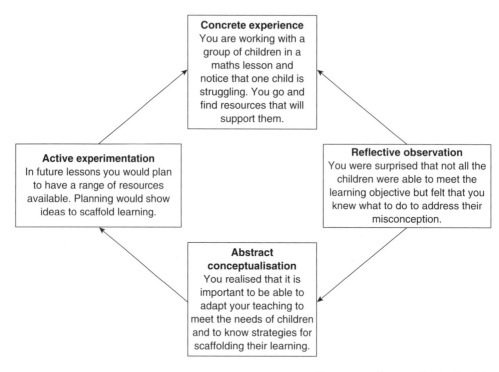

Figure 1.2 Kolb's Learning Cycle with examples

Adapted from Kolb (1984)

Kolb (1984) suggested that any situation gives us opportunity to learn, but only if we have opportunity to reflect upon it, interpret it and test out our interpretations.

Gibbs' Reflective Cycle

Gibbs' (1988) Reflective Cycle includes six stages, and again encourages learning from an experience to enable greater understanding next time a similar situation occurs (see figure 1.3).

It is important with each of these sections that you write a short account to allow you opportunity to think about each stage in the cycle, rather than briefly answering all.

- At the *Description* stage, you need to set the scene – some contextual information may be helpful here, but stick to what is relevant.

- When you come to think about *Feelings*, consider how your feelings may have differed at the time, immediately afterwards, and then a short while after the event.

- In your *Evaluation* of the situation, you should write about whether you think things went well or not.

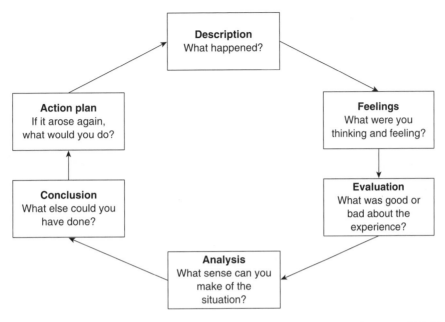

Figure 1.3 Gibbs' Learning Cycle

Adapted from Gibbs (1988)

- When you begin to engage in *Analysis*, it is useful to consider theory, thinking about different perspectives about the situation or similar situations.

- The *Conclusion* is a chance to think about whether you could have done anything differently. What have you learned from your experience?

- The *Action Plan* is the point where you consider what you will do differently next time a similar situation arises.

While Kolb (1984) and Gibbs (1988) present their stages as cycles, in practice, it could be that you are reflecting on entirely different experiences in your next evaluation of your practice, so it may feel as if the 'cycle' ends after the action plan. However, as discussed above, this will support you so that next time a similar situation arises, you will have a greater body of knowledge upon which to draw when deciding your course of action; the cycle will continue, but there may be a hiatus between some stages.

Learning through reflection

It is useful to also consider Moon (1999) and Bain *et al.* (1999) who consider how learning occurs in their processes of reflection in more linear models.

Moon's Levels of Learning and Learning Journals

Stage 1 Noticing	The student has to register the topic, event or incident as being interesting or important in some way.
Stage 2 Making sense	The student thinks more about what they have noticed and tries to understand it better.
Stage 3 Making meaning	The student starts to ask questions and to connect ideas together.
Stage 4 Working with meaning	The student makes links with other ideas and events. They would probably refer to literature and other research. At this point, reflection on the learning is likely to be taking place.
Stage 5 Transformative learning	The student has reached the point where they can formulate new ideas of their own. They know what they would do if a similar situation arose in the future.

Figure 1.4 Moon's stages of learning

Adapted from Moon (1999)

Moon (1999) suggests that it is only in the two final stages of the process that reflection on learning is likely to take place – and this was developed in her later work. She discussed the process of reflecting on specific critical incidents in Learning Journals, suggesting that deeper understanding is gained from drafting and redrafting a description of an incident while asking more in-depth questions to develop deeper analysis (Moon, 2006).

 **Find out more from . . . websites**

Examples of the reflective writing process, with analysis of each draft, as well as more information about developing reflective writing are available from:

www.cetl.org.uk/UserFiles/File/reflective-writing-project/ThePark.pdf

Accessed January 29, 2017

Bain's Framework (the 5Rs)

Bain *et al.* (1999) also proposed a similar five-stage model following research with Australian trainee teachers who were asked to reflect during their teaching placements:

Level 1 Reporting	The student describes, reports or retells with minimal transformation, no added observations or insights
Level 2 Responding	The student uses what they have reported in some way; they observe or make a judgement, ask a rhetorical question about the experience or share their emotional response to the situation.
Level 3 Relating	The student identifies aspects of the situation which have personal meaning, makes connections to current or prior experience, seeks a superficial understanding, identifies a strength/area for development and gives a superficial explanation for the reason something has happened, or identifies something they need to plan, do or change.
Level 4 Reasoning	The student integrates the experience with theoretical concepts, personal experiences and seeks a deeper understanding of why something has happened. They hypothesise, ask questions, look for answers, consider alternatives, and then attempt to explain their or others' behaviour with a greater depth of understanding.
Level 5 Reconstructing	The student engages in abstract thinking to generalise or apply their learning, drawing original conclusions from their reflections, generalising, formulating their own theory or position based on what they have learnt. They plan their own further learning based on their reflections.

Figure 1.5 Bain's framework

Adapted from Bain et al. (1999)

 Reflection and discussion activity

Reflection

Trainee, think about the models for reflection discussed above. Bolton suggests that in order to reflect, we need to write (Bolton, 2014). Over a period of a few weeks, reflect on four different experiences using each of the models above.

Mentor, consider your own reflective practice too, and take time during this period to also reflect using the models discussed. Think about four different experiences that have occurred in your role as mentor. Also, consider Bain *et al.*'s (1999) findings – provide written feedback for your trainee on their reflection.

Discussion

Trainee and mentor, consider each reflective model, and decide which aspects you found most challenging, which model or models you found most useful for you. Would you adapt any of the models or take aspects of more than one to form a reflective model that is perfect for you? How does the mentor's written feedback help?

🔦 Find out more from . . . research

There are many other models for reflection, some based on a linear or vertical model, for example those by Moon (1999) or Bain *et al.* (1999), and some which are iterative or cyclical, such as those developed by Kolb (1984) and Gibbs (1998). Others that are frequently cited and which were developed for nursing practitioners, but can also be applied to teacher training, are by Rolfe *et al.* (2001) and Johns (2009).

Rolfe *et al.*'s reflective model is based on three questions:

- What?

- So what?

- Now what?

Rolfe, G, Freshwater, D and Jasper, M (2001) *Critical Reflection in Nursing and the Helping Professions: A user's guide*. Basingstoke: Palgrave Macmillan.

Johns' model of reflection considers 'Looking out' as well as 'Looking in' and asks those who are reflecting to question the perspectives of others and the impact their actions have on others.

Johns, C (2009) *Becoming a Reflective Practitioner.* Chichester: Wiley-Blackwell.

Why reflect?

In order to 'buy into' the concept of reflection, it is important to briefly consider why we should all engage in reflective practice. Bolton (2014) summarises reasons that we should aspire to become reflective practitioners.

'Reflective practice enables enquiry into:

- what we know and wish or need to explore further;

- what we know but do not know we know;

- what we do not know and want to know;

- what we think, feel, believe, value, understand about our role and boundaries;

- how our actions match up with what we believe;

- how to value and take into account personal feelings.'

(Bolton, 2014, p.2)

However, it is also important for you at this stage in your training to think about the short-term benefits of reflective practice. When speaking to recently qualified teachers, the reasons that they suggest they do not regularly engage in structured reflective practice are that they say they have not got time to reflect, they are not clear how this will improve what goes on in their classroom, or that they find the process embarrassing or upsetting.

In an ideal world (one with many more hours in the day!), you would have the opportunity to reflect upon all aspects of your professional practice in great depth. However, a realistic approach is needed to ensure that reflective practice is valuable and meaningful, but also sustainable.

 **Case study**

Emma, who has been teaching for two years, does not write detailed reflections every day, but after developing and practising reflection during her training, she finds that she now routinely reflects on learners' progress, the success of the activities that she has planned and any problems that arose. She says that: *It is important to reflect on each lesson, be it a quick ten minute chat with teaching assistants or a more intense discussion with subject leads to support next steps. Reflecting ensures that I can deliver lessons that are engaging and specific to meet learners' needs. It also means that subsequent lessons can use a similar or alternative approach, dependent on the initial outcome. Reflecting with other members of staff is good for professional development as it can offer advice and support on structuring and teaching lessons or activities to include within it.*

Chapter summary

In this chapter, you have looked at different models that can support you in reflecting, but the model you use is up to you. Sometimes, you may want to use aspects of different approaches.

This chapter has presented the importance of ensuring that you reflect in some way to further improve your future practice.

References

Argyris, C and Schön, D (1974) *Theory in Practice: Increasing professional effectiveness*. San Fransisco, CA: Jossey-Bass.

Bain, J, Ballantyne, R, Packer, J and Mills, C (1999) Using journal writing to enhance student teachers' reflectivity during field experience placements. *Teachers and Teaching: Theory and Practice*, 5(1): 51–73.

Beaty, L (1997) *Developing Your Teaching Through Reflective Practice*. Birmingham: SEDA.

Bolton, G (2014) *Reflective Practice, Writing and Professional Development* (4th edn). London: SAGE.

Dewey, J (1933) *How We Think: A restatement of reflective thinking in the educative process.* Boston, MA: DC Heath & Co.

Dewey, J (1938) *Experience and Education.* New York: Kappa Delta Pi.

Gibbs, G (1988) *Learning by Doing: A guide to teaching and learning methods.* Oxford: Further Education Unit.

Kolb, DA (1984) *Experiential Learning: Experience as a source of learning and development.* Upper Saddle River, NJ: Prentice Hall.

Matthews, B and Jessel, J (1998) Reflective and reflexive practice in initial teacher education: A critical case study. *Teaching in Higher Education*, 3(2): 231–43.

Moon, J (1999) *Reflection in Learning and Professional Development: Theory and practice.* London: Kogan Page.

Moon, J (2006*) Learning Journals* (2nd edn). London: Routledge.

Schön, D (1983) *The Reflective Practitioner: How professionals think in action.* New York: Basic Books.

Schön, D (1987) *Educating the Reflective Practitioner.* San Fransisco, CA: Jossey-Bass.

2
Teacher presence
Rachael Paige

This chapter will

- introduce you to some strategies to help you have a 'presence' in the classroom;
- discuss what it means to have presence, both techniques and developing your own confidence in the classroom;
- support you in reflecting upon which characteristics create presence and how you can develop your skills.

Introduction: is presence the 'x factor' of teaching?

Think about someone you know that you would identify as having presence. What is it about them? The clothes they wear or the way they use their body language? Is it the way they speak or how they interact with other people? It is quite difficult to say exactly what it is that gives some people that special something, that 'x factor', which makes them stand out from the crowd or encourages other people to stop and listen to them.

To have presence can be very useful (and sometimes essential), not only in the classroom but also in meetings and situations where you want to have an influence. In fact, this phenomenon is written about in a range of fields: leadership and management (Senge *et al.*, 2004), business (Carny *et al.*, 2010) and also within the context of behaviour management (Jones, 2007). It appears to be something important in our interactions, but is quite difficult to completely define. In Chapter 9 (written by Emma Clarke and Steve McNichol), you will also read of Canter's assertive discipline approach which has an emphasis upon the direction (assertion) of the teacher towards the pupils, which can be interpreted as having a presence in the classroom. Within this chapter, I will argue that effective presence is more subtle than Canter describes, but the importance of the teacher role (which Canter, 1992, identifies) remains a theme.

In education, teacher presence is not often written about explicitly (and is certainly not framed as an approach to communication, as I shall present in this chapter), but it is talked about often. In fact, the lack of presence can be a significant barrier to trainee teachers (and qualified teachers) in having that positive influence in the classroom which inspires children to engage in the learning. In this chapter, we shall look more closely at 'what is teacher presence?' and introduce you to some techniques that can help you develop this aspect of your teacher role. For mentors, this chapter should challenge you to think about the feedback you give to trainees and ensure that vague terms, such as presence, are unpicked to support professional development.

 Reflection and discussion activity

Reflection

Before reading the next part of the chapter:

Trainee, list the qualities or characteristics that you think create presence in the classroom. You perhaps know someone who has presence so try to describe them and what it is that makes you identify them as someone with presence.

Mentor, think about when you might have used the term 'presence' in your mentoring role and unpick some of the features you are expecting to see from the trainee. Be as specific as possible.

Discussion

Trainee and mentor, now compare your lists. Start to discuss similarities and differences in the lists. Is presence something some people have, or can we learn some of these strategies?

What is presence and can it be learned?

In the first trainee and mentor reflection activity, you may have thought of someone that you would identify as having presence. It is likely that some of the characteristics are related to non-verbal communication: use of gesture, smile, position in the classroom and an enthusiastic approach, for example. You may also have listed some ways in which they use their voice: intonation, change in volume. People who are identified as having a presence often also present as confident, whether that is genuine confidence or presenting in that way (see Figure 2.2 and Amy Cuddy's work later in this chapter). These are all ideas that we shall explore together in detail throughout this chapter. As we start to unpick the concept of teacher presence, hopefully you are beginning to realise that we can learn some techniques to help us in the classroom (and other professional situations requiring influence and effective communication). It is true to say that some people do seem to have that instinctive way of asserting their presence and having an influence in the classroom. Some of this is related to confidence (genuine or presented) or a willingness to overcome any inhibitions when engaging the pupils in their learning. While identifying techniques is reasonably easy, developing your persona so that you present as confident and use an engaging style with the pupils takes more self-reflection and rehearsal. It is far more complex to truly believe in your own competence as a teacher and then present that confidence in the classroom. That is why it is so important to develop as a reflective practitioner, and the mentor role is significant in coaching trainees to become more reflective, willing to attempt new things (and sometimes fail) and develop a confidence in their own professional practice.

When considering this phenomenon – and whether techniques can be learnt or developed to increase presence – it is helpful to make a few initial assertions. First, presence is viewed by this author as a communication tool and is related to engaging others and having influence. As we look at some research and case studies throughout the chapter, you will see how this perspective is supported by others (such as Babad *et al.*, 2004; Rodgers and Raider-Roth, 2006; Korthagen and Vasalos, 2009). This perspective is important as communication is a key aspect in a positive classroom environment to enable all pupils to participate in learning. Second, within literature there is a very interesting distinction between *having presence* and *being present*. *Having presence* relates to the techniques the teacher uses and reflects a somewhat behaviourist approach to communication (see Chapter 9). Behaviourism, in its broadest sense, suggests that a certain stimulus can encourage a particular response. The use of stickers, or awards, to reinforce positive behaviour is an example. In this context of communicating through teacher presence, it could be that a positive and enthusiastic persona presented by the teacher may encourage pupils to engage and participate. Alternatively, *being present* (a concept promoted by Rodgers and Raider-Roth, 2006), has a different emphasis. While the outward communication by the teacher remains important, these authors identify that a genuine and authentic relationship with the pupils, built upon mutual respect and trust, is more important than acting or learning techniques. It is this genuine *being present* (p.271) and *in the moment* (p.279) when nothing else matters but the learning, the students and the subject matter that culminates in true teacher presence.

These two ways of viewing presence will help to shape the discussion in this chapter.

 **Case study**

David is a trainee primary teacher following a School Direct route into teaching. He is in his first term with a school he knows quite well from volunteering with them prior to starting the course. David says that he is happy at the school and has a good relationship with his mentor, Tim. David has been leading groups consistently and well during the first part of his placement. He has also led a sequence of English lessons with Tim in the classroom and working with small groups. David has felt confident leading the English lessons because English is a specialism for him and he has observed Tim leading English previously.

This week David taught a science lesson and Tim observed him. After the lesson, Tim asked David to reflect specifically upon the progress children made and their engagement in the lesson. David realised that many of the children had not been focused on the lesson, and instead were off task during practical activities. David was able to explain how he used the behaviour systems in place and he felt that the children needed to be more committed to the lesson and listen to the instructions. The following day, Tim provided David with some formal written feedback. In the areas for development Tim suggested: 'Have more presence'.

Reflection and discussion activity

Mentor, although we may feel that we have discussed a situation with our trainee and that they understand the targets set, sometimes we make assumptions. Reflect on what assumptions may have been made by Tim. What do you think Tim actually meant by 'have more presence'? When providing follow up written support to trainees, think about how you communicate those more complex concepts, such as presence or persona.

Trainee, presently in this case study we only really know what David thought and the written feedback that Tim provided. We will return to the case study later to explore what Tim said in the verbal feedback. Take time to think about the target: *Have more presence*. What do you think this might mean? What do you think may have influenced the perceived lack of presence in this lesson?

Trainee and mentor, begin to draft a more specific target that would help David progress. Perhaps your target will be linked to being confident in the science subject matter so that David can be fully 'in the moment' of learning. Or perhaps you will concentrate on his non-verbal behaviours or use of voice.

Having presence: developing techniques

You may have heard of the 'Dr Fox Effect'. This term refers to a study in the 1970s by Naftulin, Ware and Donnelly (1973) in which student evaluation ratings were given to 'Dr Myron L. Fox' for his lecture entitled 'mathematical games theory as applied to physician education'. During the lecture Dr Fox used techniques to engage the audience which included humour and giving an enthusiastic presentation. However, what the learners failed to notice (and the learners were a group of experienced educators themselves, such as social worker educators) was that Dr Fox was giving something of a nonsense lecture, with contradictions throughout, neologisms and conclusions which did not support the previous statement. You may have realised: Dr Fox was an actor. His rapport and enthusiasm had, according to Naftulin *et al.*, 'seduced' the group.

 Find out more from . . . internet clips

The Dr Fox lecture is available on YouTube: **www.youtube.com/watch?v=RcxW6nrWwtc**

Accessed January 27, 2017

While there have been some more recent studies that have criticised this idea of 'seduction' (this term is used by Naftulin *et al.* (1973) to mean that learners are seduced into thinking they have learned something by a charismatic teacher), the way you present yourself as the teacher is important. You need to show enthusiasm and interest in the subject yourself before you can expect your learners to engage. I am sure you can think of examples from sessions you have attended when the delivery of the content has been so 'dry' and 'boring' that it is very hard to concentrate however committed you are as the learner. This may seem like an obvious statement, but for trainee teachers sometimes there is so much to think about: the subject content, the pedagogical approaches you are using, ensuring positive learning behaviours and perhaps your mentor is observing. It is easy to become overwhelmed with so many priorities and consequently not communicate the love of learning and enjoyment of the subject as you would wish. Peel and Babad (2014) replicated Naftulin *et al.*'s study, and while they found that learners were not as naïve as originally presented by the original research team in thinking they learned significantly new things just because the teacher was charismatic, this recent study does support that learners value the enthusiasm and energy shown in the delivery by the teacher. Neill and Caswell (1993) call it 'nonverbal pzazz'; White and Gardner (2012) call it the 'classroom x-factor') but a key message for you is to be enthusiastic: enjoy (and show that you enjoy) leading the learning in your class.

Building upon this point that having enthusiasm and building rapport with your learners is a positive starting point, we shall start to unpick the different ways we communicate and establish a presence, including some exercises for you to try. Another familiar (mis)quoted researcher leads us to think about non-verbal communication. Mehrabrian (1972) is well known for his work in the area of non-verbal communication and it is from his 1972 work that the '7-38-55' distinction has emerged relating to when communicating attitudes or feelings: according to Mehrabrian, 7 per cent of communication of attitudes and feelings are in the words we say, 38 per cent in the way we say them and 55 per cent in facial expression. Research in this area has moved forward from this simplistic formula, and there are authors who argue fervently that words are just as important as the way we say them and the non-verbal behaviours we exhibit. However, the delivery of your words and your use of non-verbal behaviours can have a significant impact upon the presence we have in the classroom. In fact, the message you are communicating is at its strongest when your actual words, the way you say them (intonation) and your non-verbal communication are all in synchronisation.

Which non-verbal behaviours help create presence in the classroom?

There have been some interesting research studies looking at teachers' non-verbal behaviours and students' perceptions of those teachers. Some examples of this research can be found in Ambady and Rosenthal (1993), Babad *et al.* (2003) and Babad *et al.* (2004). These researchers were particularly interested in how participants who did not know the teacher rated them when only watching short clips of non-verbal behaviours with no sound content (they call these 'thin slices'). These initial ratings were compared to the overall evaluations of the actual class at the end of the teaching semester. Those initial 'thin slices' predicted the end ratings that actual classes of students gave to the teacher. It appears that we communicate a great deal through our body language and non-verbal behaviours and those initial impressions seem to remain when teaching over a longer period of time. It is important to acknowledge that these researchers did focus mainly upon high school and college students in USA and Israel but Babad, with other researchers (Babad *et al.* 1991; Babad and Taylor, 1992), also extended their work to looking at those in fourth grade, which would equate to Year 5 in the UK.

This body of research identifies three important aspects of communication in the classroom:

a) self-presentation;

b) social perception;

c) social interaction.

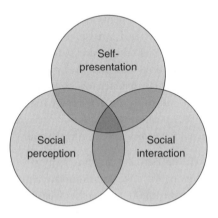

Figure 2.1 *Presence as an integrated social experience*

Adapted from Babad et al. (2004)

This provides a helpful way to view teacher presence which includes the things that you do and the way you present as a teacher (self-presentation), the way that your pupils' perceive you (social perception) and the relationships you have with your pupils (social interaction).

Later in the chapter, when we look at what it means to 'be present' and the importance of the relationships within the classroom, social perception and social interaction will be addressed. So, let's think about you as the teacher and how you can use techniques to help present yourself in a confident and influential way.

Self-presentation

One of the most important things to reflect upon is how you demonstrate a confident and calm manner in the classroom. Carney *et al.* (2010) explore how our body language can not only give the impression of confidence to the audience, but their research also suggests that when we adopt a strong and confident stance it actually impacts the genuine confidence we have in ourselves.

 Find out more from . . . TED Talks

In her 2012 TED Talk, Amy Cuddy addresses how our body language can help us in presenting as confident in high-stress situations, such as a job interview. Her research (with Carney *et al.*, 2010) asked participants to practise 'high-power' poses. Have a look at Amy's talk here:

www.ted.com/talks/amy_cuddy_your_body_language_shapes_who_you_are?language=en

Accessed March 23, 2017

Try some of these high-power poses when preparing yourself for your day of teaching.

Also, notice your own body language and when you may exhibit body language that does not exude confidence. Cuddy (2012), as you will see in the talk, uses the phrase *fake it 'til you make it*. Consider how your non-verbal behaviours, as well as your verbal behaviours, exhibit the teacher you want to be.

Which body language should we use to show confidence and presence in the classroom?

Along with Amy Cuddy, other researchers in this field (Elisha Babad, for example) agree that there are some key ways we can use our body language. A key tip is to think carefully about open and closed body language. When we fold our arms or cross our legs, this can be interpreted as closed body language and those who observe us may feel we are not approachable, or that we are very nervous. Alternatively, display open, positive body language such as some of the suggestions below:

Posture: Ensure that your posture is good by straightening your back and keeping your shoulders extended rather than hunched.

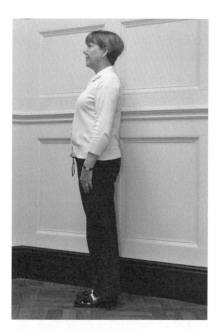

Figure 2.2 Straight back, shoulders extended

Use of gesture: Open palms are a positive way to communicate willingness to listen to others, openness to ideas and warmth towards your pupils.

Figure 2.3 Open palms

Assertive gesture: The use of 'palms down' is an assertive gesture. It can help you communicate your point strongly or show that the discussion has ended.

Figure 2.4 Palms down

Facial expression: Ensure that you have a positive expression. A smile is extremely powerful in building rapport and creating a positive climate for learning. However, recipients can tell the difference between real and fake smiles. Real smiles are also seen in the eyes as well as the mouth. Use eye contact well to show interest in what the learners are saying or doing (or to show that you have seen what the learners are doing.).

Figure 2.5 Smile!

Babad *et al.* (2004) also identified some other characteristics of good teacher behaviours when they are teaching:

- A relaxed persona with positive body language

- Stands rather than sits when addressing the whole group

- Expressive in hand, body, face and voice

- Moves around the space (but not excessively)

- Has a strong orientation towards the learners. This means that you are not just talking to an audience but that you are really engaging and noticing your learners, and allowing yourself to explore ideas deeper with your learners (rather than distracted by the next point on the lesson plan).

Grounded: When you are in the classroom use a 'grounded' stance (Churches and Terry, 2007) to show that you are confident and comfortable in front of an audience. This involves ensuring that you are standing with your legs side by side with your weight equally distributed (not leaning to one side), good posture (shoulders

Figure 2.6 Grounded stance

extended not hunched) and arms by your side (not hidden in pockets, folded or behind your back). Ensure that you are looking at the class and showing that you are acknowledging your learners.

 Find out more from . . . research

In my own research, I conducted a study with some trainee teachers at the end of their programme. In two separate focus groups the trainee teachers were asked to watch four clips of teachers teaching for 30 seconds. Unlike the studies by Ambady and Rosenthal (1993) and Babad *et al*. (2003), the participants were able to listen to the words being spoken as well as the non-verbal actions. They were then asked to discuss 'Which characteristics create presence?' Using thematic analysis (drawing out key themes from what was said) of the participants' responses, a key message that emerged from both focus groups was that confidence, or at least to appear confident, is important. From reading this chapter so far you will see that this links very closely to the work of Carney *et al*. (2010). That confidence, according to these trainee teachers, is evident in the positive body language exhibited by the teacher, the eye contact (including 'the teacher look'), and the intonation and careful use of voice to communicate and maintain interest. Also, the position of the teacher in the classroom and the way the space in the classroom is used was important.

The four categories identified in this small-scale research are helpful in starting to unpick some of the techniques that can be used in the classroom. However, while these participants were able to verbalise those

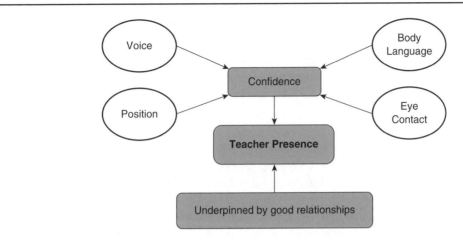

Figure 2.7 A representation of the themes emerging from the focus groups

techniques used to create a presence, or exhibit confidence, in the classroom, the importance of relationships and knowing the individuals in the class was a very strong theme. This particular group of trainee teachers felt that you could not have technique without genuine connectedness to your pupils. Kornelsen (2006, p.79) identifies a 'shift from a way of doing to a way of being' which teachers described as they progressed within their career. While the participants in my study did not describe this idea of a journey that Kornelsen found when talking to new teachers, there is definitely an acknowledgement that technique cannot stand alone when working with real children in your classroom.

 **Case study**

Let's return to the conversation between David (the trainee in the case study) and Tim (the mentor).

David had received written feedback from Tim which said: 'Have more presence'. David asked Tim to explain more of what he meant and here is an excerpt from their conversation.

Tim: When we discussed the lesson, you acknowledged that the children were not on task and they were not really taking notice of you when you gave them instructions. Your voice was very quiet and you were addressing them from the corner table, where you were working with your group. I could tell that you were getting worried about the lack of focus during the lesson because you stopped looking around the room, you just focused on your group and some of the others were not achieving very much.

David: I did realise that some of the children were not on task but I had told everyone what to do before I went to my group. The children should have got on with the task.

Reflection and discussion activity

Trainee and mentor, look at the targets you drafted earlier. Which one would you suggest now? What advice would you give to David to support his own self-reflection and support him in accepting constructive feedback?

In the case study, David is obviously exhibiting some behaviours that are demonstrating his lack of confidence in that particular session. He has not moved himself from the place where he is sitting to address the entire class (positionality), or used eye contact and positive body language to reassert himself in the classroom. In fact, from Tim's observation, it appears that David was either avoiding looking at the children (due to the fact that he was not confident in tackling any lack of engagement) or he was so engrossed in working with his group that he had lost that global view of the classroom that is so important. Tim also mentioned the use of voice. Using intonation and volume well is important. I recommend a site called Voice Care to my trainee teachers, which has lots of activities to develop your use of voice and also gives tips about how to look after your voice.

 Find out more from . . . websites

The Voice Care website has activities and tips for developing your voice: **http://voicecare.org.uk/your-voice/**

Accessed January 29, 2017

Being present

Throughout this chapter you will have realised that it is not enough to simply learn some techniques to create a presence in the classroom. You need to take time to build relationships with your learners and get to know them and how they respond to you. Rodgers and Raider-Roth define presence in teaching as:

a state of alert awareness, receptivity, and connectedness to the mental, emotional, and physical workings of both the individual and the group in the context of their learning environments, and the ability to respond with a considered and compassionate best next step. (2006, p.266).

 Discussion activity

Read the definition from Rodgers and Raider-Roth (2006). What do you think this means in terms of:

- your view of yourself as the teacher in the classroom;
- the way you interact with the pupils in your class;

- the way you structure your learning activities;

- the way you manage the classroom;

- the way you set up the learning environment?

Think about your own practice. Reflect upon how you can change any habits or practices which hinder that opportunity to be 'connected' to all aspects of the pupil's learning development.

This definition has many implications for practitioners, especially in a primary classroom. This quotation challenges us to ensure we know our pupils as individuals and the dynamics of those individuals as a class: to be sensitive and aware of any changes that may affect pupils in our care and respond to that appropriately. Schön (1983) calls this 'reflection in action': being able to think about what is happening in the here and now, and what would be the most effective action. You will also notice in the quotation that these authors use words such as 'compassionate'. The importance of our engagement with pupils on a human level, rather than being so preoccupied with getting from the beginning to the end of our plan, can set us apart as teachers who are really able to respond to our pupils and ensure they are progressing in all aspects. As Rodgers and Raider-Roth term it, to *be* present.

These authors do state explicitly that they do not agree that teaching can be reduced to a series of behaviours or techniques (p.266) but that their concept of presence (as defined above) makes the difference in the classroom. They identify four dimensions of presence:

- self-awareness or connection to the self;

- connection to students;

- connection to subject matter and pedagogical knowledge;

- the context or current situation.

Implications of the four dimensions

If we take these four dimensions as essential aspects of our professional practice, then there are skills that we need to develop beyond those that often appear in lists of professional competencies. The dimensions appear to be essential for developing that classroom presence where pupils take notice, not because you are using techniques and dramatic actions to gain attention, but because the pupils have developed respect for you and want to listen to what you have to say. This is something that takes time and has to be part of the professional identity that you develop. To build that trust and respect, pupils need to see that you are able to manage your own emotions and present a safe environment. Daniel Goleman (2006) in his book *Emotional Intelligence* identifies the importance of managing our own emotions and knowing ourselves well so that we are able to respond and behave in a measured and calm way, while still being true to ourselves. This is where there is a difference between *having presence* and *being present*. Having presence is about presenting yourself in a particular way, but it is very difficult to maintain that persona if your genuine thoughts, feelings and emotions are not in line with your outward expression. For example, you may be feeling very anxious and worried about a situation (perhaps it is an observation by your mentor). You can use techniques such as those suggested in previous sections of this chapter, and we know from the research that these are helpful techniques to influence and communicate with our class, but maintaining that character or persona can drain our energy and make us feel detached from what is really happening. This is especially true if we have to maintain this false persona over a long period of time. Pupils in our primary classes are with us for significant periods of time and will see the inconsistencies. Korthagen and Vasalos (2009), who perpetuate this definition of presence being explored in this section in their work, say that true presence is part of a 'u' model: it starts with self-reflection and self-knowledge – they call this 'open mind, open heart, open will' (p.9) – this leads to presence (as defined by Rodgers and Raider-Roth) and this enables the individual to be open in responding to situations and problems.

In summary, these authors believe that rather than learning dramatic poses and adjusting non-verbal communication, genuine behaviours and actions will flow from a reflective practitioner who brings their genuine self to the classroom, who has developed openness and an understanding of how they can just *be*. This extract from Meijer *et al.* (2009) demonstrates how a trainee teacher has this realisation during a mentoring conversation. 'Paulien' has been struggling with establishing presence in the classroom and has been using a reflection model, supported by coaching conversations with Angelo, to support her development. Here she has a significant breakthrough in her understanding of teacher presence in the classroom:

Paulien (trainee teacher): *I do believe that I am much more, that more and more I learn to **genuinely be**. It gives such a happy feeling [laughs]. It specifically comes to me in sudden realizations. Then there is this sudden insight and then BANG, **I am**. Something like that. Then I'm very aware of, well, yes, of me.*

Angelo (mentor): *And what does this mean to you, when you teach from this sense of being, or, being a teacher who's able to teach from her inner sense of being? Imagine you would always be able to teach from your sense of being, your inner self? What would this mean?*

Paulien: *Well, it would save so much of your energy. If you're really yourself – I know it's strange, but it's really hard to be yourself – but if you finally succeed in being yourself, everything just comes naturally. But I find it very difficult, when I lose touch with myself, to reconnect with myself.*

Meijer *et al.* (2009, p.306)

 Reflection and discussion activity

Read the extract above between Paulien and Angelo. There are some interesting ideas here that you can start to think about and discuss with your mentor:

- What does it mean as a teacher to 'genuinely be', as Paulien describes? Angelo begins to unpick this description by saying that it is 'teach(ing) from your sense of being'. What does this concept mean to you?

- Paulien says that when she loses touch with herself it is very difficult to reconnect. This can be interpreted as those moments in teaching when we no longer feel relaxed, or that we are able to be ourselves in the classroom because of the different pressures and distractions. Think about a situation you have had in the classroom where you have felt similar to Paulien. What were the barriers, or distractions? In those situations, how can you reconnect?

 ## Chapter summary

Within this chapter, we have thought about techniques you can use to engage learners by having an enthusiastic persona, using positive non-verbal body language and portraying an open approach to your classroom management. We have looked at some research in the first part of the chapter which suggests some effective non-verbal behaviours to support your delivery, such as open hand gestures and a good posture. We have thought about the significance of confidence, or presenting as confident until you are able to genuinely interact with your class from a place of personal security in your own competence (*fake it 'til you make it*). Finally, we have been challenged to think about teacher presence from a different perspective, away from techniques. The important place of genuine interactions (rather than a performance) and developing relationships where influence is based upon mutual respect. This type of presence takes time to build and develop, which is why I have presented in this chapter these two perspectives. Techniques can help us make initial impressions with our class (which are so important) and can help us communicate in an interesting and engaging way. However, this type of performance can quickly fade, so it is paramount that teacher presence in the long term is built upon relationships, genuine compassion for your learners and a flexibility to respond to the circumstance and in the moment.

References

Ambady, N and Rosenthal, R (1993) Half a minute: Predicting teacher evaluations from thin slices of non-verbal behavior and physical attractiveness. *Journal of Personality and Social Psychology*, 64(3): 431–41.

Babad, E, Bernieri, F and Rosenthal, R (1991) Students as judges of teachers' verbal and nonverbal behavior. *American Educational Research Journal*, 28: 211–34.

Babad, E and Taylor, P (1992) Transparency of teacher expectancies across language, cultural boundaries. *Journal of Education Research*, 86: 211–34.

Babad, E, Avni-Babad, D and Rosental, R (2003) Teachers' brief nonverbal behaviors in defined instructional situations can predict students' evaluations. *Journal of Educational Psychology*, 95(3): 553–62.

Babad, E, Avni-Babad, D and Rosental, R (2004) Prediction of students' evaluations from brief instances of professors' nonverbal behavior in defined instructional situations. *Social Psychology of Education*, 7(1): 3–33.

Canter, L and Canter, M (1992) *Assertive Discipline: Positive behavior management for today's classroom* (2nd edn) Santa Monica, CA: Lee Canter & Associates.

Carney, D, Cuddy, A and Yap, A (2010) Power posing. *Psychological Science*, 21 (10): 1363–8.

Churches, R and Terry, R (2007) *NLP for Teachers: How to become a highly effective teacher.* Wales: Crown House Publishing.

Jones, F (2007) *Tools for Teaching: Discipline, instruction, motivation.* CA: Fredric H Jones & Associates.

Goleman, D (2006) *Emotional Intelligence.* New York: Bantam Books.

Kornelsen, L (2006) Teaching with presence. *New Directions for Adults and Continuing Education,* 111: 73–82.

Korthagen, F and Vasalos, A (2009) From reflection to presence and mindfulness: 30 years of developments concerning the concept of reflection in teacher education. EARLI Conference, The Netherlands.

Mehrabian, A (1972) *Nonverbal Communication.* New Brunswick, NJ: Aldine Transaction.

Meijer, P, Korthagen, F and Vasalos, A (2009) Supporting presence in teacher education: the connection between the personal and professional aspects of teaching. *Teaching and Teacher Education*, 25(2): 297–308.

Naftulin, D, Ware, J and Donnelly, F (1973) The Doctor Fox lecture: a paradigm of educational seduction. *Journal of Medical Education*, 48: 630–5.

Neill, S and Caswell, C (1993) *Body Language for Competent Teachers.* London: Routledge.

Peel, E and Babad, A (2014) The Doctor Fox research (1973) re-revisited: 'educational seduction' ruled out. *Journal of Educational Psychology,* 106(1): 36–45.

Rodgers, C and Raider-Roth, M (2006) Presence in teaching. *Teachers and Teaching: Theory and Practice*, 12(3): 265–87.

Schön, DA (1983) *The Reflective Practitioner: How professionals think in action.* New York: Basic Books.

Senge, P, Scharmer, C, Jaworski, J and Flowers, B (2004) *Presence: Exploring profound change in people, organizations and society.* London: Nicholas Brearley.

White, J and Gardner, J (2012) *The Classroom X-Factor.* London: Routledge.

3

Principles of teaching for learning

Sue Lambert

This chapter will

- provide opportunities to think about what we mean when we say 'learning';
- see how different theories and approaches have influenced teaching for learning in the classroom;
- reflect on these; recognising when and why particular approaches may be more or less useful in the classroom.

Introduction

As teachers, it is important to remember that learning can be interpreted and defined in many different ways and that it can look different – depending on what you are trying to learn.

Reflection and discussion activity

Reflection

Trainee, how do you learn best?

- When things are presented in blocks of information?
- When things are presented in a cross-curricular or creative way?

- When you have a say in the direction of learning?

- When you use new or unfamiliar materials?

- When you are given the 'big picture' and see the purpose of the learning?

- When you work with someone else to discuss things or ask and answer questions?

- When you teach someone else?

- Does it vary? Why?

Mentor, think about how you vary your approach to teaching and learning and why. Can you think of some examples to share with the trainee? For example, when you teach in blocks, in a more cross-curricular way or when children have taken the lead in the direction of the learning?

Discussion

Trainee and mentor, discuss why the approach to teaching and learning might vary. Discuss whether you think this is important.

As a teacher you need to understand the theories and research that have influenced what you teach and how you teach it. Nothing is more important than knowing the children that you teach and what will 'hook' them into the learning and why. You need to feel confident that this is giving children the best opportunities to learn. You need to be able to reflect on the approaches that will be most successful for supporting children to make progress in their learning and to evaluate how successful these have been.

As Hattie (2012) explains:

> There is no fixed recipe for ensuring that teaching has the maximum possible effect on student learning and no set of principles that apply to all learning for all students. But there are practices that we know are effective and many practices that we know are not.

(Hattie, 2012, p.4)

There are many theories about how children learn, based on research and practice from Ancient Greek times through to the most recent theories; focusing on the importance of children having a range of skills to enable them to learn in the rapidly changing world of new technologies (connectivism) (Siemens, 2005). It is not possible to look at every approach in one chapter, but I shall present some examples and links to other materials as well as give you opportunities to reflect. Through these activities, you will be able to learn more about different principles of teaching for learning. This will help you to think about what this might look like in the classroom, deepening your understanding of how you might teach in particular ways and why. As MacBlain (2014) notes, it is important to understand historical and cultural influences that shape practice but also to recognise that new approaches or developments about learning will continue to be influential. There are lots of different ways to teach and theories about learning and some of these will be explored more fully in later chapters such as Mastery (Chapter 7) and Approaches for engagement (Chapter 6).

Reflection and discussion activity

Reflection

Trainee, think about something that you have had to learn. Was there a teacher you had that really helped you? What was it about their teaching that helped you to learn?

Discussion

Mentor, share some examples of helpful ways you have found to 'hook' children into the learning, particularly any reluctant learners. Unpick why you approached the learning in a particular way.

Trainee and mentor, discuss what you think are things that can help or hinder children being able to engage in learning and what you need to consider to successfully 'hook' children into learning.

Theories that influence classroom practice

This section will briefly discuss some theories and principles of teaching for learning and give some examples of what this might look like in the classroom. The Find out more from . . . sections have some references to further reading and websites, if you want to look at some of the things discussed in more detail.

Behaviourist theories

Behaviourist theories focus on learned behaviours, usually in response to stimuli. Exponents state that behaviours become more automatic with repeated practice or reinforcement. You may be familiar with Pavlov's dog. Ivan Pavlov conditioned a dog to respond to a bell when food was present. He did this repeatedly to the point where he could ring the bell and the dog would salivate even if there was no food, because the dog was conditioned to associate the bell with food. This is known as classical conditioning. The other area is operant or behavioural conditioning. Thorndike (cited in Shunk, 2012) and Skinner (1974) are well-known authors in this area. Thorndike found that not all positives motivated learners and negatives did not always lessen unwanted behaviours. He argued that you need to know exactly what it is you want to teach and how you want to teach it. If you know what responses you should get, you can reinforce these behaviours. Trial and error are important ways of learning. Skinner (1974) agreed with much of Thorndike's work and felt that reinforcing a behaviour through the use of rewards to promote positive behaviours or sanctions to prevent inappropriate or negative behaviour enabled children to be active learners. Repetition reinforces the behaviour that is desired through consequences for the actions. Most behaviourists emphasise the importance of positive reinforcement.

Reflection and discussion activity

Scenario

Cassie is making noises on the carpet when you are teaching the whole class about multiplying and dividing by two. This happens quite often and when you ask her for an answer to a question she gets the answer right but you do not praise her. The rest of the children do not seem to be distracted by her behaviour so you ignore it. You praise the other children for their correct answers and listening to each other. After a number of sessions, the noises stop and when asked for an answer, which she answers correctly, you praise her for the answer. If children get the answers wrong, there is no praise.

Reflection

Trainee, think about the impact of this approach on Cassie's learning and that of the other children. If it helps, think about how you responded to praise or not having efforts recognised.

Mentor, think about how you use praise for correct responses and how you address things if children give an incorrect answer. Think about when this approach may be useful or less useful for the children so that you can discuss it with the trainee.

Discussion

Mentor and trainee, think about what the strengths and limitations of this approach might be. Here are a few things to start you off. Stimulus and response does not necessarily mean understanding. Children become used to the rewards so they lose their impact. It can be useful for rote learning and where rewards can be given for correct response.

 Find out more from . . . websites and books

A short film that looks at some behaviourist theorists. Pavlov, Skinner and Watson.

www.youtube.com/watch?v=xvVaTy8mQrg

Accessed January 29, 2017

Skinner, BF (1978) *Reflections on Behaviorism and Society*. Englewood Cliffs, NJ: Prentice-Hall.

Cognitivist theories

This is an approach to learning which recognises that, for children to be successful learners, they need to be aware of their own learning and how they learn. This helps them to know how to improve their learning.

Teachers often help children to do this by modelling and explaining the learning process and expectations. Giving children a clear focus for the learning and outlining how they will know they have been successful in the learning are important. This approach also encourages dialogue: the teacher encourages children to articulate their learning, such as how they solved a worded problem in mathematics, while errors or misconceptions are used to unpick the learning. A well-known theorist in this area is Howard Gardner (1999) and you may have heard of his research suggesting that we have multiple intelligences. He believed that there is not one global intelligence but that we have a range of intelligences so our learning in one area may be stronger than in another (Muijs and Reynolds, 2007).

Table 3.1 Intelligences identified by Gardner

Intelligence	Characteristics
Bodily kinaesthetic intelligence	• Can use their body to express emotion • Can play games effectively • Can invent a game • Can choreograph dance and sequences of movement
Interpersonal intelligence	• Notices differences in people, i.e. contrasts in their moods, temperaments, motivations and intentions • Is empathetic • Can effectively lead, organise and manage
Linguistic intelligence	• Can order meanings and rhythm of words • Can decode rules of grammar • Can invent new language • Enjoys playing with words
Musical intelligence	• Is sensitive to rhythm, pitch and timbre • Appreciates timing and tone • Enjoys creating and listening to music • Can recognise melodies accurately
Visual/Special intelligence	• Can make representations of the visual world • Can create mental images • Can use visual and special awareness in unfamiliar circumstances
Logical/Mathematical intelligence	• Can work logically • Can make deductions • Can use reasoning to find answers and solutions • Is a problem solver • Can categorise, calculate and hypothesise • Likes to experiment • Can develop arguments

(Continued)

Table 3.1 (Continued)

Intelligence	Characteristics
Naturalistic intelligence (added 1999)	• Can identify and group particular plant or animal species • Can identify different weather formations and climates • Can classify natural things such as rocks, types of mountains and geographical landscapes • Can apply knowledge of nature for such as farming, landscaping, or animal training
Existential intelligence (added 1999)	• Prefers activities that allow them to choose • Looks for connections in things across the curriculum and more widely • Can develop questions to investigate because they can think reflectively • Appreciates and values the world around them • Can see things from a range of perspectives

Table based on the multiple intelligences outlined in Gardner, H (1983, 1999)

Gardner (1999) also cautions that labelling things as learning styles is not helpful and can make the focus of teaching and learning too narrow (*see* Table 3.1). You need to be aware that, for children who have different intelligences, accessing for example learning that is language heavy or mathematical learning may be challenging, so as a teacher you need to be very aware of this. As Pritchard (2009) notes:

> *individual learners have preferred ways of working, thinking and learning. If an individual's preferred approach to a learning task is ignored in the ways that a teacher expects them to work, there is a distinct possibility that their learning will not progress as efficiently and effectively as it might.*

(Pritchard, 2009, p.56)

There is a lot of debate about intelligence: whether it is fixed or changeable, and what it actually is, but there is some evidence to suggest that intelligence can be learned, developed and enhanced. It may not be helpful to see children as having higher or lower intelligence (Lazear, 2004; Hymer and Michel, 2002).

 Reflection and discussion activity

Reflection

Trainee, why might it hinder your teaching if you assume children have fixed intelligence or if children think they have fixed intelligence?

Mentor, can you think of ways that you have avoided labelling children in terms of intelligence. Can you think of children that have surprised you by what they could do because you approached the learning in a way that enabled them to 'shine'?

Discussion

Mentor and trainee, discuss the previous points and how your approach to planning and learning might take this into account.

Long- and short-term memory (which includes working memory) also need some consideration when thinking about planning teaching for learning (Sousa, 2011). There are some useful publications and links in the Find out more from . . . section. For many years, there was a focus on getting information into long-term memory so it was a permanent part of learning. Working memory is temporary and can only store, deal with or retrieve things for a limited amount of time and this varies with how old you are. Those younger than five have less capacity than between five years and adolescence (Sousa, 2011). This has implications for the amount of information we expect children to store and use.

Less is more! (Sousa 2011, p.52).

As Sousa (2011) notes, working memory needs to connect with the learner's past experiences and, depending on the answer to the two questions below, it is either saved or rejected.

> *'Does this make sense?' This question refers to whether the learner can understand the item on the basis of past experience. Does it 'fit' into what the learner knows about how the world works? When a student says 'I don't understand,' it means the student is having a problem making sense of the learning.*
>
> *'Does it have meaning?' This question refers to whether the item is relevant to the learner. For what purpose should the learner remember it? Meaning, of course, is a very personal thing and is greatly influenced by that person's experiences. The same item can have great meaning for one student and none for another. Questions like 'Why do I have to know this?' or 'When will I ever use this?' indicate that the student has not, for whatever reason perceived this learning as relevant.*
>
> (Sousa, 2011, p.52)

Sousa's questions also link learning the constructivist approach, discussed later in the chapter.

 ## Reflection and discussion activity

Scenario

You are doing a lesson about instruction writing in English. You share with the children that you are writing instructions for planting seeds, which will be part of your science lesson later. The children already know about the key features such as using the imperative verb, time connectives and writing in the second person

(Continued)

(Continued)

present tense. You begin by reminding the children about what they already know and show them a list of key features which you pin up on the wall as a reminder. You explain that they will be planting the seeds in their science lesson and that they need instructions to be able to do this correctly. You then use an example of an instruction writing frame on the interactive board to model writing instructions and talk through the process with the children as you model it, asking them for responses to questions to reinforce the key points that you want them to remember. Some children seem to be struggling to focus and engage once you start to model writing the instructions.

Reflection

Trainee, think back to the early reflection about how you learn 'best' and the discussion above about different intelligences and memory. Why might some of the children be less engaged during the modelling part of the lesson?

Mentor, think about how you have ensured children who learn in different ways have been able to access the learning. If it is helpful, link it to the scenario example, and in the discussion share with the trainee how you keep all the children engaged.

Discussion

Mentor and trainee, discuss some of the ways you involve the children in learning and how you might have approached the case study differently. How might this affect how you plan your teaching?

 **Find out more from . . . internet clips**

Howard Gardner discusses and reflects on multiple intelligences. **www.youtube.com/watch?v=I2QtSbP4FRg**

Accessed January 29, 2017

Bridging behaviourist and cognitivist theories

Albert Bandura (1977) felt that behaviourist theories provided an incomplete picture because you do not only learn from your own experiences but also from things that you observe, can imitate or see modelled. Learners also learn *where there is no immediate or apparent reward* (Pound, 2014, p.57). They can use all of this to develop their ability to problem solve and consider consequences. Bandura believed that people are able to control their behaviour to some degree and learn. This is known as social learning theory. He believed that helping learners achieve success meant that they would be better able to achieve further success and take on challenges. Observing others complete something successfully and having this reinforced motivates others to do the same. You need to role model positive behaviours, ways to solve conflicts and things such as reading yourself in class when children read so they see that you think this is important (Pound, 2014).

 Reflection and discussion activity

Scenario

You are doing a maths lesson about solving worded problems. You model an example as a class about how to solve a worded problem by looking for key words that identify what the calculation is and how to answer the question. You ask a child who is confident to come out and do the calculation, talking through the process with the child and asking them to explain what they are doing. You praise the child for the correct answer and showing the other children how he/she worked it out. You praise all the children and say that you know they will be able to do a calculation of their own now that they have seen someone else show them how to do it. The children are then asked to have a go independently at a different worded problem using the same calculation method. The children still have your example on the board and most have a go, although a few still struggle to complete it correctly on their own.

Reflection

Trainee, think about why this might be a helpful approach for children and what the issues might be for those who still struggle.

Mentor, think of examples of when this approach has been helpful in your teaching and when it has not been as helpful.

Discussion

Trainee and mentor, discuss what you have both decided are possible strengths and limitations of this approach.

 Find out more from . . . internet clips

Watch Albert Bandura talking about learning. **www.youtube.com/watch?v=PsTIJyoxOKg**

Accessed January 29, 2017

Cognitive constructivist and social constructivist theories

Constructivists think that you learn best when you build on your existing knowledge, skills and understanding and when you construct your own learning and build new knowledge. Learning is an active process and prior learning is a key feature of this approach. Muijs and Reynolds (2007) note that this means that what each child might learn from a lesson may be slightly different.

Piaget (in Piaget and Inhelder, 2000) is probably the best known name associated with the cognitive constructivist approach to learning. He developed an approach to learning based on stages of development, broadly associated with different age bands (*see* Table 3.2). This is an example of Piaget's stages of development and I have added the column to show what this might look like in practice.

Piaget also emphasised the importance of thinking and giving children thinking time (Fisher, 2005, p.13). Piaget suggested that we build links between things we know (schema) and these are added to so new schema are created all the time. The links within and across schema enable us to learn and make progress. If each

Table 3.2 Piaget's stages of development

Stage of development	What happens at this stage	What it might look like
Sensori-motor stage	Knowledge and understanding come from physical actions and senses. Children are self-centred.	Children learn by looking, listening, tasting, touching and smelling. They learn to move and experience the environment by doing things physically. They are playing with things, e.g. toys in the bath.
Pre-operational stage	Children learn to use and control their environment more. They start to use words and language for objects and this helps support ideas for play. They do not have complete knowledge, so may have misconceptions that may not be logical.	Children may use language incorrectly as they learn, e.g. 'I goed to the shops' instead of 'I went to the shops' and they may also have misconceptions about things such as all big things sink and all small things float.
Concrete operational stage	Children develop more logical thinking. This is usually only with things they can see or are concrete.	Looking at the example above, at this stage (when looking at things that float or sink), they will begin to see that size is not necessarily a factor. They can recognise that many ships are very big and heavy but still float and begin to think about other reasons for things to float and sink.
Formal operational stage	Thinking becomes more ordered and logical. This means that they can work with abstract ideas, predict and hypothesise and see the implications of their thinking and that of others.	At this stage, children and young adults can offer reasoned explanations for things. For example, they might say that two things that weigh the same but are shaped differently will either float or sink based on what they know already about water resistance, boats, seeds transported by water etc.

Adapted from How Children Learn (*Pound, 2014*)

developmental stage is not completed, then it can cause problems for further learning. Context can impact on learning too, so a child might be able to do something within the classroom but may not see how to use this learning in a different context or environment which may limit their learning. More successful learning occurs when children can link it to 'real life' situations and see the purpose of the learning.

As Pritchard (2009) notes, *Effective learning is learning which is lasting and capable of being put to use in new and different situations* (p. x). However, Gray and MacBlain (2015) note that in Piaget's work there is little emphasis on the role of the teacher.

 Reflection and discussion activity

Reflection

Trainee, think about Piaget's stages of development and the importance he attaches to completing each stage. What do you think could be issues for children and teachers if any stages are not fully developed?

Mentor, think of children who have a delay in their development. What do you do to support these children in your planning and teaching?

Discussion

Trainee and mentor, share a discussion about what the issues for children may be and the ways that your planning and teaching needs to take this into account to support children in their learning.

Within constructivist theory there is *social constructivism*. Probably the best-known theorists in this area of learning are Vygotsky (2012, in Vygotsky *et al.*) and Bruner (1977) who recognised both the role of the teacher and the impact of cultural background as key to learning. They proposed that social interaction was important for learning to be able to take place, and prior and current knowledge enabled new learning to develop from the interactions. This could be with peers, teachers, parents and carers, sometimes but not always, a *more knowledgeable other* to enable further learning to take place. Learning can take place anywhere. Usually in a school setting the teacher is in the role of the *more knowledgeable other*. You may be familiar with the term *scaffolding learning*. The teacher breaks down the learning into manageable steps for children to enable them to build new learning on what they already know. Vygotsky called this the *Zone of Proximal Development* (ZPD), i.e. a level just above the level of knowledge, skills and understanding that the children already have and where they need help to make progress. Teachers scaffold in different ways, for example, through discussion, use of resources, encouraging group discussion and targeted questioning. Repetition helps to embed the learning.

John Dewey (1916) is influential in terms of his views that children learn by doing and enquiring, and that the teacher is the facilitator of learning. He argued that learning did need to be structured and although you cannot change past experiences you can influence the present and future learning of children (Gray and McBlain, 2015). Trial and error is seen as a positive part of the learning process. This links with enquiry and investigative approaches to learning. This is explored in more detail in Chapter 6.

Table 3.3 Example of the teacher's role in enquiry-based approaches

Teachers	Pupils
• Establish the task • Facilitate the process	• Pursue their own line of enquiry • Draw on existing knowledge • Highlight learning needs • Find/collect, analyse and present relevant evidence

 ## Reflection and discussion activity

Scenario

As part of a topic about flight, you have a discussion with the children about what sorts of things they know that can fly. You ask them to think about toys they have or have seen, living things and anything else that they can think of that can fly. The children are encouraged to come up with a list with a partner, and these are then shared in a class discussion. You guide the children to look at key features of things that can fly and use questioning to make sure that they are looking at materials, shapes and key features. You then explain that they are going to make something that they think can fly and you are going to take the finished things outside to see which can fly the furthest across the playground. The children are given a range of materials and pictures of things that fly, including natural things such as butterflies and seeds as well as kites, planes etc. The children work in friendship groups of three or four. You give them some time to explore the materials and to create a design. While they are doing this, you work with each group guiding them with key questions such as 'Why have you decided to use this material?' or 'What has made you decide that this is a good shape for something that is going to fly?' Depending on their responses, you guide them to think about why choices may or may not work so they can revise and adapt what they are doing.

Reflection

Trainee, think about the importance of the teacher's role in this example. What might be the issues for the teacher in planning this approach to learning? Do you think this is a good approach to support learning? Why?

Mentor, think about how you group children and ways that you help them by scaffolding the learning with different resources, use of questions and amount of support.

Discussion

Trainee and mentor, discuss different ways of scaffolding learning and what you need to consider when thinking about how the children can access the learning.

 ## Find out more from . . . websites

Easy-to-read information about Vygotsky and Piaget with a short video about the differences between their theories of learning. **www.simplypsychology.org/vygotsky.html#piaget**

Accessed January 29, 2017

Other approaches to teaching for learning

Emotional Intelligence (EQ)

Several authors have considered the influence that emotional intelligence has on how well children progress (Alexander, 2010; Goleman, 1996). How a person 'feels' about a learning situation determines the attention it gets, so we need to use emotion intelligently (Sousa, 2011). As a teacher you need to be aware of the impact that emotion can have. Basically, if you are able to be self-aware in terms of your own emotions and manage these emotions and those of others, you are better able to learn.

Goleman (1996) identified five 'domains' of EQ; three are to do with knowing and managing your emotions and motivation, and the other two concern recognising and understanding the emotions of others and managing relationships. If emotions are not managed, learning can be inhibited.

 Reflection and discussion activity

Reflection

Trainee, think about times when children have not seemed able to learn because of something that happened, perhaps at a break time. What did you or the teacher do to help the child manage their emotions?

Mentor, think about examples of successful approaches that you have used when children were struggling with their emotions or in relating to other children.

Discussion

Mentor and trainee, think about what useful approaches you could develop to help children develop emotional intelligence.

 Find out more from . . . internet clips

Daniel Goleman introduces Emotional Intelligence. **www.youtube.com/watch?v=Y7m9eNoB3NU**

Accessed January 29, 2017

Thinking skills and problem-solving approaches

Skills-based approaches to learning and building learning around thinking skills are also ideas you may encounter in schools. These approaches provide a framework for developing thinking skills and solving problems. Learning is about understanding, so advocates of skills-based approaches and developing thinking skills promote the idea that developing the skills gives context to the knowledge. There are elements of a number of the learning theories discussed in these approaches. In the Find out more about . . . section there is a link to Belle Wallace's (2001) Thinking Actively in a Social Context (TASC) approach and Edward de Bono's (2000) *Six Thinking Hats,* which are also discussed further below. The focus becomes more about developing skills for learning rather than acquiring knowledge because the skills will enable children to find out things they need to know. De Bono developed a toolkit for ways of thinking. Each hat encourages different approaches.

Table 3.4 Six Thinking Hats

Hats	
White	This is about looking at information and thinking about what you can find out/learn from it.
Red	This is about exploring your feelings and emotions about a situation (Links to Goleman's EQ).
Black	This involves you thinking about what could go wrong in a situation.
Yellow	This involves you thinking positively about opportunities and benefits in a situation.
Green	This is about looking for solutions and problem solving. It is about exploring lots of approaches and is open ended.
Blue	This is for the person managing the process. This hat should support everyone in being involved in what is going on and raise more ideas from other hats if needed.

Adapted from How Children Learn 3: Contemporary thinking and theorists (Pound, 2009)

 ## Reflection and discussion activity

Trainee and mentor, think about the 'thinking hats' approach. Do you think there might be issues with teaching thinking skills on their own? Can you see when it could be useful in teaching?

 ## Find out more from . . . internet clips and websites

Edward de Bono talking about the impact of thinking skills.

Accessed January 29, 2017

www.youtube.com/watch?v=yUliluJrWKg

An example of de Bono's six hats in the primary classroom.

www.debonogroup.com/six_thinking_hats.php

Accessed January 29, 2017

An explanation of the TASC approach.

http://tascwheel.com/?page_id=289

Accessed January 29, 2017

Lorin et al. (2001) provided a revised version of Bloom's Taxonomy to show how thinking develops to higher levels. Bloom used his taxonomy to support his argument that learning needs to be broken down into levels – and as you develop you are able to do higher-level thinking and learning. Some schools use this to help them develop higher order questions, and this is further explored in Chapter 8 about questioning and dialogue. In the Find out more . . . section there are links to examples of Bloom's Taxonomy and a simple example of what skills might be demonstrated at each level.

 Reflection and discussion activity

Reflection

Trainee, think back to the beginning of the chapter when you were asked to think about how you learn best, reflecting on the different principles and approaches. Are there approaches that you think are more helpful to support learning?

Discussion

Trainee and mentor, discuss why it is important to know about the principles for learning and teaching, and how this may help you as you develop your own teaching for learning.

 Find out more from . . . websites and books

Examples of the levels of thinking in Bloom's Taxonomy:

www.brainboxx.co.uk/a3_aspects/pages/ThinkingBloom.htm

Accessed January 29, 2017

Gershon, M (2015) *How to Use Blooom's Taxonomy in the Classroom: The complete guide.* Charlestown, SC: CreateSpace.

Chapter summary

This chapter has given you a brief overview of some key learning theories and approaches.

You can see that a lot of the principles for learning and teaching are used within lessons to help children learn. The approach used depends on what children are learning and how you plan your teaching to make sure their learning is effective. As Hattie (2012) notes:

> *It matters what teachers do but what matters most is having an appropriate mind frame relating to the impact of what they do . . . having a mind frame in which they see it as their role to evaluate their effect on learning.*

(Hattie, 2012, p.15)

It is not really about the principles for teaching and learning per se but about knowing why you teach what you teach in particular ways. This teaching needs to be grounded in an understanding of how children learn, having the ability to reflect and having confidence in why you do what you do.

References

Alexander, R (ed.) (2010) *Children, Their World, Their Education: Final report and recommendations of the Cambridge Primary Review.* Abingdon: Routledge.

Bandura, A (1977) *Social Learning Theory.* New York: General Learning Press.

Bruner, JS (1977) *The Process of Education (1960)* (2nd edn). Cambridge, MA: Harvard University Press.

De Bono, E (2000) *Six Thinking Hats.* London: Penguin.

Dewey, J (1961) *Democracy and Education (1961).* New York: Macmillan.

Fisher, R (2005) *Teaching Children to Think* (2nd edn). Cheltenham: Nelson Thornes.

Gardner, H (1983) *Frames of Mind: The theory of multiple intelligences.* London: HarperCollins.

Gardner, H (1999) *Intelligence Reframed: Multiple intelligences for the 21st century.* New York: Basic Books.

Goleman, D (1996) *Emotional Intelligence: Why it can matter more than IQ.* London: Bloomsbury Publishing.

Gray, C and MacBlain, S (2015) *Learning Theories in Childhood* (2nd edn). London: SAGE.

Hattie, J (2012) *Visible Learning for Teachers: Maximising impact on learning.* Abingdon: Routledge.

Hymer, B and Michel, D (2002) *Gifted and Talented Learners: Creating a policy for inclusion.* London: David Fulton.

Lazear, D (2004) *Multiple Intelligences Approach to Assessment.* Carmarthen: Crown House Publishing.

Lorin W, Anderson, LW, Krathwohl, DR and Bloom, BS (2001) *A Taxonomy for Learning, Teaching, and Assessing: A revision of Bloom's taxonomy of educational objectives*. New York: Longman.

MacBlain, S (2014) *How Children Learn*. London: SAGE.

Muijs, D and Reynolds, D (2007) *Effective Teaching: Evidence and practice* (3rd edn). London: SAGE.

Piaget, J and Inhelder, B (2000) *The Psychology of the Child*. New York: Basic Books.

Pound, L (2009) *Contemporary Thinking and Theorists: An overview of contemporary educational and psychological theorists*. London: Practical Pre-School Books.

Pound, L (2014) *How Children Learn: Educational theories and approaches – from Comenius the father of modern education to giants such as Piaget, Vygotsky and Malaguzzi*. London: Practical Pre-School Books.

Pritchard, A (2009) *Ways of Learning: Learning theories and learning styles in the classroom*. Abingdon: Routledge.

Shunk, D (2012) *Learning Theories: An educational perspective* (6th edn). Boston, MA: Pearson Education. Available at: http://server2.docfoc.com/uploads/Z2015/12/26/1koY3p4pMU/5a9f4b6679bd468fb0e9a9d541487e09.pdf

Siemens, G (2005) Connectivism: a learning theory for the digital age. *International Journal of Instructional Technology and Distance Learning*, 2(1): 3–10.

Skinner, BF (1974) *About Behaviorism*. New York: Vintage Books.

Sousa, D (2011) *How the Brain Learns* (4th edn). London: SAGE.

Vygotsky, LS, Hanfmann, E, Vakar, G and Kozulin, A (2012) *Thought and Language*. Cambridge, MA: MIT Press.

Wallace, B (ed.) (2001) *Teaching Thinking Skills Across the Primary Curriculum: A practical approach for all abilities*. Abingdon: David Fulton Publishers.

4
Planning for learning
Rebecca Geeson

┌─── **This chapter will** ───────────────────────┐

- consider the reasons for lesson planning;
- become more familiar with the key aspects included in lesson plans;
- consider the reasons for including different elements in your lesson plan;
- develop your ability to plan efficiently.

└───┘

Introduction

Even if you are at the very early stages of your teaching career, it is likely that you are already aware of lesson planning. You may have been introduced to your school's or training provider's planning format, have been given lesson plans to look at or to work from, and even had a go at planning lessons already. It is also likely that when you looked at your first lesson plan, it appeared to be a confusing grid which included lots of information, and your initial thoughts were 'Do I really have to do one of those for *every* lesson I teach?'. This chapter initially aims to develop your understanding of why teachers plan so that you are able to see that the task of lesson planning is purposeful. Consideration of the elements that make up a successful plan will follow. Once you understand what you are doing, why you are doing what you are doing and what strategies you can use to help you through the process, your lesson planning will become more efficient and effective.

Why do we plan?

It is important initially to clarify the difference between *writing lesson plans* and *planning*. Quite simply, the process of planning does not require any paperwork at all; we all constantly undertake planning, or make decisions about the future. However, the writing of lesson plans, or lesson planning, involves recording the thoughts that a teacher has during the process of deciding how to ensure pupils make progress in their learning. This chapter will consider both: why teachers plan lessons, and why teachers write lesson plans.

Why plan lessons?

Standing in front of a class of pupils, probably with other experienced adults around you and teaching can seem a little daunting in your early training. However, standing in front of that audience with no idea what you are going to say or do is even more frightening. At the early stages of your training, it is likely that you will not be 'let loose' to teach a class of pupils unless you have presented a plan beforehand, so you will not yet have experienced the feeling of attempting to teach a class without having prepared. Later on in your career, you will inevitably have occasions when you will find yourself suddenly having to take over a class; it will be at times like these that you will remember how important it is to be prepared.

Many approaches to teaching suggest that pupils need to take ownership of and lead their own learning. However, these valuable approaches rely on the teacher having the knowledge and ability to skilfully lead and encourage pupils to learn new knowledge or a particular concept or to develop a skill through their chosen interest. Without this direction and encouragement from the teacher, there would be no way to ensure that pupils make progress.

The crucial thing to remember is that planning and preparing can happen in many ways (Hattie, 2012). Schools usually require lessons to be prepared *in one form or another* before the start of the lesson, and while the way that these plans are presented will differ immensely from school to school, there certainly is no 'best' way to present planning. The underlying purpose of the process of planning remains the same though: in order to ensure pupils' learning progresses, decisions have to be made.

Learning is central to the planning process. Pupils' learning and progress is at the heart of education, and school leaders are responsible for and held accountable for this progress. One of the ways that some schools monitor learning and progress in their schools is through the planning process. While it is unlikely that most school leaders sit and analyse individual lesson plans on a weekly basis, having a lesson-planning process in place serves a number of purposes, all linked to pupils' learning and progress. Lesson planning:

- ensures that pupils' prior learning is developed and built upon from lesson to lesson, between subjects, across year groups;

- allows for the learning and progress of individuals and groups to be considered;

- provides a plan for how teachers are going to assess the progress of their learners and provide a starting point for the next sequence of learning.

Luke has been teaching for two years, and sees pupil progress as the heart of lesson planning.

> *Planning has been an important tool for structuring lessons. It has helped me to organise the content of my sessions and ensures I deliver the content in the most effective way to suit the needs of the learners. Across a strand, planning enables me to see a clear progression of learning: focusing on knowledge, skills and understanding. I plan individual lessons that consider the needs of pupils with all abilities – ensuring pupils have access to learning. Subsequent lessons build on formative assessment to ensure progression occurs.*

Figure 4.1 The plan, do, assess cycle

This can be seen as a cyclical process:

Observations will form an ongoing part of your teaching career: people such as mentors in school, training providers and school leaders will come and observe your teaching. Again, the ultimate reason for this is to ensure that the pupils in your class are learning and making progress. School inspectors generally do not ask to see lesson plans.

In fact, Ofsted explicitly state that they do not require schools to provide lesson plans, nor do they specify how planning should be set out or the amount of detail it should include (Ofsted, 2016). Whether planning is effective will be evidenced elsewhere, for example, through what the pupils say, how they behave and respond to questions and the work that they produce in a lesson and over time. However, particularly during training, the lesson planning document may still be a valuable tool for supporting observers' understanding of how you plan to ensure progress in the lesson. Your analysis of the lesson plan, of a lesson in which pupils did not make expected progress, after the event can be very useful to help you work out why and plan for improvements next time. Just as importantly, you can use the lesson plan to also help you to identify your strengths.

 Reflection and discussion activity

Choose a time when the trainee can observe the mentor teaching the class.

Reflection

Mentor, ensure your lesson plan is presented with the level of detail you would expect from your trainee. Point out to them how you are planning to check progress during the lesson.

Trainee, carry out a focused lesson observation, looking particularly at how your mentor is ensuring the pupils make progress in the lesson. Are they asking questions? What type of questions? Are they working with

(Continued)

(Continued)

individuals/groups? Do they observe pupils' discussions? Are they sticking to the lesson plan that they have given you? If not, why do you think they have adapted their plans and does this relate to progress? Do they stop groups or the whole class at unplanned points to explain or clarify?

Discussion

Trainee and mentor, after the lesson, discuss how the pupils' progress was assessed in the lesson. Also, look at the learning in pupils' books together, and use this to add to your understanding of progression in the lesson.

Following the above activity, you may have seen misconceptions occur. Early on in our teaching careers, hearing pupils give the 'wrong' answer can be a worry and cause self-doubt: 'Is this because I did not explain properly? I clearly did not plan this well enough!' but this level of reflection is actually very valuable. More experienced teachers expect misconceptions, and value them. One child's incorrect response is likely to be the tip of the iceberg; others may also have not understood, and by finding out more, a good teacher can immediately respond ensuring the child's learning is back on track for that lesson, but also help identify where the learning will move onto in subsequent lessons.

Developing your understanding of planning

In Table 4 on page 61, there are some broad phases for planning as a trainee teacher.

 Reflection and discussion activity

Reflection

Trainee, where are you now? Just as you will be encouraging the pupils in your class to reflect on their own prior learning, think about your understanding of planning lessons at this point. Look at the phases described in Table 4.1 - where are you now?

Mentor, what does your trainee need now? As teachers, we know that different learners need different levels of support at different times. Before you begin to set expectations of your trainee concerning what you require from them in their planning, there is a need to consider their current level of understanding and provide them with activities that build on what they already know. Think about where you feel the trainee is now based on Table 4.1, and be prepared to provide examples/evidence to support your views.

Discussion

Discuss where both of you feel the trainee's current level of understanding is and think about what support the trainee will need in order to progress.

Here are some broad phases of planning as a trainee teacher:

Table 4.1 The development of planning skills

Stage	How does the trainee plan at this stage?	What can the mentor do to support the trainee's planning at this stage?	What does the trainee need to develop their planning skills further?
Pre-introductory phase *Mentor plans.*	Trainee uses mentor's plans to teach lessons.	Mentor's own shorthand will need explaining. Mentor will need to discuss the planning with trainee, explaining reasons for their planning choices. Mentor will need to explain pupils' prior learning in depth.	Trainee should focus on gaining an understanding of the pupils' prior knowledge. Observe mentor's teaching and annotate their plan during the lesson, raising questions to discuss after the lesson.
Introductory planning phase *Mentor and trainee work together to plan.*	Trainee uses mentor's ideas and mentor's understanding of pupils' prior learning and uses mentor's planning as a model and begins to plan aspects of subsequent lessons (parts of the lesson, group activities etc.).	Mentor can support through modelling the planning of small aspects of the lesson. Mentor may need to step in during the lesson to explain/support – sometimes what has been explained by mentor has been misinterpreted by trainee. If planning is done as a team, invite trainee to attend.	Trainee should explain and show where the planning has come from (NC, long-/medium-term plans, published schemes etc.). Trainee should attempt to assess and evaluate prior learning before moving on to planning more independently.
Developing planning phase *Trainee working more independently after initial input and before feedback.*	Through this phase, trainee moves from simply adapting mentor's plans to planning larger parts of the lesson with less need for support. Initially, trainee relies heavily upon the plans or schemes used by the school. Further through this stage, trainee adapts these to meet the needs of the class with more confidence and includes more of their own ideas and adaptations.	Trainee seeks advice from mentor before planning the lesson to ensure their understanding of prior learning is correct. Mentor should suggest initial ideas and then trainee attempts to write the plan independently. Trainee seeks advice after the plan is written for confirmation. Mentor encourages trainee to 'submit' their plans to mentor well in advance of the lesson so that mentor has opportunity to offer feedback and there is time for this process to happen more than once. Mentor should remain aware that trainee's developing confidence may be misplaced, so support will still be needed during planning.	Trainee should be beginning to build up own 'bank' of ideas, resources, approaches, strategies that can be used or adapted in lessons. Trainee should be gaining confidence with their assessments of the pupils' learning.

(Continued)

Table 4.1 (Continued)

Stage	How does the trainee plan at this stage?	What can the mentor do to support the trainee's planning at this stage?	What does the trainee need to develop their planning skills further?
Extending planning phase *Trainee works independently, with mentor checking at particular stages.*	Trainee suggests and discusses their planning verbally with mentor before attempting plans independently. Trainee starts writing individual lesson plans without a huge amount of input from mentor and is generally able to gauge prior learning accurately and independently.	Mentor supports with the ideas stage, but expects trainee to explain prior learning and expected progress of pupils.	If appropriate, trainee should work with planning team in school to consider and contribute ideas to medium-term planning.
	Trainee plans individual lesson plans independently, drawing from their own assessment of prior learning.	Trainee presents mentor with a plan which they feel is 'just about there' and may only need a few amendments. Less feedback time should be needed in advance of the lesson.	Trainee should engage with the longer term planning process within school.
	Trainee plans individual lessons with complete autonomy, making use of longer term planning in schools (where appropriate) and engaging in the creation of longer term plans.	Mentor only needs to consider plans after some lessons in order to reflect on effectiveness of teaching.	Trainee should aim to increase efficiency in the planning process.

The mentor/trainee relationship is something that requires commitment and work from both sides to ensure an effective working partnership. For you as a trainee, it is important to consider that the purpose for planning lessons is to ensure that learners make good progress. It could be that you sometimes forget that your mentor has to consider your learning and progress, too.

 **Case study**

I worked with my first trainee last year - I'll call her Sophie – and her planning was not great. It wasn't so much that what she put in the plan wasn't right; she usually had appropriate learning objectives that built on prior learning (although her success criteria weren't great), and activities she had planned were generally appropriate. The main problem was that she didn't let me see it until just before the lesson, despite me gently (and then more forcibly) reminding her that I needed to see it at least a day beforehand.

There had been some lessons I watched that frankly were unsatisfactory; hardly any progress was made by the majority of the pupils, and when I looked at her plans I could see why. There were usually different reasons for the weaknesses in the lesson; on one occasion she entirely missed out explaining some key vocabulary, on another she had tried to build on prior learning but as she was asking the pupils to apply it in an entirely different context, she hadn't realised she needed to make the link more explicit. I was annoyed that she hadn't shared her plans with me in advance. I know the class, and would have been able to give her ideas to avoid so many of the problems she was encountering in the lesson.

As I was new to mentoring, and not long out of training myself, I was quite worried about discussing this with Sophie, but I knew I had to. I was going to be held accountable for the pupils' progress during the year, and if the pupils did not make progress in the six weeks she was teaching my class, I would have problems I also wanted to make sure that Sophie's time in the school was of value. When I talked to her, it turned out that she was working at a part-time job some evenings, and getting planning done, let alone sending it to me, was a challenge. This explained things. I can remember how long lesson plans used to take me when I was training. Sophie also admitted she had not even thought about things from my perspective; she knew that the pupils' progress was the most important thing, but did not see how lesson planning supported it until we discussed it. Once she could see how to track progress through her planning and realised how it would impact on pupils' learning, things got better. It was not a fun conversation, but once things were out in the open, our relationship seemed to improve too, and thankfully, so did Sophie's teaching and the pupils' progress.

As you can see from this mentor's story, Sophie had not allowed time for her mentor to feedback to her, and support the *trainee* in her learning. The lesson plan itself is merely a record of your preparation, but particularly in the early stages of your career, the advice gained from more experienced teachers is invaluable . . . *before* you teach each lesson.

Who is the plan for?

Lesson plans can be present in many different formats, but the key point to remember is that ultimately the lesson plan is not for anyone other than you, as trainee. It is a reminder for you of your thought processes during the planning stage, so that when you are in front of the class, you will have the confidence to say that the learners are making progress.

It is very rare (and best avoided) that teachers read from their lesson plan as they are teaching. However, having an aide-mémoire can be helpful to remind you of organisational details during the lesson. For this reason, 'wordy' plans tend to be less effective – the information that needs to be found quickly is hidden within less relevant text; try succinct bullet points instead.

However, at all stages of your career, it is important to remember that while the lesson plan is mainly for you, others may also need to be able to decipher it. Along with your mentor, and perhaps the senior leadership team, teaching assistants who work in the class will need to be able to understand your plans for the lesson to ensure pupil progress. A balance, therefore, is needed between what you need to support your teaching of the lesson, and what others may need to be able to understand from the plan.

The Early Years Foundation Stage Framework and the National Curriculum

In many schools, the National Curriculum (2013) forms the basis for long-term plans as 'maintained schools are legally required to follow the statutory national curriculum' (DfE, 2013, p.5). Learning outcomes are presented in the National Curriculum, and then schools use these to form the basis of their long-term plans. Different approaches are needed depending on the subject being considered; the learning outcomes for the 'core' subjects of mathematics, English and science are presented in year-by-year detail in the National Curriculum, whereas the learning outcomes for whole Key Stages are provided for other (or 'foundation') subjects, so there is an opportunity to organise aspects more flexibly.

It is important to note that the National Curriculum is designed to provide *an outline of the core knowledge* that pupils need and is *just one element in the education of every child* (DfE, 2013, p.6). It is designed to allow time for schools to develop a wider curriculum which extends pupils' knowledge, skills and understanding beyond the National Curriculum specifications. This enables schools to have some freedom beyond the statutory requirements. However, along with other schools that are able to choose not to use the National Curriculum, a long-term planning stage supports schools in mapping out what will be taught when to ensure progress, to avoid repetition, and in the case of maintained schools, show evidence that legal requirements are met.

The Early Years Foundation Stage (EYFS) Framework is 'mandatory for all Early Years providers', whether they are maintained, non-maintained or independent (DfE, 2014, p.4) and seeks to provide quality and consistency in all settings and a secure foundation for pupils' learning and development (DfE, 2014, p.5). This means that all schools will start their planning process with the EYFS Framework, and many will begin with the National Curriculum for pupils in Key Stages 1 and 2. Whether or not schools label the subsequent stages as in the table below, they will all go through a process of gradually fine-tuning broad learning outcomes until a focused, specific, measurable learning objective can be created for an individual session.

As above, maths, a core subject for which detailed year-by-year outcomes are provided, may be approached differently from art, a foundation subject.

Table 4.2 *Learning outcomes to learning objectives*

Maths	Planning stage	Art
In year 3 *Pupils should be taught to measure, compare, add and subtract: lengths (m/cm/mm); mass (kg, g); volume/ capacity (l/ml) (DfE, 2013, p.117).*	**National Curriculum**	At the end of KS1 *Pupils should be taught to use drawing, painting and sculpture to develop and share their ideas, experiences and imagination and to use a range of materials creatively to design and make products (DfE, 2013, p.177)*
Term 1: *Lengths*	**Long-term planning in school**	Year 3 *Drawing*
Week 1: *To compare lengths (m/cm/mm)*	**Medium-term planning**	Term 1 *Drawing using a range of materials*
Individual lesson objective for one session: *To compare lengths of objects smaller than 10cm long.*	**Short-term planning**	1st lesson in the sequence of work: *To draw from experience using charcoal and chalk.*

Different schools organise the different stages of planning in different ways. Sometimes, a long-term plan may include only very brief learning outcomes and the medium-term plan will include further details. This may then be followed up with a short-term, or daily plan, and at the training stage, a daily session plan is advisable, whether or not your school does expect this of their experienced members of staff. In other cases, a long-term plan will have a great deal of depth and detail, which may make the medium-term stage less necessary. The important thing to note is that while all schools will plan in EYFS from the EYFS Framework, some schools will be basing their KS1 and KS2 curricula on the National Curriculum, while others will not. However, to ensure progress is made, a mapping process will have taken place before you come to plan your lesson.

What goes in a lesson plan?

For the purposes of this book, I have chosen to concentrate on short-term planning, the most detailed and final planning stage. Long- and medium-term planning are usually carried out well before you arrive for a training placement in school, but these stages will have taken into account many factors, including the school ethos and approach to learning. You will have the opportunity to contribute to these planning stages later in your career.

Common themes can be seen in planning that is presented in different formats, all of which relate to progression in learning. While it is important to be prepared to be flexible with timings and respond to what is going on in the lesson, it is also useful before you start the lesson to have a plan which attempts to ensure that there is neither too much, nor too little going on in a lesson.

The key aspects to consider when planning for progression in pupils' learning are:

- pupils' prior learning

- the lesson objective

- success criteria

- assessment

Each of these aspects needs to be considered based on knowledge of your class and the different needs of each child in your class.

Prior and subsequent learning

Having a secure understanding of pupils' prior learning is crucial in order to ensure their subsequent learning builds on what they already know so that you can ensure progress. It is sometimes challenging as a trainee to know your class before you plan your first series of lessons, but good mentors will support you in finding this out. Having a secure understanding of the curriculum being taught will also support you so that as you quickly develop the skill of initially assessing pupils' learning and see how they respond to your input, you will be able to adapt your plans for the lesson to ensure you start from the right point.

As well as discussing the need for teachers to have a good understanding of pupils' prior learning, Hattie (2012) talks about understanding pupils' ways of thinking (as these differ from adults' ways of thinking) and also their motivation to learn; your ability to plan for your class's progress will depend on you developing your understanding of them as learners as well as understanding what they have learned in the past.

It is also useful to consider where you aim for the pupils' learning to progress in subsequent lessons. This will ensure that you keep the learning you are working towards over time at the front of your mind when planning.

 Find out more from ... books

Hattie, J (2012) *Visible Learning for Teachers: Maximising impact on learning.* London: Routledge.

Piaget's work around the stages which pupils' thinking develops can be found in:

Piaget, J and Inhelder, B (2000) *The Psychology of the Child.* New York: Basic Books.

Learning objectives

As Hattie explains, *the more transparent the teacher makes the learning goals, the more likely the student is to engage in the work needed to meet the goal* (2012, p.46). These learning goals may be referred to as learning intentions, lesson objectives, learning aims, intended learning or acronyms such as LO (Learning or Lesson Objectives), WALT (We Are Learning To . . .). These terms all refer to the learning that is planned for the lesson.

Learning objectives should:

- be a clear description of what is to be *learned* by end of lesson (not what will be *produced*);

- be achievable in one lesson;

- build on previous learning;

- take account of pupils' prior knowledge;

- be able to be assessed.

Learning objectives are the foundation for all lesson plans and should be based around the skills, knowledge and understanding that pupils will learn during the lesson, rather than the outcome of the lesson (as is sometimes found in trainee lesson plans).

- *Skills* – can be applied in different contexts and often start with 'to be able to', e.g. to be able to solve multi-step word problems.

- *Knowledge* – pupils know something new; they often start with 'to know', e.g. to know which materials are thermal insulators.

- *Understanding* – relates to concepts or ideas and often start with 'to understand', e.g. to understand why Hadrian's Wall was built.

You should avoid linking learning objectives to the context of the learning. This is because assessment is based on the progress of knowledge, skills and understanding, not on specific contexts. If you take the first objective above and add a context, you will be able to see why: *To be able to solve multi-step word problems about the circus.*

We know that pupils make progress at different rates, and that deep learning often takes time so we know that objectives will need to be revisited. However, there is little chance that you would plan another lesson around circus-related, multi-step problems; you will want to create different learning contexts to engage the pupils and to ensure that they can apply their learning in different contexts, so to ensure that your learning objectives are not tied to one particular context.

For the same reason, it is best to avoid including what is going to be produced in learning objectives. If we amend the second objective above slightly: To wrap containers of hot water with different materials to see which keeps water hottest for longest, we can see that not only does the objective become overly verbose, but also does not allow for the learning to be reinforced, consolidated or applied in other contexts or in other lessons.

It is worth considering at the planning stage when, during the lesson, the learning objective should be shared; it might be that initially hiding and later revealing the objective during or at the end of the lesson is more appropriate, although this should be a deliberate pedagogical decision, not an afterthought. Arguably, pupils should be aware of what they are learning in order to learn effectively (Hattie, 2012), but it may be that by sharing the exact nature of the knowledge, skills or understanding in the learning objective at the beginning of the lesson will 'give the game away' and restrict opportunities for learning.

Another useful consideration is that of your choice of language. The plan, as above, is for a different audience than the lesson itself; an adult audience with experience in teaching and education will be able to understand a more complex learning objective than a group of seven-year-olds. Think about this carefully when planning the wording of your learning objective. It may be helpful to include two learning objectives on your lesson plan: one appropriate for adults, and one in 'child-friendly' language.

Success criteria

Success criteria come in different forms. Some teachers see this success criteria as a series of steps to help pupils get to the end goal (or learning objective). Others see success criteria as a measurement against learning outcomes that can support pupils in a deeper understanding of the purpose of the lesson and in evaluating their own success against the learning goal. This is supported by Hattie (2012) who explains that pupils should be aware of the learning objective, and also be able to know whether they have achieved the desired learning.

Teachers often find it beneficial for pupils to be involved in planning their own success criteria. The process of encouraging the pupils to think about their learning, or engaging in metacognition, embeds the teacher's intentions of the learning that will take place in the lesson. However, you should be prepared to steer the pupils in an appropriate direction to ensure that you keep the learning on track, if necessary.

Table 4.3 An example of 'Steps to success' success criteria and 'Learning outcome' success criteria

Learning objective	Learning outcome success criteria	'Steps to success' success criteria
To be able to identify odd and even numbers.	I will be able to identify whether a number is odd or even.	Look at the last digit in the number to check the pattern. Divide the number in two to check.
To write an effective characterisation.	Someone who reads it will feel they really know the person.	Use adjectives. Include all or some of the following, with examples: - hobbies and interests - attitude to others - what makes that person a friend.

Reflection and discussion activity

Reflection

Trainee, analyse your learning objectives; think about whether they relate to skills, knowledge or understanding. Also, consider whether context or outcomes appear, and, if so, how will this impact on assessment. Which ones do you now think would benefit from rewording?

Mentor, think about your trainee's learning objectives that you feel were not successful (i.e. resulted in insufficient progress for learners). Why?

Discussion

Considering the less successful learning objectives that you have both identified, rework these.

Also, consider the link between learning objectives and success criteria that you have used. Do they clearly convey the intention of the learning that will take place in the lesson and enable pupils to be aware of what success looks like?

Assessment

Assessment as a concept is discussed more fully in Chapter 5 by Elizabeth Farrar, so this chapter will concentrate on its place within the planning structure.

From a planning perspective, opportunities to assess are vital to ensure the assessment does happen. As a teacher, it is easy to get 'carried away' with what is going on in the lesson, and become as engaged as the pupils with interesting and exciting learning opportunities. However, your role as the teacher depends on you moving pupils' learning forward, and without assessing what is going on right now, you will be unable to plan subsequent learning.

You should plan what you are going to assess (based on the learning objective and success criteria), but also who you are going to assess and how you are going to assess. It is usually unrealistic to attempt to assess all pupils individually during every lesson. In one lesson, it may be that you plan to focus on a small group, of individuals with whom you are working; ask your teaching assistant to focus on another group and make initial judgements about the progress of the rest of the class through questioning at various other points in the lesson. Your marking of their work after the lesson will either support in-lesson assessment, or highlight misconceptions that have occurred and inform subsequent plans. Over the next lessons, it is advisable that assessment is focused on different groups. However, while this approach makes assessment manageable, it does require careful consideration at the planning stage to ensure that you gain a clear understanding of how each child's progress develops over a sequence of lessons.

Differentiation

Carefully consider, based on the different learners in your class, how to group the pupils. Ensure you are responsive and flexible between subjects and within subjects.

─── **Find out more from . . . websites** ───

BBC Active explains how differentiation can be managed through varying tasks, grouping, resources, pace, outcome, dialogue and support, and assessment. **www.bbcactive.com/BBCActiveIdeasandResources/ MethodsofDifferentiationintheClassroom.aspx**

Accessed January 29, 2017

Activities

What are you and the pupils going to do in the lesson in order to support their progress towards the learning objective? What *resources, key vocabulary* and *adult support* are going to be used and by whom? What different parts of the lesson will happen when?

Modelling, where pupils learn from things being demonstrated to them, and *scaffolding,* where pupils' learning is supported by another ('more knowledgeable') child or an adult are important learning theories to consider when planning activities. Consider where in the sequence of learning the pupils are and what the desired learning is; would it be most appropriate to introduce parts of the lesson through modelling? At what points would scaffolding deepen their understanding?

─── **Find out more from . . . educational theorists** ───

Modelling

Bandura told us that: *Most human behaviour is learned observationally through modelling: from observing others, one forms an idea of how new behaviours are performed, and on later occasions this coded information serves as a guide for action* (Bandura, 1977, p.22).

Scaffolding

Vygotsky initially discussed the need to learn from *more knowledgeable others,* as part of his work on the Zone of Proximal Development: *The distance between the actual development level as determined by independent problem solving and the level of potential development as determined through problem solving under adult guidance or in collaboration with more capable peers* (Vygotsky, 1978, p.66).

Bruner (1966) builds further on this idea and created the term 'scaffolding' to describe learning that would allow pupils to use what they had learned independently through three modes of presentation.

A useful summary of these and other key educational theorists' ideas can be found in:

Aubrey, K and Riley, A (2016) *Understanding and Using Educational Theories.* London: SAGE.

Key questions and vocabulary

In Chapter 8, John Paramore reflects on how questions to simulate dialogue will support your understanding of questioning. Many teachers find that having key questions planned before the start of the lesson enables them to 'keep on track' in terms of the flow of the lesson, and the assessment that will take place. You may want to target questions based upon your previous assessment, or providing opportunities to further deepen pupils' understanding.

It is also useful to make it clear at the planning stage what subject-specific vocabulary you are going to use in your lesson. This may involve introducing new words and phrases to your pupils, but should also be in the plan as a reminder to you to continue to embed the vocabulary that pupils need in relation to a particular objective, theme or topic.

Resources

It helps to note down on your plan what resources you need to prepare before your lesson as a reminder as you prepare for the day. Thinking this through should be done alongside your planning of activities, and also while considering differentiation.

Role of other adults

Planning for other adults should be embedded throughout other aspects of learning. You can read a detailed exploration of working with Teaching Assistants in Chapter 12 by Emma Clarke. However, in terms of planning, you should ensure that other adults are seen as a valuable resource in supporting pupils' progress, and in light of this, carefully plan for their involvement in learning throughout the lesson.

It is important not only to plan for the use of other adults within each lesson, but also plan for time for you and any additional adults to discuss the lesson beforehand, and also time to reflect on pupils' progress afterwards to inform your future planning.

Plenary

An evaluation or reflection upon the aims of the lesson supports both the pupils' understanding of their learning and your own assessment of their learning. Plenaries should not simply be a 'show and tell'; think carefully about the learning that each child will engage in during this part of the lesson. Mini-plenaries, or little reviews of learning during the lesson are often more beneficial as they give opportunity for you and the pupils to respond immediately to progress in learning. Usually, these are not planned; you need to learn to realise when a mini-plenary should be included, basing your decisions on your ongoing assessment of the pupils' learning.

Plenaries may include:

- Following up on questions that pupils have set themselves at the start of the lesson;

- Opportunities for the pupils to peer- and self-assess against success criteria;

- Asking the pupils to reflect on their learning: *What are the three most important things we have learned in this lesson? What rules or tips could we create to help us next time we are . . . ?*;

- Providing opportunities for pupils to apply their learning in different contexts, perhaps justifying choices or providing a rationale based on their learning in the lesson;

- Explaining to the pupils where their learning will develop in subsequent lessons; helping them see that their learning is an ongoing process rather than 'stand-alone' sessions.

 Find out more from . . . websites

Mike Gershon has produced a huge range of tools to support the planning process. His 'Plenary Producer' may give you some ideas to start you off:

http://mikegershon.com/resources/download-info/the-plenary-producer-ideas-ks2-ks3-powerpoint/

Accessed January 29, 2017

As you choose questions or activities for plenaries, carefully reflect on *why* the activity is supporting, deepening or embedding pupils' learning.

Reflection and discussion activity

Reflection

Mentor, it is useful to remember that your trainee may be moving to work within a different school on their next placement, so giving them the opportunity to experiment with different lesson planning formats will support their professional development.

Trainee, depending on your experience, either:

Ask fellow trainees, other teachers, your training provider to share with you different planning formats that they use. Which ones would you feel most confident to use? Choose one or two that you like best and plan lessons using these instead of the format that you have been using so far.

Or:

Create your own planning format. Make use of key aspects (as above, or as seen in many other plans).

Discussion

Consider what worked and what did not work and why, keeping in mind the main purpose: reminding you of the decisions you made to ensure pupil progress in the lesson.

Figure 4.2 Planning as a spiral process

If we add to the diagram that describes the planning process in more depth now, we see that planning is actually an ongoing or spiral process:

The process relies upon *flexibility* and *responsiveness*. Beginning trainees often ask 'Does it matter if I do not do what I have put on my plan?'. The answer, of course, is that it does not matter at all, as long as the changes made are having a positive impact on pupil progress, and in fact, responding to and adapting planning is integral to ensure the spiral continues within subsequent lessons. Part of your skills as a teacher depends on your ability to respond to the unexpected, and to learn from it (see Chapter 1 on Reflection for professional development). The secret to the ability of responding flexibly within lessons lies in your subject knowledge, both of the subject that you are teaching, and in your understanding of where your teaching fits within the curriculum, along with your knowledge of the pupils' prior learning, and them as learners (Hattie, 2012). This enables you to respond to a child's misconceptions, either by taking them to a different stage in the sequence of learning, or by discussing their ideas from a different perspective. It is useful to include possible misconceptions within your plan to help you prepare for them.

Where next? Lesson planning beyond training

A trainee teacher once complained to me that her mentor's (a teacher with 20 years' experience) planning was not 'as detailed as it should be', and asked if I could provide some examples of 'really good' plans written by good and outstanding teachers. Of course, what makes a 'really good' lesson plan varies from teacher to teacher and at different points in their careers and with different groups of pupils. Remember, lesson plans are for you, to support you in planning for pupils to make progress in their learning. Because you are at an early stage in your professional development, your lesson plans may take longer to create and include more detail than your experienced mentor would include in theirs. However, please remember that this should not always be the case Be reassured that you will not continue to spend so many hours planning in the future; you will very quickly develop your bank of ideas of different ways to approach learning and different ways to engage pupils, and your own subject knowledge will continue to grow.

Find out more from . . . Government reports

A recent DfE report from a review group who considered teachers' planning workload is available from the DfE website. This report presents findings which support schools encouraging collaborative planning and making use of high-quality, externally produced resources. It also reiterates the point that planning should serve the purpose of supporting learning, rather than be an extensive and time-consuming task.

www.gov.uk/government/uploads/system/uploads/attachment_data/file/511257/Eliminating-unnecessary-workload-around-planning-and-teaching-resources.pdf

Accessed January 29, 2017

Reflection and discussion activity

Collect examples of planning from different teachers in the school, and if possible, plans that were used in the past.

Reflection

Trainee, ensuring you remain professional, critically analyse the plans of other teachers in the school (taking care to remember their audience when writing their plans – themselves!). What appeals to you when thinking about how you would like to organise your own planning format?

Discussion

Mentor, how has your planning changed during your career? What strategies have you discovered to support efficient and effective lesson planning? Discuss this with your trainee.

However, to avoid having to wait years before things slot into place for you, it is useful to consider possible strategies to improve your lesson-planning efficiency now. I have sometimes heard very enthusiastic trainees suggesting that they have prepared a 'plan B' lesson plan. They have recognised a very important point: that having a contingency plan is useful. However, it seems a little excessive and inefficient to go to the effort of producing two in-depth plans; consideration of alternatives within one lesson plan, having good subject and curriculum knowledge, and seeking support from your mentor about the appropriateness of the plan, should be more than sufficient to ensure that you can respond effectively to unforeseen aspects of your lesson.

Other approaches that may help are:

- Team planning

  Develop supportive relationships with others in school. If there are parallel classes, share planning. However, it should be noted that you will be held accountable for what is taught in your class, so you should amend and adapt other people's plans before you use them if needed.

- Using published planning

  Making use of prepared resources can make planning a much more efficient process (Hattie, 2012; DfE, 2016). The main disadvantage of many published schemes is that they are not specific to your class, so as above, you will need to adapt them.

- Familiar activities

  Make use of activities that you have used before, but change the context or content. As well as speeding up your planning, this has the added benefit of making more efficient use of lesson time as pupils are able to get on with activities without lengthy explanations.

- Carousels

  Consider using a range of activities that can be used for all groups in the class, but just adapted slightly to provide specific support or extension depending on ability.

- Long-term and medium-term planning

  As you become more experienced, you will also have more autonomy over long- and medium-term plans. This will give you opportunity to plan ahead and have greater understanding of where an individual lesson sits within pupils' longer term learning. Spending time on this stage will also improve efficiency in your short-term lesson planning.

 **Chapter summary**

Some schools and training providers will recommend that you make use of a particular planning format. In this chapter we have considered the rationale behind planning: pupil progress should be central to the planning process, and your lesson plan is a tool to support you to enable pupils' learning and progress. It should be seen as a more valuable and authentic process than a tick-box exercise for mentors or senior leaders in school. Any planning document that you produce should work for you.

The ideas discussed above are common themes seen in many lesson plans and may provide a good basis as you formulate your own approach to planning. You may decide to use the following headings in your lesson-planning format:

- Prior learning

- Subsequent learning

- Lesson objective

- Reference to National Curriculum or EYFS framework

- Success criteria

- Assessment (how, what, who, when)

(Continued)

(Continued)

- Differentiation (how different pupils/groups of pupils' different needs will be met, how individual pupils and/or groups will be supported and challenged, how learning might be extended) including specific reference to pupils with EAL, SEND, specific needs

- Key questions

- Key vocabulary

- Resources (what and how they will be used)

- Plenary

- Timings

- Role of other adults

It is also valuable to annotate your lesson plans during and after the lesson. Again, for the purpose of ensuring that pupil progress over time, get into the habit of making quick written notes on your plans that show both:

- Pupil progress in the lessons: your assessment of pupils' learning, perhaps considering individuals or groups. Begin to think about 'what next?' for individuals and groups.

- Implications for your own learning: 'This aspect worked'; 'At this point, I had to make changes because . . .'; 'Here, I could have . . .' etc. These comments will be invaluable in informing later 'reflection-on-action' (Schön, 1983).

Keeping at the front of your mind that one of your main responsibilities as a teacher is to ensure pupils all make progress in every lesson, it is important that you should always be prepared to adapt your lesson plans as they are happening. Accept that your meticulously prepared lesson plan should be flexible and responsive, and do not stick to the plan if you see that pupils are not learning. However, alongside ensuring that your lesson plans are focused on pupil progress, throughout your career, remember to also make use of lesson plans to reflect on and develop your own teaching.

References

Aubrey, K and Riley, A (2016) *Understanding and Using Educational Theories*. London: SAGE.

Bandura, A (1977) *Social Learning Theory*. New York: General Learning Press.

Bruner, J (1966) *Toward a Theory of Instruction*. Cambridge, MA: Harvard University Press.

Department for Education (2013) *The National Curriculum for England: Key Stages 1 and 2 Framework Document*. Available at: **www.gov.uk/government/collections/national-curriculum** (accessed January 29, 2017).

Department for Education (2016) *Eliminating Unnecessary Workload Around Planning and Teaching Resources: Report of the Independent Teacher Workload Review Group.* Retrieved from: **www.gov.uk/government/uploads/system/uploads/attachment_data/file/511257/Eliminating-unnecessary-workload-around-planning-and-teaching-resources.pdf** (accessed January 29, 2017).

Hattie, J (2012) *Visible Learning for Teachers: Maximising impact on learning.* London: Routledge.

Ofsted, (2016) *School Inspection Handbook.* Available at: **www.gov.uk/government/publications/school-inspection-handbook-from-september-2015** (accessed January 29, 2017).

Piaget, J and Inhelder, B (2000) *The Psychology of the Child.* New York: Basic Books.

Pound, L (2009) *Contemporary Thinking and Theorists: An overview of contemporary educational and psychological theorists.* London: Practical Pre-School Books.

Vygotsky, L (1978) *Mind in Society.* Cambridge, MA: Harvard University Press.

5
Assessment
Elizabeth Farrar

 This chapter will

- explore different approaches to assessment to help children make progress;
- consider what formative assessment strategies might look like in the classroom;
- consider how assessment impacts upon learning objectives and success criteria;
- reflect on the part that feedback has to play in ensuring that children understand where they are in their learning and what they need to do next;
- develop your understanding of summative assessment and its place in primary education.

Introduction

As a trainee teacher you may wonder what part assessment will play in your daily practice. Will it be something that you need to be concerned with at all, or is it something that the pupils will do, maybe at some future point, such as at the end of the unit of work, the term or the year? What does it look like and why do we do it? Any of these questions, and probably many more, might have occurred to you. This chapter aims to address some of these.

Assessment in the classroom takes two forms: summative and formative. Summative assessment takes place at the end of a period of learning such as a unit of work, an academic year or a key stage, for instance. Pupils are evaluated against a standard or benchmark. SATs and GCSEs are examples of summative assessment which you will probably be familiar with. Summative assessment is carried out for the purpose of reporting the achievement of individual students at a particular time (Harlen and Harlen, 2007). Formative assessment is ongoing and takes place during the learning process, enabling you to evaluate learning needs and progress. It allows teaching and learning to be modified and adapted to better meet these needs. You will find that formative assessment is often referred to as Assessment for Learning (AfL).

Summative and formative assessment are not contradictory or conflicting practices but can be seen as complementary approaches. Clarke and Hattie (2001) employ a gardening analogy to explain this. If you think of your pupils as plants, then summative assessment would be the process of measuring them. These measurements may be interesting to compare and analyse, but they do not affect the growth of the plants. Formative assessment is the garden equivalent of you feeding and watering your plants, and therefore directly affecting their growth.

 Reflection and discussion activity

Reflection

Trainee, think about pupils you have worked with and lessons you have observed. What adaptations were being made to lessons to cater for pupils who are working 'below' and 'above' their age-related expectations?

Mentor, think about what adaptations you make for pupil progress. Share some of these with the trainee.

Discussion

Mentor and trainee, discuss the impact of the approaches in helping children to make progress that you have both chosen in the reflection.

Summative assessment

Assessment lies at the very heart of teaching, as you need to know what progress your pupils are making in order to know what you need to teach them. This is certainly not intending to imply a 'teaching to the test' approach should be taken, but rather that learning needs to be steered to ensure that progress is made towards the age-related expectations as laid out in the National Curriculum, and by individual schools. Assessment is, therefore, fundamental to the whole of your practice. There would be little point in going to swimming lessons for a year if the assessment of your progress at the end was related to your proficiency in salsa dancing, for example. Currently, the recent removal of nationally-agreed levels means that there are many methods by which schools are tracking and assessing their pupils' progress. Assessment is being looked at in lots of different ways, both using commercial schemes and also schools' own adapted assessments. There could be any number of ways in which the school you are working at has chosen to assess their pupils, and so it is neither possible nor helpful to try to explain any of these in specific detail in this chapter. However, I can discuss what the assessment system you are working with needs to be able to do.

The requirements that children need to have achieved by the end of Key Stage 1 and Key Stage 2 are specified within the National Curriculum, and so many schools and commercially produced systems have taken these and reduced them to a set of 'non-negotiables' or key skills. These have then been broken down into what children are expected to know by the end of the year. The pupils are assessed against this set of statements to determine whether they are working below, at, or above their year group (often referred to as 'age-related') expectations.

Why test?

Summative testing can contribute to learning but, for instance, teaching a skill for the first half term of the year, followed by a successful assessment, cannot be assumed to indicate that your pupils are secure with that skill and that it can be left behind, safely ticked off on your record. To be certain that the skill is secured, it should be revisited throughout the year in a range of forms to ensure that it is embedded thoroughly. To embed knowledge, understanding or skills, you must provide your pupils with enough opportunities to practise, use, revisit, consolidate and apply what you want them to learn, otherwise their long-term memory is bypassed and things are forgotten, no matter how well they seemed to know or understand them at the point of teaching. Using summative testing can be considered to help to revisit and therefore consolidate prior learning. Faragher (2014) notes that schools now operate within a standards-driven assessment culture. The introduction of the National Curriculum, Ofsted inspections, testing and league tables, along with the glut of associated strategies and initiatives, have all been driven by the intention of improving standards on the international stage as well as nationally. Powerful national bodies have taken charge of the curriculum and assessment, with teachers becoming accountable for the achievement of externally set targets. As trainees, it is useful for you to be aware of the accountability that rests with all teachers for their pupils' progress.

 Reflection and discussion activity

Reflection

Trainee, having looked at the school's systems, consider how every child's progress is being effectively tracked and what is done during daily lessons to feed in to this tracking.

Look out for examples of summative assessment being used to revisit and consolidate learning.

Mentor, consider how you can support your trainee in understanding the place of summative assessment and also the ways in which reporting is expected for accountability. Organise some opportunities to look at examples of summative assessment relevant to the age range of the pupils they are teaching (for example, past papers for year 6 SATs or year 1 phonics screening).

Discussion

Trainee and mentor, consider summative assessment preparations in your school and discuss strategies that can be used to minimise any negative effects of the pressures assessment may produce.

Formative assessment

Black and Wiliam were commissioned by the Assessment Reform Group to review the literature around formative assessment. Their findings, published in *Inside the Black Box: Raising standards through classroom assessment* (1998) were presented to the policy makers. They stated that summative assessment dominated, but that formative assessment had the most potential for improving standards of children's learning. Following this, the 'Excellence and Enjoyment' strategy for primary schools, launched by the Secretary of State in 2003, formally introduced Assessment for Learning into the national teaching and learning agenda. The stage was set for formative assessment to become a fundamental part of primary school teaching and learning.

Find out more from . . . research and publications

You can read the *Inside the Black Box* publication online. Here is a link to the document:

http://weaeducation.typepad.co.uk/files/blackbox-1.pdf

Accessed January 29, 2017

Harlen and Harlen (2007) summarise the key components of formative assessment, and these are clearly reflected in the strategies advocated by Clarke (2014). These include pupils:

- understanding their goals;

- knowing what good-quality work looks like;

- being involved in self-assessment;

- taking a role in identifying their next steps in learning;

- communicating understanding and skills facilitated by the teacher's use of open questions;

- taking part in a two-way dialogue with the teacher encouraging reflection on learning;

- being part of a classroom ethos that promotes engagement and employs learner-centred teaching.

However, as reported by Boyle and Charles (2014), research within a large national sample of primary schools showed that there is wide variety in interpretation and understanding of the term 'formative assessment'. Consequently, you will see lots of different approaches in different schools but all practitioners are focused upon supporting children in moving forward with their learning. You can learn a great deal from a variety of practice.

The 2014 curriculum

The curriculum introduced in 2014 provides a slimmed-down outline of the fundamental knowledge, skills and understanding to be taught, but gives the freedom to shape the curriculum so that it caters for pupils' needs within individual schools. The current *Ofsted School Inspection Handbook* (2015, p.48) specifies that good teachers should *plan learning that sustains pupils' interest and challenges their thinking.* In order to do this it is important to know what your pupils are interested in, and by involving them in the planning process this is easily achievable.

To discover what was happening in schools prior to the 2014 curriculum, read the Find out more . . . section at the end of the chapter.

 Reflection and discussion activity

Reflection

Trainee, look at some of the learning objectives you have seen being used; think about whether they reflect what the children did learn in that lesson, and how knowing the objectives helped to move the learning forward.

Discussion

Mentor and trainee, discuss together the success criteria for a particular lesson and consider how these have been arrived at.

Discuss the Learning Objective(s) for a particular lesson and look at the National Curriculum to see where the objectives have been drawn from.

Formative assessment in the classroom

The use of formative assessment strategies can be planned into all lessons, allowing these techniques to become embedded in your practice.

These are some formative assessment strategies you could include in your planning:

- Ensure that you have factored in time to allow the pupils to have input when possible; a 'knowledge harvest' before planning begins means that you are aware of what the pupils know and would like to know about a particular topic and can then plan with these factors in mind.

- Sharing of the learning objective ensures that pupils are all aware of the expected learning and focus on 'learning' rather than 'doing'.

- Shared success criteria, ideally developed with pupils. This should also include analysis of examples of 'good ones', possibly as compared to 'less good ones' (you will see some schools call this a WAGOLL: What a good one looks like).

- Effective questioning to be used, both to gauge prior knowledge and to check current understanding throughout the lesson; also to elicit misconceptions and this may result in you discovering the need to adapt the lesson for all, groups or individuals.

- Collaborative improvement during the lesson. This can take the form of mini-plenaries (bringing the whole class back together to review learning so far mid-lesson) which allow for modelling by the teacher or redrafting to better achieve the success criteria using an example from a pupil's work, followed by peer assessment carried out by all pupils facilitated by the example shown (this strategy is further explained later in the chapter).

- A plenary which provides time and opportunity for children to self-assess, or peer assess, against the learning objective and success criteria, then reflect on their learning and consider their next steps.

Along with the strategies above which occur at certain points before and within the lesson, feedback should happen *throughout* the lesson, with pupils being involved in self- and peer-assessment as well as adult-led assessment and feedback. All feedback, oral and written, should be directly related to the learning objectives and success criteria.

 Reflection and discussion activity

Reflection

Trainee, think about the strategies listed above. Find some real examples of these strategies.

Think about which ones you could use effectively in the next lesson you teach.

Mentor, look at an observation you have undertaken and consider how you can give focused feedback to your trainee on the strategies listed above.

Discussion

Mentor and trainee, share the outcomes of both your reflection activities and begin to forward-plan next steps for developing competency in this area.

Formative assessment techniques cannot simply be imposed upon a class of pupils to achieve instant success. For the strategies to make a positive difference, rather than just become an imposition, the learning environment has to be right.

How do I create a positive learning environment?

The learning environment is created by a wide range of elements. There are the physical aspects, such as the placement of the tables, wall displays, the arrangement of resources and the lighting. There are also the intangible aspects, including the rules, the way learning activities are organised, the sounds and the energy in the room. The teacher's attitude also affects the pupils' response to the environment they find themselves in. Having a teacher who is negative or uninterested (in either the pupils themselves or the subject matter of the lesson) is unlikely to produce a positive emotional environment, no matter how creative and artistic the appearance of the room. A good environment can be seen in pupils' involvement and reaction to the ethos of the school, and in how they conduct themselves, including their courtesy, respect and manners towards one another. It also shows in pupils' respect for the school's amenities and equipment, which includes the presentation of work in books, and their observance of any school uniform policies. A poor learning environment can be signalled by an untidy or chaotic classroom, and also by pupils' lack of engagement and persistent low-level disruption which contribute to reduced learning and progress.

Wall displays deserve a mention here: be careful what you choose to put on the wall. There is a temptation to select the 'best' work, but think about the message this gives to your pupils. Which pupils' work do you value? Is it only the higher attaining pupils' pieces, or do you recognise that some pupils have put in great amounts of effort, despite not having achieved quite the same outcome as others? If you do not demonstrate that you value everyone's efforts, then some pupils may well not try as hard the next time.

It is often a good idea to allow the pupils themselves to be in charge of creating at least one display in the classroom to ensure that they feel involved in the formation of their own learning environment. Working walls are a useful way not only to include everyone's contributions, but also to assist and promote learning. These displays are interactive, and can be used to record, support and visualise learning. They should reflect the teaching sequence and be built up over time, including good examples of work, key vocabulary, targets, success criteria, cross-curricular links and questions. These displays contribute clearly to building a vibrant and welcoming classroom climate which values learning highly.

The classroom environment contributes a central role in helping pupils to be engaged and successful in their learning. As the teacher, you can take control and adapt the environment to achieve these results. Moving the tables around to achieve a better seating plan, or even altering the lighting or the temperature can improve the effectiveness of learning in the classroom.

Clarke (2014) explains how vital it is to achieve the appropriate learning culture, which includes enabling children to develop an awareness of their own knowledge and how they learn, as well as having 'growth mindsets' (this concept, introduced by Carol Dweck (2012), is explored in detail in Chapter 7) and not being grouped by ability.

Why is a growth mindset important?

The current primary curriculum works on the principle that all pupils can achieve. If the teacher is going to succeed in enabling all the pupils in their class to achieve the necessary requirements for that year group, as set out in the curriculum documents, then it is vital that they believe this is possible for all pupils. With the exception of a small minority (around 2 per cent of children who potentially cannot achieve in line with their peers due to severe learning impairments), all pupils will be able to reach the goals set. Some pupils will need more time and opportunities for practice, may need more input and support for longer, and will definitely have to invest more effort than their peers, but given these they will succeed. A pupil whose current assessments suggest they are lagging behind in maths may well be level with, or ahead of, their year group in science or art or PE, for example. To have a growth mindset is to believe that all can achieve, that intelligence is not fixed, and to embrace a belief that there is no 'glass ceiling' preventing pupils from achieving. For example, a child who is not in line with their peers in maths this term, or this year, could catch up and exceed peers at a later stage in their maths learning journey. However, there needs to be a belief (by the teacher and the pupil) that this is possible. Labelling pupils as 'low ability' can be unhelpful and effectively gives them a golden ticket to stop trying; removing their self-belief and damaging their self-esteem so that it becomes a 'self-fulfilling prophecy'. This brings us back to the importance of establishing a growth mindset with both pupils and staff, and wherever possible, parents too. Hattie suggests that the most powerful influence on pupil achievement is their own opinion regarding their chances of success (2008, p.43). This can then become a barrier if pupils only achieve to an expectation which they have formed that is lower than their true potential. Bearing this in mind, it is easy to see how important the promotion of a growth mindset and a positive self-belief is in enabling our pupils to succeed.

 **Case study**

It appeared that Tom was not achieving as well as his peers throughout Key Stage 1. Maths was a particular area where he was underachieving, and he always worked in a group supported by a teaching assistant. He ended Year 2 well below age-related expectations (as a Level 1 on the previous system). His parents were unconcerned, stating that they 'could not do maths' and did not expect him to be any different. During Year 3, the school launched an initiative to promote a growth mindset. Tom was seen to identify himself as a 'poor learner' and during circle time spoke of how he believed that he was 'no good' at maths. When the class discussed growth mindset and the concept of how intelligence was not fixed, but developed like muscles, Tom cried and said that he had not known that he 'could make himself be cleverer' (*sic*). Over the next two years the class teacher removed ability groupings and ensured that over the course of a half term, every child had worked together. Opportunities were given for self-selection of activities and tasks, and also the long-term absence of the teaching assistant meant that Tom was no longer able to rely on adult support in maths lessons. In Year 5 Tom would choose to work with older pupils on a regular basis and was keen to challenge himself, regarding failure as an opportunity to learn. The mixed-age group class meant that he was often seen tackling Year 6 tasks. His maths SATs result was one mark away from a Level 5 (using the previous old system of levels), which placed him well above age-related expectations, but also meant that his progress since Key Stage 1 was not only the best of the cohort, but well above average nationally.

Reflection

•   Think about how you present differentiated work to children and whether you may be inadvertently putting a 'ceiling' on their learning.

Learning objectives and success criteria

Children need to know the reasons for the lesson and what is expected of them. The learning objective serves to identify this clearly. By constructing the learning objective at the planning stage, as the teacher you will have had to think through your own expectations of the learning journey you wish the pupils to take. By starting a lesson plan with a precise view of what the outcome needs to be, the planning will be more focused, the purpose of activities and tasks will be clear and, if this is clear in your own mind, then a successful outcome is much more likely. Giving the children access to your own expectations of the learning will keep the lesson focused firmly on the required learning (Briggs *et al.*, 2003, p.25).

In Chapter 4, Rebecca Geeson has explored in detail the key aspects of a successful lesson plan and there are some helpful examples of learning objectives. Learning objectives should be carefully constructed to ensure that they focus on the transferable skill. For example, setting the learning objective of 'We are learning to write a poem about snow' overlooks the fact that, by writing the poem, the pupils are learning specific poetry skills which they can then use to write poems about any given topic. The learning objective should not be context based, but must focus on what the transferable skills are that they are expected to learn in that lesson or unit of work (Clarke, 2014, p.79).

 **Case study**

Freddie had planned a lesson for his Year 3 class with the stated learning objective 'We are learning how to measure how tall we are'. All the children understood what they were expected to do and spent the lesson engaged in the activity, using various methods of measuring each other and recording their heights. Some time later, thinking of this lesson, Freddie planned another lesson for the children to go outside and measure the sunflowers they had grown, along with the goalposts, fences, walls and other objects in the playground. The children's behaviour rapidly deteriorated and Freddie knew that this could not be due to them working outside as this was a regular feature of his lessons. Gathering the children back for a mini-plenary, his open questions soon uncovered the fact that the children were not relating this activity to the lesson about measuring each other, and were very confused about what needed to be done. The learning objective was changed to 'We are learning to measure heights', and the success criteria were focused clearly on how to successfully measure heights of any objects with the children. The links were made with their previous learning and the pupils completed the lesson successfully. Later in the year, Freddie planned another lessons on measuring to allow him to assess the pupil's learning away from the point of teaching – and this demonstrated that the transferable skills required for measuring height had been acquired and retained by most pupils.

Reflection

- Ask pupils what they are learning and see if you get the response you expected.

The use of success criteria follows on from the creation of learning objectives for lessons or units of work. Having decided on the end result, the success criteria then provide a clear path from the pupil's prior learning, so current level of knowledge, skill or understanding, to where they are required to be by the end. To use a road analogy, you are guiding the pupils from point A to point B on the map and the success criteria act as signposts along the way to ensure that they take the appropriate route. The success criteria help pupils to identify when success has been achieved, or where things have gone awry, and support them in discussing ways of improving (Clarke, 2014, p.81). By providing children with examples of good (and possibly weaker) work, it is possible for them to consider the features of these and then construct their own success criteria as they analyse what is required to produce the desired outcome.

Questioning

The use of questioning in the classroom is discussed at length elsewhere in this book (see Chapter 8 by John Paramore). However, as Clarke (2014) and Hattie (2008) state, ongoing effective questioning produces the most important feedback, which is *what teachers learn from students*. The responses you get illuminate your knowledge of the pupils' understanding, thus guiding the lesson and allowing you to plan for individual needs.

In respect of assessment for learning, Dylan Wiliam places a great deal of importance upon what he terms *hinge point questions*. He discussed these in his keynote speech given at the 2007 Association for Learning Technology Conference in Nottingham, England. These questions are a diagnostic tool which provide data on your pupils' learning within the lesson and enable you to pinpoint misconceptions so they can be addressed quickly. They are questions which pupils can answer in no more than two minutes, and which the teacher can look at and interpret the responses in less than 30 seconds. Every pupil answers, usually by holding up an individual whiteboard, unless you have access to an electronic voting system which is ideal for this type of question. These questions, and the multiple choice answers, need to be planned carefully to elicit any likely misconceptions. The possible alternative answers need to help the teacher to see the problems some pupils are having with their reasoning.

 Find out more from . . . internet clips

Listen to Dylan Wiliam speak about hinge point questions here:

www.youtube.com/watch?v=Mh5SZZt207k

Accessed January 29, 2017

 Reflection and discussion activity

Reflection

Trainee, choose a lesson you are about to teach and see if you can devise a hinge point question to use. Come up with multiple choice answers which will demonstrate clearly some possible misconceptions. Check if it is possible for a pupil to get the answer correct using wrong reasoning.

Discuss the responses you got with your mentor after the lesson. Consider whether the hinge point question helped you to adapt the rest of your lesson to meet the pupils' needs.

Discussion

Trainee and mentor, discuss the thinking that a child has used to arrive at each of the following answers, and what you would do next to address their misconception.

Question: 45 + 9 =

Answers: (a) 459 (b) 56 (c) 54 (d) 5

Question: What do plants need most to survive?

Answers: (a) Light (b) Soil (c) Food (d) Water

Feedback

Throughout the literature about assessment for learning, feedback is consistently viewed as a vital element. Hattie acknowledges that, of all the influences on achievement, feedback seems to be among those that have greatest effect. There is a challenge in establishing what is precisely meant by the term feedback, and equally many types of it are to be found (2008, p.173). Hattie's findings suggest that the most powerful feedback is when it is from the pupil to the teacher, as this helps make learning 'visible'.

Feedback is defined as *a consequence of performance* (2008, p.174). Feedback given by the teacher needs to result in improvement, and if it does not, then it has been a waste of time and effort on the part of those producing it. Some types, such as the celebratory 'Well done!' and 'Good work!', give no indication to the learner as to what was good, or why they are deemed to have done well. If the feedback you are giving does not indicate what to do next to improve the work, then it serves little purpose other than to demonstrate to someone (parents or carers, line manager, headteacher, inspector) that the pupil's work has been read. Accountability means that teachers do often feel obliged to write copious amounts in books which will not have an impact on learning, but is there to just show it has been done. When marking is done well, comments will identify what has been done successfully, what needs improvement and how to go about making that improvement. Do be aware that the addition of a mark or grade has been suggested to take pupils' attention away from any comments, and in the case of lower-ability children to demotivate them (Black *et al.*, 2003, p.43).

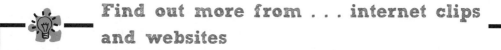

Find out more from . . . internet clips and websites

Dylan Wiliam conducted an experiment looking at the use of grades. He found out some interesting things about whether grades lead to improvements (which usually they do not) and how pupils respond to a lack

(Continued)

(Continued)

of grading (which initially they did not like). In these clips there are also examples of assessment strategies in action (in a secondary school). See his work here (this is the second episode where teachers use comments not grades):

www.youtube.com/watch?v=1iD6Zadhg4M

Accessed January 29, 2017

Remember that the key indicator that feedback has been successful is when students have responded to it and made the necessary improvements to their work. If the same mistake is being made continually and teacher comments are repeated, then this is likely to be picked up during book scrutinies and the effectiveness of feedback will, quite rightly, be called into question. Feedback must produce progress.

 Reflection and discussion activity

Reflection

Trainee, make sure that you are familiar with the school's feedback and marking policy. Consider examples of where you have seen this policy being implemented and look at these to see if you can identify improvements that have appeared as a result.

Discussion

Trainee and mentor, find and discuss some examples of feedback in books which have had a clear impact on learning. Compare these with some examples of feedback the trainee has produced and see if you can identify any ways the trainee teacher could make their feedback more effective.

You need to give your pupils opportunities to employ self-assessment and peer-assessment during lessons. Collaborative improvement is a strategy advocated by Clarke in which the use of the visualiser enables pupil's work to be displayed at any point in the lesson and improved collaboratively. Success criteria are used to provide a framework for the assessment, so your pupils can identify effective parts and explain why they are positive. Improvements can then be suggested for the work. After this modelling process, pupils can work in pairs to find good points and to make improvements. The sharing of ideas should be promoted and this co-operative feedback will produce a quality of discussion which is often absent from just swapping books (2014, p.123). The reflection on learning that this process enables is an important element of AfL: it promotes independent learning, communication and support in the classroom. This can start from the Foundation Stage where there should be an emphasis on building an open, reflective climate in which adults model appropriate language and behaviour. It should then be developed throughout the primary phase with peer- and self-assessment and evaluation, which start off as oral comments in the Foundation Stage and then extend to include written comments as pupils move up through the Key Stages. This assessment cycle enables children to reflect on what has been learned and, when appropriate, judge it against a set of criteria. Evaluation describes the process children use to gain an understanding of how they are learning. Both are equally important for your pupils' development and should be ongoing within your daily teaching.

 **Case study**

Natalie was becoming frustrated with the lack of progress her Year 5 pupils were showing with their writing skills. She spent many hours writing extensive amounts of feedback into their books, but it was apparent that little improvement was resulting from it. Her school provided her with a visualiser and explained the concept of collaborative improvement. She showed the class examples of writing that had been produced by a previous Year 5 class and asked them to identify the good points. They constructed a list of success criteria and the class began to draft their own work. At various points during this process, Natalie selected a pupil through her random 'lollipop stick' system (This is where all pupils' names are on lollipop sticks and the teacher pulls out names to respond to questions) and together the class assessed the work so far. As it was clear to the pupils that this was a draft, they were happy to share ideas and accept suggestions for improvement. These were marked on the work using the interactive whiteboard and then copies were printed off and circulated around the room for reference. Good parts were highlighted in pink and points to redraft were highlighted in green. The pupils then worked in pairs to replicate the process themselves. Although initially the improvement in the standard of writing was quite limited, Natalie persevered until the way of working was embedded and the pupils would actively request an 'improvement stop'. The feedback became very precisely related to the success criteria and the standard of writing rose rapidly across the entire class. Natalie reduced her own marking to specifically commenting on the criteria, to suggest an improvement and to model an example of what she required. Time was then put aside each week when the pupils would respond to the marking and demonstrate the required improvement.

Reflection

- Consider whether your marking is related to the success criteria of your lesson, and whether you are giving your pupils time to read and respond to any marking you do.

What have we found out?

In conclusion, you have seen that you need to collect information at the start, at the end, and throughout the lesson. Opportunities to discover misconceptions need to be planned for and you need to have a range of options ready to rectify these. The information must be used to enable you to adapt lessons and decide how best to cater for your pupils' learning needs. If there are problems – and pupils are not making the expected progress – explaining it all again, but louder, may not be the best solution Alternative strategies could include the provision of more examples, giving concrete apparatus, if appropriate, giving opportunities for reteaching another child, asking for an explanation of their thinking or giving more time for practice. To be effective you need to structure your lessons to incorporate all the key elements of the assessment cycle that we have discussed in this chapter. With the framework of formative assessment in place, including the use of learning objectives and success criteria, which are fully understood along with feedback directly related to these, delivered in a suitable learning environment, you should find that positive outcomes are accessible for all of your pupils.

 Find out more from . . . history

What was happening prior to 2014/15?

So that you can contextualise the current situation and know a bit about what is most likely being referred to in staffrooms around the country, it is useful for you to be aware of what has happened in schools over recent years, with all the changes which your mentor and other school staff you will be working with have seen. Since the introduction of the new National Curriculum in September 2014, there has been removal of the National Curriculum levels. Previously, pupils were assessed against a set of standards, which placed them at a point within these levels (commonly 1–5 in primary schools), which were further subdivided into sub levels of a, b and c (for example 2a, 2b, 2c). There was also a points system which ran alongside the sub levels (the Average Point Score (APS)) with each sub-level having 2 points attributed, to allow a very fine analysis of progress to be made. Children were expected to achieve at least Level 2 by the end of Key Stage 1 and at least Level 4 by the end of Key Stage 2. Progress, as well as attainment, was tracked as it is now. Initially, any grade of Level 2 to any Level 4 was deemed sufficient, but as progress began to be focused on more closely, particularly by Ofsted, a child achieving a Level 2b by the end of Key Stage 1 would have to achieve a 4b to have made satisfactory progress. Subsequently, this was raised so that the expectation became that 2b would have to convert to 4a to be seen as good progress. This continued in the same manner with the result that schools were placed under constantly increasing pressure to race children up through the levels to achieve ever more highly. The consequence of this approach was that children could be moving on to cover the requirements of the next sub level with only a tenuous grasp on what they had previously learned.

What happens now?

In response to this moving through the levels and superficial learning, levels were removed. The emphasis now is on children achieving mastery of the given set of requirements for the year group they are in and achieving 'age-related expectations'. Ashley Compton explores Mastery in Chapter 7, with a particular emphasis upon mathematics. However, a key aspect is that pupils need to be given time to learn to apply the knowledge and skills they have learned and so achieve a deep level of learning, with the idea being that having experienced this deep learning (or mastery) they will then retain this as they move on through their school career.

References

Black, P and Wiliam, D (1998) *Inside the Black Box: Raising standards through classroom assessment*. London: School of Education, King's College London.

Black, P, Harrison, C, Lee, C, Marshall, B, Wiliam, D, and Press, OU (2003) *Assessment for Learning: Putting it into practice*. Maidenhead: Open University Press.

Boyle, B and Charles, M (2014) *Formative Assessment for Teaching and Learning*. Los Angeles, CA: SAGE Publications.

Briggs, MS, Woodfield, A, Martin, CD and Swatton, PJ (2003) *Assessment for Learning and Teaching in Primary Schools: Meeting the professional standards framework for QTS (Achieving QTS)*. Exeter: Learning Matters.

Clarke, S (2014) *Outstanding Formative Assessment: Culture and practice*. London: Hodder Education.

Clarke, S and Hattie, J (2001) *Unlocking Formative Assessment: Practical strategies for enhancing pupils' learning in the primary classroom*. London: Hodder & Stoughton Educational.

Dweck, CS (2012) *Mindset*. London: Robinson.

Faragher, S (2014) *Understanding Assessment in Primary education*. London: SAGE Publications.

Harlen, W and Harlen, PW (2007) *Assessment of Learning*. London: SAGE Publications.

Hattie, JAC (2008) *Visible Learning: A synthesis of over 800 meta-analyses relating to achievement*. London: Routledge.

Ofsted (2015) *School Inspection Handbook*. Available at: **www.gov.uk/government/publications/school-inspection-handbook-from-september-2015** (accessed January 29, 2017).

Wiliam, D (2007*) Assessment, Learning and Technology: Prospects at the periphery of control*. Available at: **www.alt.ac.uk/sites/default/files/assets_editor_uploads/documents/altc2007_dylan_wiliam_keynote_transcript.pdf** (accessed January 29, 2017).

6

Approaches for engagement

Andrew Dickenson

This chapter will

- introduce you to some approaches that you may consider using to engage pupils, with practical ideas for your class;
- discuss four approaches for developing opportunities for engagement;
- support you in examining which elements of the approaches you may wish to incorporate into your own practice;
- reflect upon the characteristics of each approach.

Introduction: what approaches can be used to support the learning of pupils?

Ideas change over time and teachers implement approaches to learning in different ways for their pupils. Sometimes certain approaches (such as a topic-based approach) are seen in schools, or a specific theme that takes its lead from a National Curriculum subject (such as Space, or Victorian times). Within this chapter, I shall discuss some specific curriculum approaches: a cross-curricular approach, immersive learning, an enquiry-based approach and Forest Schools. However, in schools, you may see other approaches such as the International Primary Curriculum (topic), Mantle of the Expert (role play), Take One Picture, Montessori philosophy (play based) and active learning, to name a few.

Consider the lessons you deliver. What is it about them that engages the pupils? Is it the lesson structure? Is it the opening presentation, a 'hook' into learning or the range of resources you have developed? Usually within a lesson, there are many factors that contribute to the engagement, or disengagement, of your pupils.

Having a range of engagement tools in your armoury is very useful to ensure that pupils are fully engaged in the learning experience, and are given opportunities to construct their own understanding. As an initial introduction to this chapter, I shall set out some very practical ways you can engage pupils well.

- **Practical activity**

  Pupils gain a range of experiences through practical enrichment of lessons. For example, in a topic about the Romans, pupils could construct their own full-scale Roman soldier shields in DT and art lessons, and then use these outside the classroom to re-enact the battle formation of the tortoise. If you are really adventurous (and your mentor agrees), water balloons can be thrown to develop further experiences of being in battle that the pupils can talk and write about. By taking an approach like this, the children have opportunities to explore their feelings and develop empathy.

- **Pupil investigation**

  Pupils can become more competent in beginning their own investigations if you give them the tools and opportunities to develop these skills. A positive way to develop independence in investigation is to use technology to enable pupils to follow a specific line of enquiry, or for them to construct their own response to an investigative question. However, support younger pupils by having some suggested sites and build older pupils' understanding of reading sources critically through specific skills-based lessons.

- **Pupils generating their own questions and responding to peers**

  Allowing pupils to discuss what they have discovered, throughout a lesson, will often lead to discovery of the most relevant questions being asked by the pupils, unprompted and sometimes without your involvement. A way to capture these questions is to use a 'Post-It' wall, where pupils add questions, and can also add the answers as they discover new knowledge. This develops an excellent peer-support approach and continues to develop curiosity in learning as well as to build independence. For example, if a pupil asks if a scorpion is an insect or an arachnid, others should be given the opportunity to respond and prove their answer is correct. The pupils will begin to create ideas and scaffold knowledge for each other based on evidence from their own investigations or observations.

 Reflection and discussion activity

Reflection

Trainee, in the next part of the chapter we are going to consider some different approaches to engagement. Think about what you have seen in school so far in terms of pupil engagement.

Consider the different environments learning takes place in (outside, classroom including role play areas, or classrooms completely transformed for a topic or a 'wow' experience).

Think about how the teacher structured the learning (setting a question to investigate, creating role-play experiences, etc.).

Mentor, think about the different approaches you tend to use in your classroom and consider why you take this particular approach (it may be a school or team decision). How can you support your trainee in understanding that there are different approaches and developing critical thought about the range of approaches? Are you able to source some different opportunities for your trainee (and you) in partner schools?

Discussion

Trainee and mentor, talk together about the approaches you have been reflecting upon. If possible, make time to observe other approaches together in colleagues' classrooms and talk about how these approaches enable learning, independence and resilience in learners.

The next part of the chapter will start to introduce you to some very specific ways that some schools organise their curriculum. I will start with a common, and well-established, approach in a topic-based curriculum, and will conclude this section by presenting a less well-known approach called immersive learning.

Topic- or theme-based approach

Adopting a topic- or theme-based curriculum is very much about finding concrete links between discrete subjects based around a specific topic or common theme. It can seem a bit overwhelming if you are starting from the very beginning of planning and resourcing lessons for a topic, as this can take a lot of work. However, it is also extremely rewarding and gives opportunities for you to be creative. Working within teams of colleagues can also help to share the workload and build the enthusiasm for a topic.

A topic or themed approach can be very child-centred and if you know the pupils in your class well, then elements of the topic can be linked to their interests, meaning they are more likely to be motivated and engaged.

 **Case study**

Here is an example of how one teacher developed their topic:

Helen had a topic to prepare for: it was Superheroes! As a starting point, she set the room out so there was a heroes' cave, arch villain's lair and a cityscape. As soon as the children entered the room they were excited to see the new additions and were curious to know how these would be integrated into their learning. Helen was able to link many subjects easily, for example, writing and art. In maths, the pupils were building up their skills to take measurements of the characters. However, Helen made sure that she taught explicit skills first, in using different measurements, calculating time and distance. It was only once these aspects were secure that Helen applied the knowledge in a topic context.

(Continued)

(Continued)

There were also opportunities for the arts: creating costumes and developing role play. The pupils also created artwork based on that of Roy Lichtenstein, looked at superheroes from legends or from around the world, and even their gymnastics techniques were framed as superhero training.

In the case study above, Helen had thought carefully about how she could link several subjects to the topics. However, she recognised that some lessons would need to be discrete. Make sure that you are building skills and knowledge so that pupils are able to apply their learning appropriately. Do not shoehorn the topic in to everything you do, if it is not appropriate.

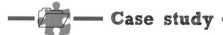 **Case study**

Another example of a themed approach is the use of children's books as the starting theme for a range of activities and lessons. A school in Cleethorpes, North Lincolnshire, used Roald Dahl's *The BFG* as its theme, linking the giant to maths/DT by measuring ingredients and cooking food from the book, comparing the heights of the giants to areas around the school, writing letters to the Queen, researching where legends of giants exist around the world and discussing the role of good and evil, linked to SMSC.

 Find out more from . . . websites

Find out more about the International Primary Curriculum, which uses theme-based learning, from this website:

www.greatlearning.com/ipc/

Accessed January 29, 2017

Reflection and discussion activity

Reflection

Trainee, consider the planning that you have seen in school. Is there any element of this that may be a themed/topic-based approach? Have you been able to see concrete links between curriculum area that would allow you to build a common theme?

Mentor, if you use a topic-based approach to teaching, what successes can you share with the trainee? Is there long-/medium-term planning available that would allow the trainee to see how themes can develop purposeful learning? If you use another approach to planning and delivering the curriculum, discuss how themes can scaffold learning.

Discussion

Trainee and mentor, now compare what you have seen. Discuss how themes can help learning from one subject to support another, provide scaffolding from prior learning to new learning, and inspire pupils to extend their development away from the classroom.

Immersive learning

Immersive learning is an approach that you may have seen in different intensities, from schools that adopt this approach fully to others that have experience weeks or days. There are several definitions explaining what immersive learning is. According to Gartner (2012), immersive learning environments can be *learning situations that are constructed using a variety of techniques and software tools, including game-based learning, simulation-based learning and virtual 3D worlds* (2012, p.1). Within a dedicated classroom, at a school located in Lincolnshire, pupils use one such multimedia environment to allow them to visit rainforests, travel around our solar system and engage with a storyteller to look at the story of Jack and the Beanstalk from the giant's perspective. This school links the immersion to 'adult world' or 'real world' through projects, as they consider purposeful learning that is connected to outside the classroom, and as a technique for involving adults at home.

The other main definition for immersive learning stems from the less technologically based use of the classroom. Here the walls and floor space are decorated and utilised to create an environment where the pupils become immersed in the theme in a much more theatrical way, almost becoming actors on the stage of their own learning. Within the context of this style of learning, there is often removal or moving of tables and chairs: the pupils choose their own learning space and work to produce the objectives of the lesson in a variety of ways, whether on tablets, on paper, in books or as a collaborative piece.

When considering the use of an immersive approach to teaching and learning, there are several aspects which need to be thought through. First, adopting the immersive learning approach fully will usually be a whole-school decision, especially as it is quite heavily reliant upon resources. As a space, your classroom should be set out so that the pupils can find areas to contemplate and work. The spaces for learning also need to have a firm link to the topic or theme. This may sound similar to the topic-based approach, but with immersive learning the entire room is transformed (not just areas for role play) to re-create as realistic an experience as possible.

The learning spaces are specifically designed so that the pupils become part of the experience and in some cases the teacher assumes a role that encompasses the theme. A successful immersive space should allow pupils to engage fully in the topic they are learning. Where success has been evident, environments have been created so that classrooms have become pirate ships, oceans and factories where props are available to add to the overall reality of the immersion. Immersive learning spaces help establish a realm of cross-curricular learning opportunities and support the progress of pupils' spoken language, reading and writing.

Here is an example of what you might do when considering a theme for immersive learning. Starting with the theme of Space, the class can be divided into groups that focus on travel, landing/surface, planets and moons. Rockets, lunar landers, rovers, launch pads, planets' surfaces and dark space are specific items that spring to mind for this topic. Remember, some items can be purchased for easy inclusion, whereas some will need to be constructed. In immersive learning, having the resources is important.

 **Case study**

Charlotte is using a book *The Lighthouse Keeper's Lunch*, by Rhonda and David Armitage, as the focus for her learning this term. This provides an idea for an immersive learning environment. Charlotte creates a display with the lighthouse on one side of the class and a string running to another wall, so that items can be sent to the keeper. She also creates areas to work in, building two boats and creating a sea and rocks area to sit on, as well as having gulls hanging from the ceiling.

She notices that the children in her Year 1 class are more engaged during the lessons, as she delivers each curriculum area by using the classroom environment and the book as the stimulus. The pupils discuss elements of the book with ease, pointing to the parts of the book they can see around them and are happy to answer questions linked to the curriculum and the illustrations. They see the environment as somewhere to engage. Although the pupils see that learning is fun, Charlotte reminds them that they are learning together. Questions and planning relates to the book and directs the pupils to where they need to sit (some in the boats, others on the rocks).

 Reflection and discussion activity

Reflection

Trainee, consider the classroom you are working in and the current theme/topic that the class is studying. What elements of the topic could be used to create an immersive learning environment? How could you then link these to planning exciting lessons to involve the pupils in using these resources? What adjustments to planning would allow for the immersive style of engagement to be used?

Mentor, think about your current topic. How could you utilise immersive learning to create a classroom setting that allows for the pupils to become completely 'immersed' in the theme? How would this impact planning and teaching?

Discussion

Trainee and mentor, now discuss and compare your ideas. Start by comparing those elements that are similar and that could form the basis for a more immersive nature to the room. What resources would need to be created, to be able to integrate the immersion? Do your ideas have a common theme? What approaches to teaching and learning would need to be considered to enable immersive learning to take place? What adjustments to planning would allow for the immersive style of engagement to be used? Is there a theme/topic in the future that could lend itself to an immersive approach?

Enquiry-based learning

This is an approach where pupils analyse evidence in order to form and test hypotheses, which may use a teacher-guided enquiry method. Here, the teacher facilitates the learning by guiding the pupils to discover the answer to questions that the pupils may have raised, based on what they already know and what they want to find out more about. For this approach, the lesson can begin with an investigation, a starting point activity or demonstration that can provide inspiration and inspire curiosity, so that the children want to learn more. This could also provoke questions from the pupils. As a class, or within small groups, the pupils (possibly along with the teacher) create a question to investigate and start designing a method to answer that question. In most instances, the initial ideas are created with teacher guidance, before narrowing down the areas to one specific focus. This can save time and add a more directed focus to the overarching theme of the lesson. There is a distinct difference between investigation and enquiry. With investigation, the teacher's questions, or the learning objective for the lesson, directs pupils from a starting point towards acquiring the knowledge necessary to find a result: the teacher leads the pupils along a pathway and uses a series of specific prompts to facilitate the 'correct' answer. Within an enquiry-based learning environment, the pupils create their own questions, such as 'How did the Romans arrive in Britain?' or 'Where does soil come from?'. They will use a series of personal observations or conjectures to formulate a response. In such cases the pupils become, what Vygotsky would call, *the more knowledgeable other*, sharing what they have already gathered as evidence with others. The website, **learning-theories.com**, crediting the work of Vygotsky, states that *The more knowledgeable other is someone or something who is perceived to have better skill or understanding of a task, process, or concept.*

 **Case study**

When studying the Egyptians, Daniel's Year 4 class were asked to think what they wanted to know more about. He shared stimuli: pictures of the pyramids, farming along the Nile, a map of Egypt and hieroglyphs. He asked the children what they already knew and what they wanted to find out more about. One group wanted to know how the stones for the pyramids were moved into place. They were able to look at modern construction techniques, selecting resources to find out how the pyramids may have been built today. Once this had been presented to the class to show what each group had learned, Daniel moved his class on to discovering how archaeologists consider the stones were moved and they were given materials, such as broom handles, rope, string, wool and textiles. Working in small groups, the pupils were asked to move a brick across a sandpit. Throughout, the group were reminded to write questions that they needed to consider, placing these on 'Post-It' notes in a journal and some recording these on an iPad, using Book Creator, to document their progress. They were asked to test a wide variety of materials and then find a solution to the original question 'How might the Egyptians have moved large blocks of stone to build the pyramids?'

As with the case study above, a teacher may choose a theme or aspect of a subject that is pertinent to the lesson they are teaching, or link to a previous session so that the pupils are actively building on their prior learning. The students need to be engaged in the enquiry, so they will need to be provided with a range of information that enables them to form an initial hypothesis. They should be able to select from a range of resources, documents and other sources that offer different viewpoints and evidence: these will then support the investigation of the enquiry question.

Some other examples of how you could create a starting point for an enquiry-based approach include:

- introducing a topic with basic information, told as an exciting, vividly explained account – e.g. a letter from a sailor on Christopher Columbus's ship;

- using a thrilling video clip;

- using a breath-taking image to inspire curiosity to find out more;

- showing a photo from the Hubble Telescope and then asking 'What do you think might be in space?' or 'What do you already know about . . . What else would you like to find out?'

Pupils should be encouraged to share all their thoughts, so that these can be narrowed as they begin to narrow the question to something they can inquire about. By eliciting pupils' initial ideas as a class, asking them to share their first tentative questions and ideas, they begin to formulate plans to help them answer the inquiry question and to think about what resources they may need to do this. After the pupils have been presented with evidence to sift through, they can be given opportunities to analyse evidence, and time needs to be allocated to allow enquiries to be revised.

It may be beneficial to use elements of immersive learning alongside this enquiry approach, for example by utilising a police incident room, placing 'Post-It' notes on a board where hypotheses can be shared and then discussed later. Creating an element of detection can instil a greater focus for the pupils. If they could act as 'reflective detectives' (this is where discussion of progress between peers takes place, feedback is given and pupils are given an opportunity to act on this) the pupils should be able to ask for the opinions of others, and assess the strengths and areas to develop in their own work, and provide feedback that supports their peers.

 Find out more from . . . websites

In this website, you will see some of John Hattie's work on visible learning and the place of feedback:

http://visible-learning.org/2013/10/john-hattie-article-about-feedback-in-schools/

Accessed January 29, 2017

So, what benefits are there from an enquiry-based approach?

As a starting point, the pupils begin (sometimes with support) to reflect on and take responsibility for their own learning. In many cases the use of an enquiry model helps to build resilience and persistence: where the ability to formulate and ask their own questions to clarify and confirm the accuracy of their understandings helps to deepen the level of understanding. Pupils also begin to use higher-order thinking skills (see John Paramore's exploration of higher order questions in Chapter 8) to solve problems and make judgements about their own work and that of others; they learn about alternative models or points of view, as well as begin to understand the importance of unbiased evidence when building reasoned arguments and viewpoints.

Find out more from . . . websites

Learn more about higher order thinking skills through Bloom's (revised) taxonomy:

https://cft.vanderbilt.edu/guides-sub-pages/blooms-taxonomy/

Accessed January 29, 2017

When enquiry-based learning is used in the classroom, students may demonstrate different behaviours in how they approach the task in hand. Pupils may enjoy the process of posing their own questions and exhibit a new-found focus on independent learning. In science, the pupils may show an interest and use their imagination in the subject of the lesson when asked to act as scientists, as researchers or investigators. Again, with a link to immersive learning, some settings provide white coats and safety glasses to create a laboratory for learning. As a teacher, using this approach to learning, you aim to ensure that the pupils connect new knowledge to prior learning in assembling a reasonable answer to their original question, from all the evidence that they have accumulated over the lesson(s). You will also encourage in the pupils a greater confidence in their learning, to take risks and try things out, make and learn from mistakes, and persevere. Furthermore, the pupils can also make decisions as to how to communicate their answer and the process of their pathway in response to the original question.

Case study

The following is taken from work by Hart (2016):

I painted my first lab coat and wore it into the lab. My students were enthralled. It wasn't long before each brought in Dad's over-sized shirts and began painting their learning on them using fabric paints. We wore our lab coats outside the classroom, through the building, and back from lunch. Along the way, everyone stopped my students to ask them about their lab coats. As they discussed their work, I realised they were

(Continued)

(Continued)

giving other students and teachers a quick review of the science content I had hoped they had learned. The lab coats became a powerful visual tool for our science program.

www.plt.org/educator-tips/lab-coats-paint-a-thousand-words

Accessed January 29, 2017

Enquiry-based learning can be used in specific lessons that lend themselves to incorporating the elements of this style of learning. However, it is unfair to ask learners both to understand new material and instantaneously apply it to a particular problem. Kirschner *et al.* (2004) suggest that enquiry-based learning can prevent learning and that minimally guided learning does not enhance student achievement, comparing the style as having the same effect as *throwing a non-swimmer out of a boat in the middle of a lake* to support learning to swim (p.4). This is why you need to support learners in building their confidence in using an enquiry-based approach, and teach them the skills associated.

 Reflection and discussion activity

Reflection

Trainee, think about how you would encourage the pupils in your class to be more independent discoverers of knowledge. How could you begin a lesson with a stimulus and then feel confident that the pupils will begin their enquiry?

Mentor, consider a lesson where an enquiry-based approach engaged the pupils. How might the trainee develop a lesson plan so that they are confident to deliver in this way?

Discussion

Trainee and mentor, discuss your answers. Consider planning a session together to examine how enquiry-based learning can be used. Once the lesson has taken place, analyse it and see how this lesson faired against a more directly teacher-led session. What were the responses? What progress was made? What positives/negatives did you see?

 Find out more from . . . websites

For further information about this approach, see these websites:

www.edutopia.org/practice/inquiry-based-learning-teacher-guided-student-driven

www.inquiringmind.co.nz/FinalResearchReportJMK.pdf

Both accessed January 29, 2017

Forest schools

It may seem odd that a school would have uncaged fires, make pupils use outdoor toilets, openly encourage pupils to experiment with tools, and hold lessons outside in all weathers. I remember a head teacher who told the staff 'There is no such thing as wrong weather, just wrong clothes' and it seems that this is something forest schools fully believe. The ethos of forest schools has spread across the UK over the last few years: maintaining a focus on using all the senses, embracing the outdoors, and a philosophy of child-led learning where discovery and learning go hand in hand. It may seem to the untrained eye that with pupils examining insects with awe and wonder, through magnifying glasses or sitting in treehouses or tents to read and complete work, that this is nothing more than disorganised play. However, the seminal author Vygotsky (1978) put the child at the centre of his own experiences and learning. The importance was that when pupils experience the world around them, with appropriate levels of support, they explore without preconceptions and directions: the teacher's input is a vague starting point but the learning develops as the pupils discover through the use of the world around them and through the use of the natural environment.

The forest schools' philosophy states that pupils should be encouraged to take more risks, be more active and have more independence in their learning. Pupils are encouraged to think outside the norm, use their imagination and develop hypothesis through discovery. It also focuses on the emotional, social and developmental benefits of education. The use of nature encourages the pupils to better understand the world around them and have a greener approach to life. To fully embrace the forest school approach, teachers are asked to minimise the use of technology, so the natural world drives the learning and pupils look through their own eyes, rather than through a screen. A key phrase of the forest school mantra is 'positive outdoor experiences', where pupils are free to experience learning within a 'safe' outdoor classroom. This is important. Even if the setting seems to flow in a very natural manner, the areas for learning are prepared so that injuries can be minimised (remember: for all outdoor learning environments, to be safe for the pupils, a risk assessment should be completed as an important part of planning the lesson).

Research shows that there is a direct link between forest schools and creativity. Fjørtoft (2005) found that natural surroundings of forest schools are pivotal in increasing the cognitive development of pupils who participate in creative and inventive play. The link between Early Years learning and forest schools is incredibly strong, linking with fine and gross motor skills. Fine motor skills are small movements, such as picking up small objects, holding a pen or crayon and using scissors. These use small muscles of the fingers, toes, wrists, lips and tongue. Gross motor skills are the bigger movements which use the large muscles in the arms, legs, torso and feet, and are actions such as sitting, standing and throwing a ball. The links are also seen in independent and group play, as well as social interaction: all elements of the developmental stages that can be enhanced by learning in an outdoor environment. As later key stages see the benefits of the physical nature of forest schools, they also see the enhanced opportunities of outdoor classrooms, providing overt links to the world outside the familiar four walls.

The biggest issue with the forest schools' approach is the lack of natural space available to some schools or where an urban environment lacks flora and fauna which impacts on the ability to utilise these to assist in learning opportunities. Here, many schools create a 'nature zone', usually linked to a pond,or they make use of local parks, so that pupils can experience the natural world and its learning possibilities. I have seen spaces in urban environments that use large raised beds which contain trees, dustbins, buckets and recycled lorry/tractor tyres as the method for growing plants within the school confines. With this idea, the pupils plant seeds, learn to look after plants and reap the benefit of observing elements of nature close at hand. There is also the use of bird/bat boxes and items that encourage or attract insects of all varieties.

 Reflection and discussion activity

Reflection

Trainee, are there any lessons that you have observed being taught in an outdoor setting? What did you see that could be added to your own practice? Is there a lesson you have delivered that could equally be at home outdoors as in? What could you have altered to allow you to do this? Where in the school grounds could a forest school approach be put into practice?

Mentor, can you think of lessons you have delivered and that the trainee observed which have used an element of outdoor learning (other than sports). Consider how the pupils reacted to the natural environment. What impact did the outdoor classroom have in the lesson? Is there anywhere within the school grounds that would allow contact with nature to impact learning in a positive way?

Discussion

Trainee and mentor, discuss the use of a forest schools' approach to learning and how it could be used during an upcoming series of lessons. Examine the short-term plans and then design a set of lessons that utilise the forest schools' ethos, within the school surroundings. What areas could you use? What outcomes would you expect to achieve?

 Chapter summary

Some of the approaches presented in this chapter may require a mind shift, or at least the willingness to try new and different ways of teaching and learning. The design of the classroom – if learning takes place within the classroom – as well as the way you plan experiences for learning, may require a major change from what you have been doing, or from what you understand a lesson to look like (perhaps from your own education). Of course, at the centre of any approach has to be the progress of the children and for those schools who have adopted a particular approach, they will have looked closely at and considered carefully their curriculum and pedagogy. With some of these approaches where it is a little more difficult to quickly measure progress (such as the immersive learning approach) some academics argue that there is the potential for children to fall behind, and that this may not be evident to the teacher quickly enough. This is why you need to think carefully about how you will ensure that you are able to continue to be accountable for the progress of children in your classroom, while making learning engaging, stimulating and fun.

A final example of how to support children in developing independence was evident in my own development of roles within a topic I was leading. The topic was Earth in Space, and it provides an example of where immersion and inquiry can be used together to engage and promote autonomous learning. I used a simple technique of printed stickers for each child with specific tasks/roles within the class to reinforce the roles we are all taking, and the responsibility of that role. Here are the roles, which you are welcome to replicate.

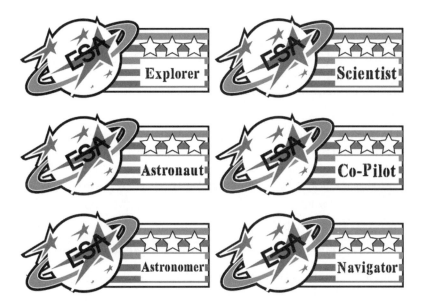

Figure 6.1 Sticker designs for science lessons

Providing specific roles focuses the pupils on their task and it also provides knowledge growth. As the pupils become more proficient, they are able to transfer skills across from other subjects.

 Discussion activity

Trainee and mentor, discuss a topic that can utilise any of the different approaches: combinations of two or mix of all.

Then consider:

How could you create an immersive learning environment to match the topic and tasks that will take place? Are costumes available? What equipment do you need to gather to make the space effective? How will you arrange the furniture? How will you plan to reflect the immersive learning experience?

(Continued)

(Continued)

If you are considering enquiry, what stimulus can you use at the beginning of lessons so that the pupils will make progress during the whole topic? What links to learning can the pupils make? How will you differentiate to ensure all pupils make progress?

If the forest schools' approach is the one you would prefer, how does the outdoor learning environment impact on the expected outcomes? What is the benefit to the progress of the pupils by taking them into an outdoor classroom? What resources will you need, how will the pupils record their progress and how will you ensure that the expected results can be recorded?

Within this chapter you have examined a few of the different ways to engage pupils by looking at specific approaches. Not all pupils learn in the same way and so, having a variety of approaches is a good way to build your own resource. Each of the approaches shown are adaptable, to suit the needs of the topic, lesson and pupils. Plan carefully to begin utilising the techniques and above all, enjoy discovering alongside your class.

References

Armitage, R and Armitage, D (2014) *The Lighthouse Keeper's Lunch*. London: Scholastic.

Dahl, R. (2016) *The BFG*. London: Penguin Books.

Fjørtoft, I (2005) Landscape as playscape: the effects of natural environments on children's play and motor development. *Children, Youth and Environments*, 14(2).

Gartner (2012, July 31) Immersive learning environments (ILEs): Gartner IT glossary (*All Definitions*). Available at: **www.gartner.com/it-glossary/immersive-learning-environments-iles/** (accessed November 12, 2016).

Hart, R (2016) Lab coats paint a thousand words: Elementary (3–5). Available at: **www.plt.org/educator-tips/lab-coats-paint-a-thousand-words/** (accessed December 1, 2016).

Kirschner, PA, Sweller, J and Clark, RE (2004). Why minimal guidance during instruction does not work: an analysis of the failure of Constructivist, discovery, problem-based, experiential, and inquiry-based teaching. *Educational Psychologist*, 41(2): 75–86.

Vygotsky (1978) In Wyse, D, Davis, R and Jones, P (eds) (2015). *Exploring Education and Childhood: From current certainties to new visions*. London: Taylor & Francis.

7
Mastery
Dr Ashley Compton

 This chapter will

- provide definitions of mastery;
- explore how to ensure that all pupils can achieve;
- demonstrate how using representations can help to develop deep understanding for pupils;
- introduce you to 'intelligent practice';
- share ideas for differentiation and intervention.

Introduction

In this chapter you will learn more about the principles of mastery and how this approach can be managed in the classroom. Although mastery as a teaching approach has existed for many years, a renewed emphasis has been placed upon this approach to learning. This approach links with the intended application of the National Curriculum that all should have the opportunity to master skills and knowledge to ensure depth of understanding, and that learning is embedded rather than rushing on to the next objective. This has serious implications for ideas about ability and differentiation. The influence of Singapore maths and Mathematics mastery is particularly evident in primary schools and, this chapter aims to explore the benefits and challenges of this.

What is mastery?

Mastery is not a new concept. Around 50 years ago, Bloom (1968) was promoting the concept of mastery learning and researching the different conditions in which this would work. This approach spread in the

United States and beyond during the following decades, although it was not tightly defined. In the 1970s, Bloom tried to synthesise the various definitions:

> *There are many versions of mastery learning in existence at present. All begin with the notion that most students can attain a high level of learning capability if instruction is approached sensitively and systematically, if students are helped when and where they have learning difficulties, if they are given sufficient time to achieve mastery, and if there is some clear criterion of what constitutes mastery.*

(Bloom, 1976, p.4)

Bloom (1968, 1976) noted that mastery learning required a change in thinking for both teachers and students: you need to believe that the vast majority of students can achieve mastery rather than thinking that only some of the pupils will achieve, and that some pupils will never achieve. He felt that aptitude for a subject was not about whether a student could learn something but about how long it would take them. Thus, students with a high aptitude for a subject would learn quickly. These are the students who are now referred to sometimes as 'fast graspers'. Bloom (1976) compared the process of mastery learning to working with a personal tutor who would respond to your individual needs, adapting the teaching as necessary and allowing you the time you need to learn. Unfortunately, this is hard to do in a school situation where one teacher has to cater for the individual needs of 30 pupils in the class during the lesson time allocated. In order to respond to the individual needs of the pupils and achieve mastery, Bloom (1968, 1976) said you need to:

- have focused objectives with clearly defined outcomes;

- be aware of the prerequisite knowledge and skills for the new learning;

- have frequent formative assessments to check progress in learning;

- be prepared to adapt teaching in response to the formative assessments:
    - by providing alternative explanations
    - more concrete illustrations
    - additional examples
    - varying the degree of independent versus highly structured learning
    - altering the type and quantity of positive reinforcement
    - finding more motivating contexts.

When the formative assessments show that the pupils are ready, you then undertake a summative assessment as a final check. These are usually written tests (for subjects like mathematics and history) but could also be physical tasks (for subjects like PE and art). Bloom (1968) suggested that the formative and summative results be described as mastery or non-mastery rather than being given grades such as A or C. Those who had not achieved mastery would get feedback that provided specific advice on what aspects still needed to be addressed and how to achieve these, while those who had already achieved mastery would be given enrichment activities. It is perhaps significant that Bloom talked about mastery learning rather than mastery teaching. In addition to the teaching strategies outlined above, Bloom emphasised the importance of the student's willingness to learn and respond to feedback and perseverance in overcoming difficulties.

England has seen a renewed interest in mastery teaching following international comparisons with areas like Singapore and Shanghai, which ranked highly in mathematics and science in the 2009 PISA tests. NCSL (2013) organised a research trip for UK teachers to Shanghai and Ningbo, China to study how they taught mathematics and science. Some aspects they discovered were about conditions for teachers: less curriculum content; subject specialist teachers were used for mathematics and science; all teachers took part in Teaching Research Groups and observed other teachers to learn from each other; and teachers spent only about 25 to 30 per cent of their time with the class, allowing them ample time for planning, assessing and providing individual support. About 20 per cent of the pupils got this individual support, which took place at lunchtime, after school or during planned intervention time. During the lessons there was a mastery approach with teacher explanations, class and group discussions, and individual practice, where all pupils did the same activities using national textbooks. Although there was evidence of over-learning, through repetition of the same concept, the delegates did not see the rote approach they had expected. Instead, they found an emphasis on pupils explaining their thinking rather than just giving answers.

Concepts were developed through the use of manipulatives, alongside informal and formal written methods. Oral rehearsal was practised as a whole class, in pairs and as individuals. Practical resources were used such as stick bundles to support the development of division calculations, reinforcing the understanding behind calculations and written recordings. Pupils were routinely expected to share their work with the class, articulate their understanding clearly and respond to questions and comments from their peers. This approach seems to lead to deep learning.

(NCSL, 2013, p.21)

Skemp (1976) presented two approaches to mathematics: instrumental understanding, which is following rules to answer questions; and relational understanding, which is understanding why these rules work. The learning witnessed in the Shanghai schools was relational, with pupils explaining their thinking. This type of understanding is required by the three aims for mathematics in the National Curriculum for England (DfE, 2013). The first aim refers to fluency with mathematics with developing conceptual understanding, while the second aim is about reasoning. The inclusion of non-routine problems in the third aim also requires relational rather than just instrumental understanding.

The National Curriculum does not use the term mastery but this is implied:

The expectation is that the majority of pupils will move through the programmes of study at broadly the same pace. *However, decisions about when to progress should always be* based on the security of pupils' understanding *and their readiness to progress to the next stage. Pupils who* grasp concepts rapidly should be challenged through being offered rich and sophisticated problems *before any acceleration through new content. Those who are not sufficiently fluent with earlier material should* consolidate their understanding, including through additional practice, *before moving on.*

(DfE, 2013, p.99)

The National Centre for Excellence in the Teaching of Mathematics (NCETM) has produced a collection of materials to support teaching for mastery. Their explanation for mastery fits with Bloom's mastery learning and the expectations of the National Curriculum. It is split into four aspects:

Mastery approach – belief that all pupils can learn mathematics;

Mastery curriculum – that all pupils should access the same curriculum;

Teaching for mastery – keeping the class together while simultaneously addressing individual needs;

Achieving mastery – having a deep conceptual understanding that allows the pupil to apply the concept in new contexts.

(Askew *et al.*, 2015, pp.5–6)

Some schools in England trialled a programme called Mathematics Mastery in Year 1 and Year 7, based on mastery teaching from Singapore. The programme involved keeping the class together until mastery was achieved, using objects and pictures to represent mathematical concepts, emphasis on problem-solving skills, relational understanding, high expectations and a growth mindset (see Research box). Keeping the class together was a big change for many of the schools that were used to having different objectives for different ability groups. In order to keep the class together, all pupils had the same objectives. Those who struggled with them were given same-day interventions, with extra teaching and practice, so that they did not fall behind the class. Those who understood the objectives quickly were not moved on to the next topic but given problems to deepen their understanding of the objective, through considering it in different contexts. The evaluation after one year of implementation found that there was a small increase in progress compared to the control group (Vignoles *et al.*, 2015). The evaluators noted that the study was limited because it looked at only one year of implementation – immediately after it was finished, so could not say what the impact would be in the long term after pupils had followed the programme throughout Years 1 to 9.

💡 Find out more from . . . research

Carol Dweck (2012) has conducted a large number of research studies related to perceptions of intelligence with students from school entry to university graduation and with adults outside education. Her key finding has been about fixed and growth mindsets. Fixed mindsets are when you believe that your intelligence (and other qualities, such as personality and moral character) are born in you and cannot be changed. Growth mindset relates to the belief that you can develop intelligence and other personal attributes through your own effort and perseverance. These mindsets are important because they influence the way we react to challenges and feedback. Pupils with a fixed mindset about their ability see success as a judgement about themselves as a person. If they do well at a test it is because they are smart. This might not seem like a bad thing. Unfortunately, when they fail at a test they then see themselves as failures. Therefore, in order to protect their images of themselves they avoid any challenge where they think there is a risk of failure. They also perceive subjects as things they are either naturally good at or not. I have encountered this with mathematics. At parents' evenings, parents would excuse their child's difficulties in mathematics by saying that they had never been good at mathematics themselves, implying that there was a maths gene that did not run in their family. In contrast, people with growth mindset would see that they needed to work harder in subjects that they found difficult.

Pupils' mindsets can be influenced by their parents and teachers, for example, through praise. Praise like 'You're so smart', 'You're excellent at art' or 'You're a natural at football' emphasises a fixed mindset and has been shown to have a negative impact on pupils in the long run. Beneficial praise, related to a growth mindset, focuses on effort and strategy: 'You clearly studied hard'; 'You really learned from your previous mistakes' or 'You have found a way of multiplying that you understand and works consistently'. Haimovitz and Dweck (2016) studied parents' beliefs about failure and how this impacted on the children's mindsets. Those parents who saw failure as something to be avoided promoted a fixed mindset in their children, while parents who saw failure as a learning opportunity promoted a growth mindset.

Can all pupils do maths?

Ability grouping is common in UK education (Boaler, 2009; Boylan and Povey, 2014), especially in English and mathematics, where pupils are often grouped within the class, using terms such as HAP, AAP and LAP. The initial letters stand for High, Average and Low, and the final letter means Pupils. The middle A sometimes means Ability and sometimes means Attainment. This labelling can contribute to a fixed mindset in both the teachers and the pupils. Boaler (2009) concluded from her research in the UK and USA that in these countries there was a belief that only some people are able to do mathematics, which was reinforced by ability grouping and setting for mathematics. She found this was particularly damaging for those in the bottom groups due to low expectations, a limited curriculum and pupils believing the label meant they could not do mathematics. However, it also limited the progress of pupils in the top group, who felt under pressure to always have the right answer to keep their reputation as being good at mathematics. Marks (2013) did research in an English primary school that had a reputation for mixed-ability teaching. In two of the three classes she studied there was still within-class ability grouping for mathematics and the pupils identified themselves by their ability group. The teachers reacted differently to the pupils in the different ability groups, with high expectations for the top group, and low expectations and an emphasis on behaviour rather than learning for the low group.

A classic study by Rosenthal and Jacobson (1968) on the Pygmalion effect found that teacher expectations had an impact on student performance. The teachers were told that some of the pupils in their class had been given a (mythical) test which showed that they were going to have an intellectual growth spurt during the year. These pupils were chosen at random but IQ tests demonstrated that these pupils did make more progress than the control group. This was especially true for the younger years (Years 1 and 2) and for the reasoning aspects of the IQ test. Although this study was conducted a long time ago, the findings from Boaler (2009) and Marks (2013) suggest that this is still relevant today.

Jerrim and Choi's (2014) analysis of the TIMSS and PISA results that sparked the renewed interest in mastery showed that the attainment gap between England and the East Asian countries began during primary school. However, this analysis was based on results from the 2003 TIMSS for Year 5, so may have limited relevance to the current primary curriculum. They also noted a gap between rich and poor pupils which increased with age. They suggested that ability grouping in English primary schools could be contributing to the increasing gap between rich and poor students. This is supported by OECD findings (2012) that in countries where pupils were grouped by ability there was a disproportionate amount of pupils from low socioeconomic groups in the lower ability groups and teachers had lower expectations of them. OECD (2012) contrasted this with higher achieving countries that did not group by ability, but instead provided additional support and early intervention to those who needed it so that they addressed any gaps in attainment before they could widen. This is one of the key ideas in mastery teaching.

 Reflection and discussion activity

Both mentor and trainee, think about the following and discuss together:

Examine your own beliefs about mathematical ability.

Do you have a fixed or a growth mindset for yourself? For the pupils you teach?

Think about the way you group pupils, your expectations for them, the way you praise them. Do these relate to a mindset?

Is this the same for other subjects?

How do you develop deep understanding?

One aspect of mastery teaching in Shanghai and Singapore is the use of textbooks. The Department for Education has promoted this in England (Gibb, 2016) by providing money for buying textbooks based on the south Asian model. One of the features of these mathematics textbooks is the Singapore bar model with its Concrete – Pictorial – Abstract (CPA) approach (*Inspire maths*, 2016; *Maths no problem!*, 2016), which is based on the work of Jerome Bruner. Bruner (1966) had a theory of learning with three ways of representing concepts: enactive, iconic and symbolic. Enactive was action-based and is called Concrete in the CPA model. This involves manipulating actual objects and is the first approach with a new topic. Iconic or Pictorial involves the use of pictures to represent the concept. The final stage is Symbolic or Abstract. For Bruner, this was language- and symbol-based, whereas in the Singapore bar model it involves using the more abstract bar image to understand what mathematics is needed in the question. This could be a simple question like 'How many sweets are there altogether?' Figure 7.1 demonstrates the different stages of the CPA and Singapore bar model in answering this question. Teachers in England may be more familiar with the Haylock and Cockburn model (2013) that connects Context (real life, practical); Mathematical image or picture; Language and Symbols in a pyramid and which emphasises the importance of teachers making connections between these different aspects to deepen understanding.

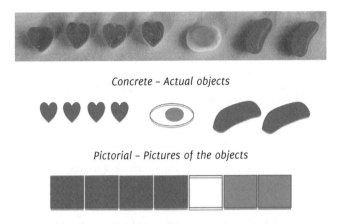

Concrete – Actual objects

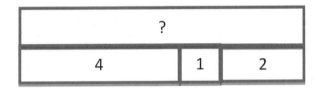

Pictorial – Pictures of the objects

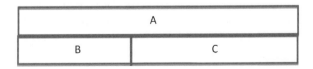

Pictorial / Abstract transition – Pictures of blocks representing objects

?		
4	1	2

Abstract – Bar model for How many sweets are there altogether?

Figure 7.1 The Singapore bar model

The Singapore bar model relies on understanding part and whole relationships and recognising that mathematical problems involve knowns and unknowns. In the bar model in Figure 7.2, the bar labelled A represents the whole, while the B and C bars are the parts. If our known quantities are B and C then it is an addition question. If the known quantities are A and B or A and C then it is a subtraction question. You can also have more than two parts to make up the whole (as in Figure 7.1), which allows more complex addition and subtraction problems but also multiplication, division, fractions and ratio.

This is easier to understand with an example. Miss Westwood has a mixed Year 1 and 2 class which is three-fifths Year 1. If there are 30 pupils in the class, how many are in each year group? The *knowns* in this case are that the whole class has 30 pupils and that 3/5 are in Year 1. We were not told but can easily work out that Year 2 is 2/5 of the class. The *unknowns* are how many pupils those fractions represent. The bar model in Figure 7.3 shows the class split into fifths, with 3/5 Year 1 and 2/5 Year 2. So you then have to work out how many pupils represent one fifth ($30 \div 5 = 6$) and multiply it by the numerators for the year groups ($3 \times 6 = 18$ pupils for Year 1 and $2 \times 6 = 12$ pupils for Year 2). The bar model does not work out the answer for you but it tries to give a picture of what needs to be done.

A	
B	C

Figure 7.2 Understanding whole and part relationships

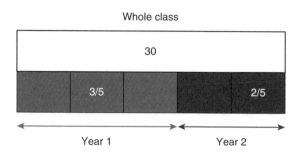

Figure 7.3 A worked example of the Singapore bar model

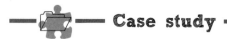 **Case study**

Charlotte is a mastery specialist teacher in mathematics and teaches a Year 6 class in a junior school. Although the school has introduced mastery in mathematics, they are unable to apply it fully because the pupils have been used to a differentiated objective approach to mathematics and the existing gaps in understanding are too large. Charlotte has been doing outreach work on mastery with the feeder infant schools and hopes that in a few years the pupils will come to the junior school without huge differences in attainment.

What Charlotte has found most effective about mastery are representation and discussion, which she calls *Show Me* and *Convince Me*. She gets the pupils to use different types of equipment, like place value counters, Dienes base 10 blocks, interlocking cubes, bundles of straws and Cuisenaire rods, to show her how to perform calculations. The pupils also draw pictures or models, like the Singapore Bar, to show the calculation. In addition to the pictures, Charlotte encourages the pupils to develop mental images so that they can use these during tests where physical equipment is not allowed. For *Convince Me*, Charlotte insists on the pupils giving full explanations orally, using precise mathematical vocabulary. A pupil explaining their working out for the question in Figure 7.3 might say:

> I know the whole class is 30 pupils and 3/5 of them are in Year 1. The Year 2 pupils have to be 2/5 of the class because 3/5 + 2/5 makes a whole. The 5 in the denominator tells me how many parts the whole is divided into so I do 30 divided by 5 to find one part. That gives me 6. The numerators tell me how many parts are in each year group. There are 3/5 in Year 1 so that is 3 × 6, which is 18 pupils. I could find out how many Year 2 pupils there are either by doing 2 × 6 or by subtracting the 18 pupils in Year 1 from the whole class of 30. Both ways give me 12 pupils, which is a way of checking my answer.

Charlotte has found that some of the Year 6 pupils who can calculate easily struggle to represent or explain the calculation. These pupils have learned the rules for using algorithms to calculate without understanding why they follow those steps (instrumental understanding). She has found that insisting on the representations and discussions frustrates the pupils initially but ultimately results in a deeper understanding of the mathematics involved.

Reflection and discussion activity

Reflection

Mentor, what equipment does your school have to represent mathematics? Is there a policy on how this is used throughout the school? How do you decide what representations to use?

Think about a time when you have worked with pupils who struggle to represent and explain their thinking. How do you help them?

Trainee, think about which mathematical equipment you are confident in using. Do you understand how different resources help to explain different mathematical concepts? Explore the mathematical equipment the school has and find out how to use it for different purposes.

Discussion

Trainee and mentor, discuss two or three forms of representation you could use with the pupils in an upcoming mathematics lesson. Plan a lesson that involves the pupils comparing and contrasting how the different representations help them understand and explain the mathematical concept.

What is intelligent practice?

Rowland (2014) talks about the importance of choosing examples carefully to demonstrate the general concept or particular aspects of it, including counter-examples. If you have limited examples this can limit the pupil's understanding of the concept, so variation is important. For example, if you always show pupils squares with the bottom line parallel to the bottom of the page, this can lead them to believe that if you tilt a square it is not a square any more. Marton's variation theory (Marton and Tsui, 2004) involves considering the ways or dimensions in which the concept can vary while still meeting the definition of the concept. This can include the different contexts in which a mathematical concept can be applied. Think about the concept of a half. This could be half of a shape, half of a group of objects, half of a measurement, 0.5 on a number line, ½ written as a fraction or the act of dividing something into two equal parts. Consider the different representations of a half in Figure 7.4. What is the same and what is different about them? What do they tell you about the meaning of a half?

According to Askew (2016), variation is an important factor in the Shanghai and Singapore textbook construction and leads to intelligent practice. Intelligent practice involves a series of questions which lead the pupils into reasoning and Skemp's (1976) relational understanding rather than just using an instrumental approach. Look at the sets of questions in Table 7.1. In these examples Dimension 1 is multiplication. It is the obvious aspect and is common to all three sets. Dimension 2 is doubling and halving. This relates to sets A and B but is less obvious and depends on the pupils making connections between the patterns. However, pupils usually find doubling and halving easy so, they are likely to notice the relationships. Dimension 3 is recombining factors. It applies to all three sets but is the least obvious because pupils do not tend to think about doubling

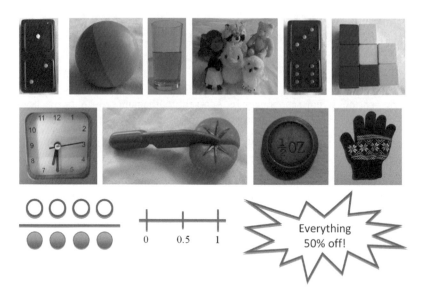

Figure 7.4 Representations of 'a half'

and halving in terms of the factor 2. You can use the questions *What do you notice?* and *What is the same? What is different?* to help focus pupils' attention. An advantage to using a Singapore-style textbook is that mathematical experts have already designed the intelligent practice for you.

What does differentiation look like in mastery?

George (2014, p.65) talks about the importance of 'equity rather than equality' in mathematics teaching, with teaching more tailored to individual needs but with an expectation that all can succeed. Earlier in the chapter, I presented studies which indicated that grouping pupils by ability did not promote success for all, so how can we differentiate for individual needs? In the Shanghai example this was done through individual support by teachers who had considerable non-contact time, although the NCSL report (2013) pointed out that around 80 per cent of the pupils were also getting private tutoring outside school. These levels of staffing and parental support are unlikely to be found in most UK schools so other options must be considered, especially for same-day interventions.

Table 7.1 Sets of questions

Set A	Set B	Set C
8 × 10	4 × 6	3 × 12
16 × 5	8 × 3	9 × 4
32 × 2.5	2 × 12	1 × 36
4 × 20	1 × 24	3 × 3 × 2 × 2

If we go back to Bloom (1968, 1976), several of his suggestions can be planned into the lesson by preparing alternative explanations, additional examples, motivating contexts and concrete illustrations. These are things that would help those struggling with the concept, while providing reinforcement for those who have already grasped it. Remember that those who have grasped the concept quickly might not yet understand it deeply. Another suggestion was varying the degree of independent versus structured learning. You could undertake a quick assessment of understanding after some individual practice and then follow up with an open-ended problem for those who understood, allowing you to work more closely on a structured task with those who were struggling. The key to avoiding the problems related to ability grouping and low expectations is to base your support on assessments of that concept on that day and not on more generalised beliefs of the pupil's abilities.

 Case study

Southwood school has introduced mastery teaching in mathematics, which has involved changes to the school timetable. In Neha's Year 2 class, the mathematics lesson is from 9:30 to 10:05. This involves direct teaching with the pupils completing a small number of examples independently. There are marking stations where the pupils can check whether they have the correct answers. The pupils also self-assess to indicate how confident they are about the work. From 10:05 to 10:20 the Teaching Assistant leads some practice activities, focusing on counting, number bonds or times tables while the teacher checks the pupils' work from the lesson. At 10:20 the pupils go out to play while the teacher plans the next steps for the pupils she has identified as needing further intervention, either because they were making mistakes or because they lacked confidence. After playtime, the pupils have another 20 minutes of mathematics, either as part of the intervention group or the deepening group. The deepening group apply the key idea from the lesson in a new context or in a problem-solving activity that was planned by Neha before the lesson.

St Hugh's school has taken a different approach to timetabling for mastery in mathematics. In Ian's Year 3 class the mathematics lesson is at the beginning of the day. However, Ian spends the first ten minutes with a small group of pupils he has identified from previous lessons as being likely to struggle with the day's objectives. During these ten minutes, Ian goes over aspects from previous lessons which are necessary for today's learning and explains key vocabulary. The rest of the pupils have a silent reading time. On Tuesdays and Thursdays, Ian plans longer interventions based on the assessments from Monday and Wednesday's lessons. The pupils who do not need the intervention will apply the concept in varied contexts. On Fridays all of the pupils work on investigations, applying the concept in varied and less predictable contexts, using a variety of representations.

Forster school has embraced the idea of mastery across the curriculum. In the core subjects (English, mathematics and science), they have lessons that are 75 minutes long. The usual structure is to teach the whole class 'ping-pong' fashion for the first half hour, which means there is a series of the teacher giving short explanations or demonstrations with the pupils trying an example, which is then discussed. This is followed by 15 minutes of intervention for some pupils, based on a quick assessment of the pupils' understanding, while the rest of the class do further exercises. The last half hour is spent with the whole class on deepening by working on a single large problem or by applying the concept in varied contexts. The approach is less tightly structured with the rest of the curriculum. There is an emphasis on teachers observing and assessing while the pupils work so that they can intervene quickly during the lesson with individuals, small groups or the whole class depending on the needs identified.

Reflection and discussion activity

Reflection

Trainee, you might find that planning is a complex and time-consuming process. Most mastery intervention models require a quick planning response to the misconceptions that the pupils present during the lesson. What preparation could you do before the lesson to help you make this quick response to your assessment of the pupils during the lesson?

Mentor, what organisation do you think would work best for interventions for you and your school? Do you feel a mastery approach with quick interventions to prevent pupils falling behind is appropriate for all subjects?

Discussion

Trainee and mentor, work together to plan a lesson that includes or is followed by a quick intervention. Think about the roles of each adult, how the pupils will be assessed and what the pupils who do not need the intervention will be doing.

Chapter summary

Mastery hinges on a belief that all pupils can and should succeed in learning if given enough time, individualised support, frequent formative assessment, quick interventions and an appropriate curriculum with common, clearly defined objectives. This differs from an ability grouping approach with differentiated objectives, and may require a change in mindset from both teachers and pupils. Although there is some evidence in the UK and abroad demonstrating good progress through a mastery approach, implementing it in the UK comes with many challenges, such as how to deliver quick interventions without substantial non-contact time.

References

Askew, M (2016) *Transforming Primary Mathematics*. Abingdon: Routledge.

Askew, M, Bishop, S, Christie, C, Eaton, S, Griffin, P, Morgan, D and Wilne, R (2015) *Teaching for Mastery: Questions, tasks and activities to support assessment*. Oxford: Oxford University Press.

Bloom, B (1968) Learning for mastery. *Evaluation Comment*, 1(2), 1–12.

Bloom, B (1976) *Human Characteristics and School Learning*. New York: McGraw-Hill.

Boaler, J (2009) *The Elephant in the Classroom: Helping children learn and love maths*. London: Souvenir Press.

Boylan, M and Povey, H (2014) Ability thinking. In Leslie, D and Mendick, H (eds) *Debates in Mathematics Education*. Abingdon: Routledge, pp.7–16.

Bruner, JS (1966) *Toward a Theory of Instruction*. Cambridge, MA: Belkapp Press.

Department for Education (2013) *National Curriculum in England*. London: HMSO.

Dweck, CS (2012) *Mindset*. London: Robinson.

George, P (2014) Made for mathematics? Implications for teaching and learning. In Leslie, D and Mendick, H (eds) *Debates in Mathematics Education*. Abingdon: Routledge, pp. 7–16.

Gibb, N (2016, July 12) South Asian method of teaching maths to be rolled out in schools. Press release. Available at: **www.gov.uk/government/news/south-asian-method-of-teaching-maths-to-be-rolled-out-in-schools**

Haimovitz, K and Dweck, C (2016) What predicts children's fixed and growth intelligence mind-sets? Not their parents' views of intelligence but their parents' views of failure. *Psychological Science*, 27(6): 859–69.

Haylock, D and Cockburn, A (2013) *Understanding Mathematics for Young Children: A guide for teachers of children 3–8*. London: SAGE.

Inspire Maths (2016) *Mastery with Inspire Maths*. Oxford University Press. Available at: http://fdslive.oup.com/ **www.oup.com/oxed/primary/maths/inspiremaths/InspireMaths_and_mastery.pdf?region=uk**

Jerrim, J and Choi, A (2014) The mathematics skills of school children: how does England compare to the high-performing East Asian jurisdictions? *Journal of Education Policy*, 29(3): 349–76.

Marks, R (2013) 'The Blue Table Means You Don't Have a Clue': The persistence of fixed-ability thinking and practices in primary mathematics in English schools. *Forum: for Promoting 3–19 Comprehensive Education*, 55(1): 31–44.

Marton, F and Tsui, A (2004) *Classroom Discourse and the Space of Learning*. Mahwah, NJ: Lawrence Erlbaum.

Maths no problem! (2016) The Singapore bar model. Available at: **www.mathsnoproblem.co.uk/model-method**

NCSL (2013) *Report on Research into Maths and Science Teaching in the Shanghai Region*. Available at: **www.gov.uk/government/uploads/system/uploads/attachment_data/file/340021/report-on-research-into-maths-and-science-teaching-in-the-shanghai-region.pdf** (accessed January 29, 2017).

OECD (2012) *Equality and Quality in Education*. OECD Publishing. Available at: **http://dx.doi.org/10.1787/9789264130852-en** (accessed January 29, 2017).

Rosenthal, R and Jacobson, L (1968) Pygmalion in the classroom. *Urban Review*, 3(1): 16–20.

Rowland, T (2014) The role of examples in mathematics teaching. In Leslie, D and Mendick, H (eds) *Debates in Mathematics Education*. Abingdon: Routledge, pp.7–16.

Skemp, RR (1976) Relational understanding and instrumental understanding. *Mathematics Teaching in the Middle School*, 12(2): 88–95. Originally published in *Mathematics Teaching*.

Vignoles, A, Jerrim, J and Cowan, R (2015) *Mathematics Mastery Primary Evaluation Report*. London: Education Endowment Foundation.

8

Questioning to stimulate dialogue

John Paramore

This chapter will

- analyse and understand the motives for asking questions;
- examine the sorts of questions that teachers ask;
- begin to understand how opportunities to extend dialogue can be exploited or missed;
- develop your understanding of the key requirements for asking effective questions.

Introduction

There is plenty of useful advice available for teachers on questions and questioning as there is on the development of a dialogic classroom. Such practical advice is, necessarily, underpinned by theories or beliefs about how children learn and how we, as teachers, can best facilitate that process.

Questioning seems the natural thing for teachers to do. So much so, that we probably do a lot of it without thinking too deeply. Consequently, when we reflect on lessons – as teachers or observers – It may be that we don't always give a great deal of detailed attention to the effect that asking particular questions had on the learning, and how a different question may have altered the course of the learning. However, practitioners who demonstrate unplanned and/or poorly reflected-on practice can come across, to an experienced observer, as merely 'playing at teachers' in some of the implicit assumptions they make about pupils and their learning. The quality and balance of questioning exhibited by a trainee teacher is a clear indicator of the difference between authentic professional practice and superficial mimicry. So, then, if we're not asking questions for the sake of it, what are we asking questions for? In other words, what might our motives for questioning be?

At this stage, it should be noted that we won't be considering the sort of managerial and rhetorical questions that we often use when we're busy 'organising' everything and everyone – 'why did you do that?' or 'would you like chips or mash?', for example. Here we will focus exclusively on questions and answers that are connected with the learning intentions of a lesson/session.

It might be worthwhile pointing out, therefore, what this chapter does and does not set out to achieve. There have been many attempts down the years to classify and categorise questioning and some of those classifications are more useful than others. Indeed, we will look briefly at the 'grand-daddy' of them all, Bloom's taxonomy, below. I will, inevitably, draw on some of these ideas with what I'm offering here but, the aim is to simplify matters rather than offer a comprehensive synthesis of everything that is out there at this time. In so doing, I will, hopefully, offer some focus and clarity for trainees not necessarily available elsewhere. The point of this chapter, therefore, is not simply to present a rehash of all the different questions you might ask and entreat with you to ensure there is a balance between such questions in your teaching. The point is to enable you to link the questions you ask to what you're trying to achieve learning-wise in the classroom. To do this we will start by unpacking why you would want to ask questions in the first place and link that to the effect of asking different sorts of questions. We will look closely at what I consider to be just as crucial as asking a good or appropriate question in the first place – that is, what you do with the response(s) you get. Here we will make the connection between the beginnings of dialogue and dialogic teaching and questioning.

That said, there is a long-standing and ongoing problem with the balance of questioning in our teaching in that we're consistently told, by research, that teachers still dominate classroom talk and ask too many closed questions. However, planning to ask higher order or open questions is all well and good and, indeed, you would be well advised to do this as a trainee, but, in the long run, this approach can feel a little stilted and unresponsive unless the level and balance of your questioning becomes almost second nature. The development of this skill is dependent on three interconnected requirements, illustrated in Figure 8.1, below, to which we will return in the summary. First, the depth of your subject knowledge is crucial to your ability to ask good questions, as is your knowledge of individual children as learners. In addition, you need to be as highly engaged with the content of your teaching as you would want your pupils to be. Thus, you need to ask yourself, as you go along, as many questions as you actually ask out loud – such as 'how might I model/scaffold this differently to overcome Lucy's misconception?' or 'does Sam really understand that? – I'll ask him to explain how he did it'. In other words, you should be actively engaged in making sense of the children understanding their learning, and it is as important to develop this disposition as it is to be aware of the sorts of questions available to you. Some call the practice that characterises this attentiveness 'reflection-in-action' (*see* Schön, 1991) but others would say, more simply, that you need to be 'switched on' and 'in the zone'.

Incidentally, in the classroom, the evidence of your deployment of these three requirements is what will distinguish you as a professional and enable you to overcome the potential embarrassment outlined in the first paragraph. Nowhere is your professional autonomy more apparent than when you're in the heat of the action making informed decisions, on the hoof, about how you might best progress children's learning: day-by-day, hour-by-hour, minute-by-minute.

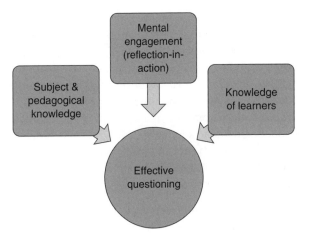

Figure 8.1 Requirements for effective questioning

 Reflection and discussion activity

Think about a trainee who has struggled to make progress. To what extent, in your experience, did gaps in the requirements for effective questioning in Figure 8.1 contribute to that lack of progress?

Motives for asking questions

 Reflection and discussion activity

What do you think the teacher wants or is trying to achieve by asking each of these questions? How do the questions differ in their purpose?

• When was the Great Fire of London?

• Can you explain how you did that?

• In your investigation, what have you found out about triangles?

• What did you find difficult about that?

• Do you like this painting? How could it be improved?

As implied above, the question that teachers don't ask often enough is what might be called the 'meta-question' (i.e. we don't ask enough questions about our questions). We do acknowledge the importance of questioning and, in an attempt to become more effective and add a veneer of sophistication to our questioning, we dip into, say, Bloom's taxonomy (sketched out below), to locate where and how we might throw some higher order questions into our repertoire. Thus, we often talk, in educational contexts, quite loosely about 'open' and 'closed' questions, 'high-order' and 'low-order' questions without spending a great deal of time unpicking what these ideas mean. As is usual in the professional academic sphere, we can go to the literature and unearth any number of articles unpicking questioning in a sophisticated way. But, in reality, we don't spend a great deal of time brushing up on definitions of a variety of relevant concepts before we head off to work in a morning. Thus, we tend to use terms that denote concepts in an 'everyday' simple sense and make necessary assumptions about what our audiences (the people we are talking to and emailing etc.) are going to understand by them.

To illustrate this point, I asked, informally, 56 postgraduate trainee teachers how they understood the four terms mentioned above. 'Closed' questions are generally taken by trainees to be ones that require one correct and mostly 'one word' answer, whereas 'open' questions either have 'more than one right answer' or answers that are 'a matter of opinion'. Low-order questions tend to be equated with closed questions and high-order questions are either synonymous with open questions and/or they are questions that 'make you think', or ones that require the use of 'complex reasoning skills'. Trainees also recognise that for some (generally lower order questions) 'you either know the answer or you don't' and for others (i.e. the ones that require 'complex reasoning') you can construct a response on the spot by synthesising information you already have or that you have been provided with. For questions that boil down to a 'matter of opinion', including questions with a moral dimension, we ideally use the information we already have to hand to make a balanced judgement. However, if we are particularly prejudiced in a certain way then we may have already made up our minds on some questions, despite evidence to the contrary.

Trainees and qualified teachers are often guided towards the categorisation I've already mentioned called Bloom's taxonomy, and/or its subsequent revisions, as an aid for developing their own questioning techniques. The taxonomy is, basically, a hierarchical classification of cognitive (and other) processes which, at its most basic level, involves us 'remembering' certain knowledge and, at its zenith, sees us synthesising or 'creating' new knowledge. As you can see on the left-hand side of Table 8.1, there are four other levels of cognitive activity in between – i.e. 'evaluating', 'analysing', 'applying' and 'understanding'. These are easier to understand in relation to questioning if we relate each level to a set of verbs and a particular question, as I have done in the other two columns.

Over its very long lifespan, the taxonomy has been tweaked a little, but the basic structure is still recognisable and I strongly recommend it to anyone interested in unlocking the true power and potential of questioning in a dialogic classroom. There are much more comprehensive (and colourful) guides to this taxonomy available in books and via the internet which give a far greater range of verbs and associated questions and activities. However, many of these, useful though they are, can be rather too much to take in at once – particularly in the context of all the other new information that trainees have to assimilate in a short space of time.

So, at this point, you might say that our work here is done, as this table could be all you need to enhance your questioning skills and repertoire. Well, not quite, because we don't just ask 'higher order' questions for the sake of it. Here, therefore, I offer a simpler categorisation of questioning based upon our motives for wanting to ask those questions in the first place. So, instead of giving you a copy of Bloom's taxonomy and letting

Table 8.1 The basic structure of Bloom's taxonomy

Category	Key verbs	Examples of questions
Synthesising (creating)	adapt, predict, design, imagine	How could you adapt and improve on this design?
Evaluating	judge, weigh up, assess, test	What do you like about this painting and why?
Analysing	sort, organise, classify	What have these shapes got in common?
Applying	show, represent, demonstrate	Can you give me an example of how evaporation can be helpful to us?
Understanding	explain, compare, contrast, rephrase	Can you explain what happens if you put salt into water?
Remembering	show, tell, recall, recite	What are the colours of the rainbow?

(See, for example, Anderson, LW and Krathwohl, DR (2001) for further reading)

you decide how you apply it to what you want to achieve in the classroom, I will begin with the things we commonly do in our classrooms and link those to the sorts of questions we might ask. Furthermore, I'm very much interested, in this chapter, in what we do in the crucial moments *after* we've asked a question as much as I am in how we go about asking the right questions in the first place.

Here, for simplicity's sake, I will argue that our motives for using questioning tend to fall into three broad categories that I've termed *motives*. First, we might want to acquire information on the current state of pupils' learning; second, we might want to use questioning as an opportunity to develop that learning further; third, we might want children to evaluate the knowledge they already have, both about themselves and the wider world. Either way, responses to questions should provide you and your children with information about what to do next. If you now go back to the reflection box at the end of the introduction, can you see how the questions given reflect one or more these three motives? You may or may not have thought of other reasons to ask questions – but they ought to fall into the very broad areas I've described. The table below summarises *the three motives* and the educational purpose which they serve.

Motive 1: to test and probe knowledge and understanding

By asking questions with this motive in mind you are collecting useful assessment information (*see* Chapter 5) on what knowledge children have already got or have acquired as a result of your inspirational teaching. Learning in this context is often observed as the replication of a desired behaviour or, in other words, via the supply of a correct answer. This information could, if you do anything with it, help you to decide who needs

Table 8.2   Motives for questioning: a summary

Motive: I want . . .	Purpose: in order . . .	Questions: by asking . . .
1: Questioning to test and probe knowledge and understanding		
. . . to **test** pupils' knowledge and explore reasoning through 'probing' understanding . . .	. . . to plan the next steps accurately and identify gaps in knowledge. This is an opportunity for pupils to recall previous learning at beginning of a lesson or recap as part of plenary or mini-plenary. Probing is necessary to elicit clarification and to enable pupils to cement their understanding through articulation.	What is the name of . . . ? Where/What/When . . . ? Can you remember . . . ? Can you explain why . . . ?
. . . to enable pupils to **apply** given knowledge in a new situation in order to solve problems . . .	. . . to give pupils opportunity to demonstrate that they can apply technical skills and knowledge in a new context. Demonstration of this ability is indicative of independent working and pupils' level of understanding.	Can you use what you know about X in order to solve Y? What does this tell you about . . . ? Can you explain that using these words in your answer?
. . . to enable pupils to **analyse** phenomena (e.g. numbers, words/texts, objects, sounds) based on given/defined properties . . .	. . . to ensure that pupils are able to recognise and sort members of particular groups (e.g. even numbers, mammals, fiction, planets). At this level, the teacher defines the criteria for sorting (Can you show me all the yellow ones?) or does the sorting herself (What have these got in common?). Here we establish the 'ground rules' that can enable success in the next section. For example, we need to recognise the key characteristics of a haiku or a piano symphony before we can create our own by applying the technical skills we are developing.	Can you sort these objects according to these characteristics? What have these got in common? Why is X an example of Y? Can you *find another* example of X?

Motive: I want ...	Purpose: in order ...	Questions: by asking ...
2: Questioning to generate knowledge		
...to help pupils to generate/**create** (i.e. **synthesise**) their own classifications and/or examples of phenomena ...	...to enable children to make choices and use their **judgement** so that they can: - explore and choose appropriate alternatives - reject inappropriate choices - explore connections between and among groups - generate their own examples	Can you *find a better example* of X (e.g. an adjective, an appropriate material) and explain why it is better? Can you *create* another or different example of X (e.g. a haiku, a waterproof shelter, a number sequence)?
...to lead pupils to **investigate** a range of alternative possibilities and draw conclusions from their findings (**i.e. test hypotheses**)	...to hand the questioning over to the pupils so they can discover things for themselves. Investigations across the curriculum where pupils and teachers ask the question **'what if I change this?'** or **'what is the effect of doing (or not doing) that?'** are possibly the most powerful questions in the generation of new knowledge.	What if I change X? What can you tell me about ...? How have you come to that conclusion?
3: Questioning to problematise knowledge		
...to enable pupils to **self-evaluate** and reflect on the learning process as well as the content ...	...to promote independence through the development of pupils' self-awareness as learners. ...for pupils to become aware their strengths and areas for improvement. They should be encouraged to articulate their needs as learners. They need to be clear when they have met the learning intentions.	What did I find hard about that? How do I know I've met the success criteria? What could you (or I) do better next time?
...to enable pupils to **interpret** and weigh up contradictory evidence	...to explore issues where there are differing points of view can be explored and resolved through **dialogue** (as opposed to debate).	Why do you think ...? What is the evidence for ...? What is your opinion on ...?
...to enable pupils to make **judgements** based on moral reasoning.	...to promote moral development. This can be overlooked and is a topic in itself. Pupils should be given opportunities to understand that 'right' and 'wrong' are not absolutes or givens but are negotiated in social and cultural contexts.	What would you do in this situation? Is it right that ...?

further help and who is ready to take the next steps you've planned for their learning. In this sense you are *testing* their knowledge. You might decide, as a result of your testing, that some of the answers, although correct, didn't give you enough information to satisfy you that the respondents really did know their stuff. Or, in other cases, you might have received a completely wrong answer. Either way, you might then engage in asking *probing* questions in order to ascertain the depth of their knowledge or the nature of their misconception.

• *When you are asking 'testing' questions, ensure that you also ask children, where appropriate, to explain how they arrived at their answers – i.e. don't forget to 'probe'.*

At other times, you might want to explore the pupils' ability to select and apply the knowledge you're reasonably confident they have through giving them a *problem to solve*. Here, you could either expect children to respond in a particular way, or you could accept more creative solutions. The ability to select and *apply* knowledge and resources in a new context is a powerful indication of understanding. Pupils need to make the connection between knowledge and skill acquired in relatively abstract circumstances, and how such learning may be applied to solve 'real-life' problems.

• *When you are asking questions that demonstrate the ability to apply knowledge, ensure that you have also helped pupils to develop strategies for problem solving in a range of contexts.*

The application of knowledge can also be extended to classification activities where children sort objects or phenomena into groups according to identifiable characteristics. For example, they might have learned that triangles are shapes with three sides and you might ask them to extract all the triangles from a group of polygons. However . . .

• *When asking children to engage in classification activity, be clear, with yourself, what the purpose of the exercise is.*

This is because the motivation for asking children to classify could be to get them to apply what they have already learned (Can you find all the triangles?), it could be to lead them towards a specific conclusion (What have these got in common? Can you sort these into two groups? Which is the odd one out? etc.) or it could be to generate new knowledge by giving children the responsibility for the sorting criteria (Can you explain how you sorted these?).

Motive 2: to generate knowledge

Do note here, then, that there is not an absolutely clear cut-off between probing knowledge, extending knowledge and generating new knowledge as your questions may have the effect of facilitating all three at once – just be clear about what you want your questions to achieve. Your prime motivation for questioning in this category is to develop critical learning that has already taken place or to promote completely new learning altogether. Learning here is seen as a process of intra-mental activity (i.e. thinking on your own to make sense of the world) and/or inter-mental activity (i.e. things shared among groups of learners who learn from each other). Thus, in the fullness of time, pupils should be asking others and themselves at least as many questions (both out loud and 'inside their heads') as they are asked in the course of their learning.

When basic factual knowledge has been established and probed, children can be encouraged to become creative with it and extend it further. That is to say, when they are beginning to know where 'things fit' through classification activities our further questions can help them to:

- explore and choose appropriate alternatives – e.g. choosing the right materials for a project;

- reject inappropriate choices – e.g. substituting one word for a better one;

- explore connections between and among groups – e.g. food webs, nouns and adjectives;

- generate their own examples – e.g. now you know how a torch works, can you design and make your own?

Such activities are connected with the development of particular technical skills – crucial if creative activity is going to produce anything with purpose and value.

Thus, the implication in using questioning to extend and generate knowledge is that teachers do not simply (in the words of the Teachers' Standards) 'impart knowledge' and then test it, but that, through our questioning, we *facilitate* an environment where pupils can co-construct 'new' knowledge among themselves. Investigations are potentially the most powerful activity for the creation of this new knowledge and the most powerful question of all questions supports this motivation – the one that starts with *'What if . . . ?'*

A *'What if . . . ?'* question is applicable across all curricula, for all age groups and is one that learners should be given the opportunity to ask themselves and each other regularly. It relates, in terms of Bloom's taxonomy, most closely to the idea of 'synthesis' and the creation of new knowledge. *'What if . . . ?'* questions are also connected with 'exploratory talk' where children are not afraid to tentatively explore their own and others' ideas where, in addition to *'What if . . . ?'* they also, typically, use language (or exploratory actions associated with such language) such as:

- *'I wonder if it would be better to do it like this?', 'Perhaps we could try . . . ?', 'Could we add another . . . ?'* or *'What about using . . . ?', for example.*

Investigating is associated with *possibility* which, in itself, is associated with *changing variables*. Most obviously, this applies to maths or science investigations where we might be encouraged to ask such questions as:

- *'What if I change the amount of x?'* or *'What if I flip the shape over?'*

But it applies across the whole curriculum. In English we might ask:

- *'What if the story didn't end like this?'* or *'what if I use a different adjective here?'*

Or, in music:

- *'What if we use a tambourine to represent the wind?'*

Of course, there is more to extending and generating knowledge than asking, or getting children to ask, *'what if . . . ?'* questions. However, the incorporation of authentic opportunities for children to engage in investigative exploration has the power to unleash the potential of creativity and independence that is so often missed when teachers simply 'impart knowledge', test it and move on.

Motive 3: to problematise knowledge

Discovering new things about the world through investigation, even when supported by high-order questioning, can still be about right and wrong answers. There is nothing wrong with that, but we may, from time to time, require children to *make a reasoned decision or judgement* on a question that does not, necessarily, have a right or a wrong answer. Here, we are asking children to engage with knowledge as *contingent*. This means understanding (or beginning to understand) that our beliefs about aspects of the world are dependent upon what we know at any one time and that, with new knowledge, those beliefs are open to change. This idea is linked closely with moral development. Also, the previous section mentioned children engaging in 'exploratory' talk, but here, for the first time, we meet the idea of learning as a sociocultural process being driven exclusively through dialogue. 'Dialogue', which we consider in the next section, in a social context, should enable pupils to form and re-form their ideas through listening to and taking into account the ideas of others. 'Others' might be 'experts', those directly affected by the issues in question or neutral observers. Whoever they are in dialogue with, we should provide opportunities for pupils to interpret contradictory evidence on issues, particularly issues important to them, by asking:

- *What would you like to happen here?, Why do you think . . . ?, What is the evidence for . . . ?, What is your opinion on . . . ?, Is it right that . . . ?*

We should also give children opportunity to begin to make *moral judgements*. They should be enabled to understand that, ultimately 'right' and 'wrong' are not absolutes or givens, but are negotiated in social and cultural contexts. To answer the question, '*Why is it wrong to run on the corridor?*' the respondent could either refer to a higher authority and reply '*because Mrs X says so*' or '*because it's against the rules [which were given to us by Mrs X]*' or she/he might deploy some reasoning as to why this might not be a good idea. Although '*because I say so*' is an expedient justification in certain circumstances, how would you want educated citizens to weigh up more controversial issues such as abortion, gay marriage, assisted dying, the death penalty, etc.? Would you want them to have carefully considered the arguments from all sides, or would you be content for them to defer completely to the 'higher' authority – for example, the law as it stands, politicians, elders, religious and community leaders?

Alongside this process we need to enable children to *self-evaluate* and reflect on the learning process as well as the content. Children need to be aware of their own strengths and areas for improvement. They should be encouraged to articulate their needs as learners and they need to be clear about when they have met the learning intentions. In other words, we should encourage children to ask themselves questions like:

- '*What did I find hard about that?*', '*How do I know I have met the success criteria?*' or '*What could I do to improve?*'

Asking the right questions for the right reasons and at the right time is crucial, but what happens next, after a question has been asked, is at least as important and deserves similar attention. In the next section we will explore the opportunities and pitfalls associated with promoting dialogue in the classroom.

Improving talk for teaching and learning

The Education Endowment Foundation have, at the time of writing, a dialogic teaching research project underway which is 'designed to improve the quality of classroom talk as a means of increasing pupils' engagement, learning, and attainment . . . It emphasises dialogue through which pupils learn to reason, discuss, argue and explain, in order to develop their higher order thinking and articulacy'.

You can follow the progress of the project via the EEF website at:

https://educationendowmentfoundation.org.uk/evaluation/projects/improving-talk-for-teaching-and-learning/

Accessed January 30, 2017

Responding to answers: supporting exploratory talk and dialogue

One issue that can emerge as the result of a barrage of quick-fire *Motive 1 questioning* (which can appear to the casual observer as a pacey, engaging, interactive episode) is that the opportunity for extending learning is closed right down or neglected altogether. In an attempt to get 'coverage' and full participation, we forget to probe children's understanding and their ability to apply it. It would be much better, and potentially more effective for everyone, if we spent longer exploring individual responses and giving children chance to reason. In recent years, many teachers have increased 'wait time' for children to respond to questions and have also used 'talk/response partners' to help children to do their reasoning with each other *before* they respond. Thus, the time given with questions tends to be 'front-loaded' in the sense that much of the reasoning is meant to take place before the response is given. There are, however, problems with this approach, especially when it is taken by trainees. First, if the question requires a right/wrong answer or a one-word answer (such as 'what is 3 x 4?' or 'can you give me an example of an adjective?') there is, potentially, not a lot there to talk about. Second, and linked to the first problem, when one partner supplies the answer immediately because they 'just know it', then again, there is not a lot to talk about.

- Don't be a slave to coverage – having lollipop sticks with names on to make sure you have asked everyone a question is fine, as is the idea of 'talk partners' – but don't let uncritical use of these techniques get in the way of learning.

For the purposes of this section I will refer to two sorts of talk (although there are, arguably, more) that we may engage children in. I have already mentioned 'exploratory talk' where pupils play with ideas, think out loud and make suggestions etc. This sort of talk becomes 'dialogic' when there is a *reciprocal* aspect to it. By this I mean that dialogue is a two-way street of *contribution* and *accommodation*. As such, not only should those engaged in dialogue be contributing their ideas and thinking to the talk, they should also be accommodating, or, at least, open to accommodating ideas shared by the other(s).

Dialogue, then, is more than mere talk or conversation, and it is quite difficult to facilitate. However, if we do equate it with 'talk' (as we often tend to) then we are not likely to ask questions that can lead to productive dialogue. First of all, then, think, before you ask a question, '*How or where* is the response to this going to be found by those being asked?'

- Is it already there in some way (i.e. something you assume/hope they've already learned)?

- Are you looking for open-ended, exploratory talk, leading to the creation of a new idea?

- Does it demand reasoning, and, if so, present an opportunity for dialogue?

- Or, are you just 'fishing' and/or will guessing be the order of the day?

This thinking will determine the 'mileage' you are going to get out of your questions in terms of dialogue and learning through dialogue. However, dialogue is also difficult because of the assumptions it makes about those engaged in it. As we've defined it, there is an implication that all parties will have something to contribute and all parties will take on board new knowledge as a result of the interaction. That said, we are going to concentrate here on those moments after a question has been posed and how we might facilitate, rather than stifle, extended talk and reasoning as a gentle way in to a dialogic approach. For a start, let's take this conversation (the children have been learning about the seasons):

Teacher: *Tom, what's your favourite time of year?*

Tom: *Christmas.*

Teacher: *Why do you like Christmas?*

Tom: *Presents.*

Teacher: *OK, Tom. Laura, what's your favourite time of year?*

Laura: *Christmas.*

Teacher: *Hands-up if your favourite time of year is Christmas.*

   [Everyone puts their hand up]

Although the teacher attempted to get Tom to share his reasons, his focus on Christmas and the subsequent, rather unproductive conversation meant that a learning opportunity was closed down rather quickly. The teacher's role has been quite passive, Tom has (quite innocently) usurped the agenda, and the opportunity for productive talk has closed right down. Now, leaving aside issues of democracy, power and manipulation, we do need to *engineer* and *steer* classroom talk towards productive enquiry – or, in other words, *dialogue*. Below is an example how the talk might have facilitated reciprocity:

Teacher: *Tom, remember we have been learning about the seasons – look at the posters we've been using. So, Tom, what's your favourite time of year – what's your favourite season?*

Tom: *Winter.*

Teacher: *Laura, what's your favourite season?*

Laura: *I like the autumn.*

Teacher: *Tom, explain to Laura all the things you like about winter. When you've done that, Tom, Laura will explain to you why she likes the autumn and what's special about it.*

[A couple of minutes later]

Teacher: *Laura, what did Tom tell you about the winter? Did you agree with him?*

There is no dialogue per se evident in this extract, but the important thing to note is how the teacher has taken the time to set up the possibility of reciprocity – i.e. an exchange and modification of views. In order to do this, she has:

- Recapped previous learning briefly to jog memories and give a focus/context;

- Anticipated deviation or blind-alleys by clarifying the subject matter;

- Provided opportunity for children to share their personal knowledge and opinions derived from that knowledge;

- Provided opportunity for children to go on to share reasoning and, possibly, learn or consolidate something and modify a previously held viewpoint.

This example gives children the opportunity to *analyse* the information they already have and *synthesise* it with new information provided by their partner. Thus, Laura could, potentially, remind Tom or even introduce him to aspects of autumn that cause him to *re-evaluate* his view of it. As such, the teacher's motive for setting up this exchange sits across the categories of 'extending' and 'evaluating' knowledge described above.

Although it is more difficult to achieve, dialogue can also generate completely new, factual knowledge about the world, particularly if children are engaged, initially, in exploratory talk using the '*What if . . . ?*' approach. On the other hand, some things are quite pointless to pursue through dialogic means – in school, at least.

Reflection and discussion activity

Reflection

Which of these *facts* (i.e. none of these things are a matter of opinion) about the world could, in theory, be *discovered* by primary-age pupils through practical activity and dialogue?

- The need to move from non-standard to standardised measures in maths;

- The relationship between the circumference and diameter of a circle;

- The workings of a volcano;

- The number and fate of Henry VIII's wives;

- How to mix orange paint.

The first two examples in the reflection and discussion activity I've seen done, successfully, in Key Stage 2. The third example would probably require doctoral level science/geology and enormous resources, although there's nothing wrong with asking 'How do you think this works?' The answer to the fourth item is never going to emerge through the power of reason alone – it simply requires a book or a broadband connection. Learning to mix orange paint is certainly exploratory in nature, but whether you would promote extended dialogue through it is debatable.

Establishing factual/practical knowledge through dialogue can be a relatively lengthy process and, for many, too risky and haphazard. For example, giving children a ruler and getting them to measure things in centimetres will get much quicker results than setting up a dialogical scenario where children need to come, eventually, to the conclusion that we need to standardise our measuring system. As professionals, we have to make choices. But, do be aware, as I mentioned at the beginning of this section, of the difference between *interactive pace* (i.e. how much seems to be getting done in the classroom) and *cognitive pace* or how thoroughly things are getting done.

 Chapter summary

In this chapter we have related the sorts of questions we ask to our motives for asking those questions. These motives are based upon the educational opportunities we wish to promote in our classrooms. However, merely asking the right questions does not necessarily maximise these opportunities, so how we are able to follow up on children's responses becomes just as crucial. Below is a summary of some of the obstacles trainees can face when trying to promote learning through questioning and extended talk, and how they might be overcome. It is clear that to surmount some of these obstacles you will require skills developed through life-long learning and experience – but this is a good place to start.

My children are reluctant to contribute

Spend time developing the right classroom climate for open talk by:

- Modelling yourself as a learner/co-learner;

- Promoting enquiry-based learning – plan to take the opportunities described in this chapter;

- Actively encouraging contributions – take all of them seriously and model respect;

- Giving time for pupils to answer *and* ask questions.

They do contribute – but are not very good at explaining their answers

- Know when you're merely testing knowledge already acquired – and get a balance. Children will not develop this ability if they are not given the opportunity;

- Be clear exactly what you want from questioning and classroom talk – is it dialogue you're after and, if so, think how your questions facilitate (or inhibit) dialogic talk?

I sometimes don't know how to respond to a misconception effectively

There is no getting round the fact that, to be effective in your questioning, you need good subject knowledge – beyond the level at which you're teaching. This will develop in time but, in the meantime:

- Research the subject matter you are going to be engaging with. Don't 'wing it';

- Be ready with alternative resources to model, scaffold or present ideas in different ways;

But, beware! Supposedly knowing (or not knowing) your stuff can lead to a one-dimensional approach driven by your own 'superior' knowledge of the subject and where *you* think the children need to go. Some children will see things in different, yet legitimate, ways.

My children seem to 'go off at a tangent' when answering questions and investigating

We often close opportunities down – from the pressures that are on us to 'move on', but also from our own insecurity (see previous points on misconceptions): what can seem to be off-topic or plain 'wrong' contributions.

- Always ask children to explain themselves – they might even know more than you!;

- Take time to 'tune-in' and explore where the respondent is 'coming from' and run with their line of thinking – keep an open mind-set;

- Be as engaged with the thinking process as you expect your pupils to be.

Thus, to come across as a 'natural' you need to develop the ability to think on your feet. There is only a certain extent to which questioning and dialogue can be pre-planned. The key to this whole chapter has been *recognising and exploiting opportunities*. Hopefully, you will, in your practice, begin to recognise more and miss fewer.

Find out more from . . . research

Alexander, RJ (2008) *Towards Dialogic Teaching: Rethinking classroom talk*. York: Dialogos.

Alexander, RJ (2015) 'Dialogic teaching and the study of classroom talk: a developmental bibliography' (online)

www.robinalexander.org.uk/wp-content/uploads/2012/10/Alexander-dialogic-teaching-bibliography1.pdf Accessed January 30, 2017

Dawes, Lynn (2014) Organising effective classroom talk. In Teresa Cremin and James Arthur (eds) *Learning to Teach in the Primary School* (3rd edn). London: Routledge.

Eaude, Tony (2015) *New Perspectives on Young Children's Moral Education: Developing Character through a Virtue Ethics Approach*. London: Bloomsbury.

References

Anderson, LW and Krathwohl, DR (2001) *A Taxonomy for Learning, Teaching, and Assessing* (abridged edn). Boston, MA: Allyn & Bacon.

Schön, D (1991) *The Reflective Practitioner*. Aldershot: Ashgate Publishing.

9
Behaviour
Emma Clarke and Steve McNichol

◆ This chapter will

- consider the expectations set out in the Teachers' Standards (2012) relevant to managing pupils' behaviour (Standard 7);
- support you in developing an understanding of how to establish a 'Framework for Discipline' using rules, rewards and sanctions to manage pupils' behaviour effectively;
- challenge you to consider alternative perspectives, by exploring the benefits of adopting restorative and solution-focused approaches to managing behaviour.

Introduction

Promoting positive behaviours within the classroom has been a priority for many years in education. In fact, it is something that new teachers state as an aspect they worry about when starting with a new class. Teachers must create a classroom in which pupils feel safe and learning can take place effectively. When considering success in achieving this, much is determined by how you *manage* the behaviour of the pupils within the classroom, keeping disruption to a minimum and on-task behaviour to a maximum. This chapter will introduce some main approaches to achieving this, taking into account both theory and practice.

First, it is important to make clear the inextricable link between the quality of teaching and pupil behaviour. If lessons are not engaging and pupils are asked to complete work that is too difficult or too easy, it is likely that pupils will display problematic behaviour of one kind or another, regardless of the behaviour management systems or strategies that are used. Therefore, behaviour management should not be seen in isolation. It is an integral part of the 'jigsaw' of being a teacher, other pieces of which are outlined in other chapters of this book. Often, improving the quality of planning, delivery, questioning, differentiation, the 'pitch' of activities and assessment will lead to as much improvement in behaviour as employing new behaviour management techniques or strategies.

The current Teachers' Standards (2012) identify the key expectations of teachers when it comes to managing pupil behaviour. These state that teachers must:

- have clear rules and routines for behaviour in classrooms, and take responsibility for promoting good and courteous behaviour both in classrooms and around the school, in accordance with the school's behaviour policy;

- have high expectations of behaviour, and establish a framework for discipline with a range of strategies, using praise, sanctions and rewards consistently and fairly;

- manage classes effectively, using approaches which are appropriate to pupils' needs in order to involve and motivate them;

- maintain good relationships with pupils, exercise appropriate authority, and act decisively when necessary.

This chapter will, therefore, address how you, the trainee teacher, can work towards meeting these expectations and how school mentors can support you to meet these requirements. It will identify key themes from the Teachers' Standards and explore how these can be developed so that you can demonstrate competence and confidence in this area to support your journey towards becoming an effective teacher.

Establishing a 'Framework for Discipline'

One of the requirements of the Teachers' Standards (2012) states that teachers must 'establish a framework for discipline with a range of strategies, using praise, sanctions and rewards consistently and fairly' (standard 7). This is very much in line with a behaviourist approach (discussed briefly in Chapter 3 by Sue Lambert), often seen in practice through Canter's Assertive Discipline approach. This approach was first published by Marlene and Lee Canter in 1976 and has become firmly established as the most common systematic approach to behaviour management in schools, based on a structure of creating rules, rewarding pupils for following these rules, and applying sanctions to any pupil who breaks the rules. It is likely that as a trainee teacher you will be working within this framework for managing behaviour, as the principles of Assertive Discipline have become so engrained in the practice of schools and teachers (so much so that many teachers do not even realise the origin of the system that they are implementing!). Due to the prevalence of Assertive Discipline, this chapter will consider how trainee teachers can effectively implement a system of rules, rewards and sanctions as a framework for managing behaviour.

 Reflection and discussion activity

Reflection

Trainee, read your school's behaviour policy. What aspects of Assertive Discipline are used in your school? How important are rewards and sanctions?

Mentor, consider the different versions of Assertive Discipline you have seen or used in different schools/classrooms. Which reward systems seemed to be most motivational for pupils?

Discussion

Trainee and mentor, focus on the rewards system in the class. When is this mostly used? Are there any times in lessons when rewards are used less often? Do you think there is a reason for this?

 **Find out more from . . . books**

Canter, L (2010) *Lee Canter's Assertive Discipline: Positive behavior management for today's classroom* (4th edn). Bloomington, IN: Solution Tree Press.

Rules

Often, schools can seem full of rules. Classroom rules, whole-school rules, playground rules, lunchtime rules and uniform rules are often all found in one school? But who decides the rules? How should the rules be worded so that they are clearly understood? How many rules should there be? This section will explore these questions so that you have a clear understanding of how to use rules effectively. It will focus on the writing of classroom rules, as this is the place where you are most likely to be setting expectations through the use of rules.

The first thing to decide upon when writing school rules is who should be involved in the process. Essentially, this comes down to two choices – do you, as the teacher, take full control, or are the pupils involved?

The framework of Assertive Discipline very much encourages the use of *teacher-formulated* rules on the basis that pupils need to know what expectations you have of them. These rules should then be communicated to pupils with no potential for alteration or adaptation. Tom Bennett, recently the chair of the ITT Behaviour Working Group and government-appointed 'behaviour tsar', also supports this approach on the basis that *I know [as the teacher] what they need because I am an adult. This is not a democracy* (Bennett, 2016). However, in many schools teachers are now encouraged to *involve pupils* in the writing of class rules to support and encourage their contribution to the classroom environment. It can be argued that when pupils are involved in creating the rules, they are more likely to comply with them. Often, this leads to a renaming of expectations from 'rules' to 'Class Agreement' or 'Code of Conduct', to reflect the fact that pupil voice has been taken into account when setting class expectations. It is for the teacher to decide how they choose to approach the process of setting rules when they have their own classroom in which to do so, but it is worth giving consideration to how other teachers in the school go about this and, which approach you feel is most appropriate.

─── 🧩 ─── **Case study** ──────────────

Sophie is a School Direct trainee teacher who has a Key Stage 2 class. On her first day with the pupils, she asks them to write down key words to describe the kind of behaviour they think makes coming to school enjoyable. When Sophie collects the pupil's ideas, words such as kind, helpful, considerate, polite, honest, respectful, careful and gentle feature prominently. As a result, Sophie uses these words to write a 'Class Agreement' on a large piece of gold paper:

We are gentle.

We are kind and considerate.

We respect other people and all property.

We are honest and always tell the truth.

We help other people.

We are always polite.

The next day, Sophie asks each pupil in the class to paint their thumb and print on to the Class Agreement as a sign that they agree to follow this.

When writing classroom rules, either teacher-formulated or collaboratively with pupils, it is important to consider how these are going to be worded. There are two main ways of wording rules – *positively* (things you want the pupils to do) or *negatively* (things you don't want the pupils to do). For example, 'be kind to others' (positive) could also be phrased 'do not be mean' (negative). Assertive Discipline encourages the use of both positively stated and negatively stated rules, such as 'follow directions' (positive), 'no teasing or name calling' (negative) and 'no swearing' (negative) (Canter, 2010, p.23). Others claim that rules should always be 'phrased in a positive rather than a negative way' (Cowley, 2014, p.158) as negative rules instruct pupils what *not* to do, rather than what *to* do. This is more likely to lead you to over-use sanctions rather than promote positive interactions with pupils. Because your primary responsibility involves the creation of positive behaviour, rather than the elimination of negative behaviour, it is therefore our opinion that it is preferable to use positively stated rules.

It is also worth considering the balance between the two main types of rules found in schools. *Moral rules* are aimed at promoting behaviour that is socially acceptable and these rules aim to tackle behaviour that is inherently wrong (and is wrong in all situations) such as abuse, violence and vandalism. These rules provide the moral framework of 'right and wrong' that pupils need to develop during their time in school. *Procedural rules* are aimed at ensuring the smooth running of a particular time or area within school, such as walking down a certain side of corridors or not entering classrooms during break times. Breaking these rules is not inherently and morally wrong, but they outline to pupils the behaviour expected of them at specific times and in specific places.

It is our view that moral rules should be given a higher status in schools than procedural rules. This means not rewarding pupils for following procedural rules, nor sanctioning them too heavily (if at all) for breaking them. This allows the focus to be on promoting the moral expectations that have the most impact on the long-term behaviour of pupils. Praise, rewards and sanctions should be centred on these moral rules so that this supports pupils in developing their own 'moral compass' of right and wrong rather than pupils simply perceiving rules as a means of control and restriction, which they are often tempted to rebel against. However, as a reflective teacher, you will make your own decision about the best way to approach this as you gain experience, see other practice and develop your own educational philosophy.

 Reflection and discussion activity

Reflection

Trainee, look at the rules in the classroom. Are they stated positively or negatively?

Mentor, when you observe trainees and comment on behaviour management, do you focus on moral or procedural rules?

Discussion

Discuss the rules you feel are most important in the classroom and in the school as a whole. How can you communicate this to pupils in the class? How can a trainee teacher model and reinforce expectations during lessons?

 Find out more from . . . books

Rogers, WA (2012) *You Know the Fair Rule: Effective behaviour management in schools* (3rd edn). London: Pearson Education.

Rewards

As with rules, often schools have many different 'rewards systems' that aim to promote and reinforce good behaviour. Often these include a mixture of:

- *Individual rewards* such as merits, stickers and individual 'points'. Often these are 'collected' and prizes given to pupils who reach set amounts. However, one-off rewards such as certificates (perhaps called 'Star of the Week') are also commonly used. Other reward systems rely on a 'raffle', with pupils earning individual tickets for a set period of time and the 'winning' pupil earning the prize when the raffle is drawn.

- *Group rewards* such as table points, whole-class rewards and whole-school house systems. Often, these are collected by pupils and combined together, with a prize being given to a 'winning' team at a certain point in time (usually at the end of a term) or when a set amount is achieved.

As much as all of these reward systems may appear to be promoting good behaviour, they have to be carefully considered as they can have a detrimental impact on behaviour if not used thoughtfully. Indeed, the concepts behind some of the systems are inherently flawed. For example, pupils quickly realise that raffle ticket reward systems rely more on luck at the point of the draw than on their behaviour, and that in a class the probability of winning is extremely low. Likewise, group rewards can often cause resentment among pupils. First, group reward systems reward pupils who may not have earned any of the 'points'. Second, group reward systems fail to reward pupils who have earned a significant number of points but are not in the winning 'team'. This often makes group reward systems unfair in the eyes of pupils.

Therefore, we would encourage you to consider individual reward systems as these are more likely to have a positive impact on pupil behaviour. This is supported by Canter's Assertive Discipline approach which states that 'positive reinforcement has the potential to be one of the most potent strategies teachers can use to motivate students' (Canter, 2010, p19). Research by Shreeve *et al.* (2002) also supported this and found that 78.6 per cent of pupils stated that being given rewards for acceptable behaviour was motivational.

 **Case study**

Kingfisher Primary School uses a reward system based on merits. All pupils have a 'merit card' which has 50 small boxes inside. Each time a pupil demonstrates behaviour that is above and beyond the expectation, staff sign one of the boxes. When all the pupil's boxes have been signed, they earn a badge that they are able to pin on their school uniform or take home, which is presented in a whole-school assembly.

Over their time in school, pupils 'build up' their merits and badges.

Table 9.1 Building up merits and badges

Number of merits	Badge
50	Bronze Shield
100	Bronze Star
150	Silver Shield
200	Silver Star
250	Gold Shield
300	Gold Star

This system motivates the pupils to strive for the next badge and maintain good standards of behaviour.

However, rewards must be managed carefully. First, it is important not to over-reward. If too many rewards are given out, they quickly lose value and pupils will come to expect to be rewarded for simply doing what is normally expected. It is also important to only give a reward when a pupil shows behaviour *above and beyond* what would normally be expected of them. Second, over-rewarding poses the very real risk of stifling pupils' intrinsic motivation. If pupils are only behaving positively in order to achieve a reward, once the reward is removed, so might be the inclination to behave in this manner. Of course, under-rewarding is also detrimental as pupils will soon 'give up' if they feel the rewards are unlikely to be given even when they display positive behaviour. Getting the balance right is the key to a reward system, but there is no hard-and-fast rule that can be applied, as no two groups of pupils are the same.

A common, non-tangible reward is that of pupil praise. This is the main reward pupils actually experience in school (Cowley, 2014) and it is well established that teacher praise can have a positive impact on behaviour (Floress and Jenkins, 2015). As with tangible rewards, it is claimed that positive praise will motivate pupils to repeat appropriate behaviour and so reduce disruption (Porter, 2014). However, as with tangible rewards, it is important not to praise too frequently as this can soon become undervalued, less powerful and therefore less likely to impact on behaviour. Similarly, it is important not to exaggerate praise ('Wow, you are sitting on that chair brilliantly! Amazing! Fantastic! I have never seen anyone sit on a chair as well as that in my life!') as pupils will soon realise that your praise is false and, therefore, will not value it.

In conclusion, reward systems and praise can be a powerful tool in promoting positive behaviour in the classroom. However, choosing the correct system and getting the balance right in terms of tangible rewards and praise is the key to success in this area.

 Reflection and discussion activity

Reflection

Trainee, observe your mentor (or another teacher).

How do pupils react when they are praised or given a reward?

Ask some pupils how much they value the rewards they are given.

Look at this reward system (**www.classdojo.com**). Do you think this is an effective reward system? (Accessed January 30, 2017)

Mentor, observe the trainee and record the frequency of rewards and praise used. Do you think the balance was right? What was the impact of the rewards and praise on pupil learning?

Discussion

Trainee, talk to your mentor about how you felt pupils reacted to earning a reward or being praised. Mentor, discuss with the trainee the impact that rewards and praise had on the pupils during the lesson you observed.

 Find out more from . . . Research

Payne, R (2014) Using rewards and sanctions in the classroom: pupils' perceptions of their own responses to current behaviour management strategies. *Educational Review.* 67, 483–504.

Sanctions

The final element to the 'framework for discipline' in most schools is that of sanctions – enforcing negative consequences when a pupil breaks the rules with the aim of deterring them (and others) from doing so again. As with rewards, there are a number of different systems used by schools to apply sanctions to pupils who breach the rules:

- a hierarchical system, where the severity of the sanction depends on the seriousness of the pupil's behaviour;

- a cumulative system, where the severity of the sanction increases each time a pupil displays unwanted behaviour (this is favoured by many schools);

- a zero-tolerance system, where the same (usually severe) sanction applies when a pupil displays any unwanted behaviour.

Whichever system is used, the first important element to any sanctions system is that you communicate it clearly to pupils and parents. The aim of this is to avoid any notion that some pupils are sanctioned differently from others and therefore prevent any perceived 'unfairness' in the system. Pupils need to know what the sanctions system is and what the consequence of poor behaviour will be prior to it being imposed. One way to do this is to publish the system in advance, such as the one suggested by Canter's *Assertive Discipline* that outlines the sanctions used in a cumulative system:

First time: *Warning.*

Second time: *Five-minute time out away from other students.*

Third time: *Miss free choice time.*

Fourth time: *Call parents.*

Fifth time: *Send to office.*

(Canter, 2010, p.35)

Once the sanctions have been communicated to pupils and parents, it is then important that you approach implementing them with fairness and consistency. Pupils will soon notice if some are sanctioned for certain behaviour and others are not. This can quickly breed resentment and damage teacher–pupil relationships. However, in the desire to be seen to be fair, teachers can often fall into the trap of public sanctioning.

The original 1976 edition of *Assertive Discipline* encouraged teachers to write the names of pupils 'on the board' when they displayed unwanted behaviour, putting a 'cross' next to their name for each time the pupils subsequently repeated the behaviour (or behaved in another unwanted manner). However, it was soon noticed that this 'public sanctioning' often led to more conflict and damaged pupil–teacher relationships, and the following edition of *Assertive Discipline* in 1992 advised teachers to keep track of this privately rather than publicly. Unfortunately, by this time *Assertive Discipline* had become so popular that teachers did not respond to this change and continued to apply public sanctioning (which is often still the case today). We strongly advise that you avoid public sanctioning and encourage trainees to keep track of unwanted behaviour on paper where it cannot be seen publicly. It is also important to *avoid group or whole-class sanctions*. Punishing innocent individuals for the behaviour of a minority (or even the majority) of pupils is inherently unfair and is one of the quickest ways to damage relationships with pupils.

As with rewards, there are potential pitfalls to sanctions. Issue them too often for minor breaches of procedural rules and there is a risk of create a negative classroom atmosphere that is not conducive to learning. There is also the likelihood that pupils will begin to resent the teacher, leading to an increase in undesirable behaviour and perhaps even provoking retaliation against the teacher (Porter, 2014). This may lead to a climate of 'staff v. pupils' rather than a climate of 'staff + pupils', which is so important to creating a positive learning environment. However, allowing pupils to display increasingly poor behaviour and failing to intervene by applying any sanctions is likely to lead very quickly lead to a further deterioration in behaviour. Once again, the key is in choosing a system that is appropriate for each class of pupils and implementing this fairly and consistently.

 Reflection and discussion activity

Reflection

Trainee, observe your mentor (or another teacher). What informal strategies do they use to deal with minor misbehaviour so that they do not have to use formal sanctions?

Mentor, how can you support your trainee to develop informal strategies for dealing with minor misbehaviour?

Discussion

Mentor and trainee, discuss the strategies that can be used to address minor misbehaviour without using formal sanctions. What type of behaviour can be dealt with using informal strategies? What type of behaviour should always be dealt with using formal sanctions?

So far, this chapter has outlined the system of Assertive Discipline and how trainees can work within this to establish a framework for discipline using rules to establish expectations of behaviour and how rewards and sanctions can be used effectively to maintain this.

Reflection and discussion activity

Reflection

Before reading the next part of this chapter:

Trainee, what are some of the advantages and disadvantages of the above approach?

What is a key aim of this type of approach? How does it fit with your own personal values and beliefs, both about the role of a teacher, and of education more widely?

Mentor, what are your own views on the role of the teacher?

Can you support the trainee in identifying the advantages and disadvantages of this approach?

Discussion

Discuss some of the strategies that you use which, the trainee might have observed which come under this umbrella.

The approaches discussed above form the 'bread and butter' of strategies for managing behaviour that you will undoubtedly have seen, used, or even remember having experienced. However, despite continued support from the government there have been issues raised which regard to these types of approaches. Criticisms include the lack of focus on emotions and the emphasis on teacher power. Although these approaches can be helpful to teachers in the short term, as they provide a very clear framework, they have been criticised for their oversimplification and mechanistic views of behaviour.

It is also very easy, particularly if you are nervous or have a challenging class or pupil, to quickly fall into the trap of focusing on sanctions rather than praise. It is all too easy to focus on what pupils are doing 'wrong' than see the pupils who are doing exactly what they have been asked.

Discussion activity

Mentor and trainee, discuss whether you have ever seen or experienced this focus on sanctions yourself. Can you remember what the initial behaviour was? How did the situation end? How would you do things differently now?

Because of the issues with a 'rewards and sanctions' approach, some schools have begun to manage behaviour in a way that takes some account of feelings and emotions. These approaches support pupils in developing the skills they need to manage their own behaviour and, therefore, shift the emphasis away from teacher control. The recent review of Initial Teacher Training (Bennett, 2016) suggested that *It is imperative that new teachers have a full and varied toolkit of strategies at their disposal*. This highlights the need for a wide range of approaches to take into account the diverse needs of pupils and the issues with a 'one size fits all' approach to managing behaviour. Sproson (2004) described a 'behaviour suitcase' that all teachers needed, from which they were able to use mixed and varied strategies. He believed that pupils fill their own 'suitcases' and begin to manage their own behaviour through watching the teacher model different strategies. However, if behaviour is managed using only rewards and sanctions, some pupils will have very empty suitcases.

Two very different approaches will now be discussed: restorative approaches and solution-focused approaches. Both of these shift the emphasis away from teacher control, which has been shown to reduce self-esteem and intrinsic motivation (Kohn, 1993), and towards empowerment, for both pupils and teachers.

Restorative approaches

Restorative approaches (RA or Restorative Justice as it is also known) are used by the police, probation service and youth workers as well as schools. Hansberry (2016) suggested restorative approaches distinguish between 'managing behaviour' and 'managing relationships'. At the core of RA is not modifying behaviour, but changing the way pupils 'see' and 'feel about' each other, which in turn influences their behaviour. The focus of RA is through pupils 'putting things right', rather than simply being punished as might happen in a rewards and punishment-based approach. However, using RA to manage behaviour is not something which you can do in isolation: it needs to be built into a whole-school plan and ethos. However, once it has been established, it can be used with individuals, groups or even whole classes.

Table 9.2 Contrasting 'authoritarian' and restorative approaches

Authoritarian approaches *The focus is on:*	Restorative approaches *The focus is on:*
Rule-breaking	Harm done to individuals
Blame or guilt	Responsibility and problem-solving
Adversarial processes	Dialogue and negotiation
Punishment to deter	Repair, apology and reparation
Impersonal processes	Interpersonal processes
and, as a result:	*and, as a result:*
The needs of those affected are often ignored	The needs of those affected are addressed
The unmet needs behind the behaviour are ignored	The unmet needs behind the behaviour are addressed
Accountability = being punished	*Accountability = putting things right*

Adapted from Hendry, R, Hopkins, B and Steele, B (2011) Restorative Approaches in Schools in the UK. Swindon: Economic and Social Research Council.

Reflection and discussion activity

Reflection

Before reading on:

Trainee, what skills do you think you would need to support pupils in 'putting things right'?

What skills do you think pupils would need to develop? How can that be encouraged in the classroom?

Mentor, consider how you can support the trainee in developing short PHSCE sessions or activities that will encourage the development of the skills identified.

Discussion

What might be the advantage of pupils repairing the problem, rather than adults punishing? Are there any issues with this type of approach?

Hendry *et al.* (2011) stated that RA were based on several key tenets which made it distinct from other approaches. These include: genuineness, valuing people, empathy, responsibility, accountability and optimism. You can see that these qualities could help to develop pupil's self-actualisation and skills for life, and are quite distinct from the focus on 'controlling' pupils' behaviour that you may have seen in other approaches. RA helps to develop skills, in both pupils and teachers including:

- active listening;

- emotional literacy;

- patience;

- objectivity;

- anger management;

- dealing with difficult situations.

In practice, these skills are nurtured, and accountability is provided through 'restorative conversations' or 'restorative meetings', as opposed to rewards and sanctions. The meetings are based on a scripted series of questions which provide support for both the teacher running the meeting and the pupil attending. The meetings (also known as conferences) or conversations can be large or small, formal or informal, but they rely on all staff using the process consistently. The same questions are asked to both the pupil who has caused the 'harm' and to the pupil who has been 'harmed'.

- *Can you tell us about what happened and how you became involved?*

- *If necessary: What happened next and/or what else? (Ask this until their story unfolds).*

- *What were you thinking at the time this happened?*

- *What have your thoughts been since?*

- *Who has been affected/upset by this and in what way?*

- *What has been the hardest thing for you?*

(www.restorativejustice4schools.co.uk)

At the conference, when the questions have been asked and answered, a conference agreement is drawn up. This is a record of the initial problem or incident, what has been agreed between the pupils at the conference, as well as possibly a section detailing what will happen if the agreement is broken or the incident happens again. An important next step is to set a time to review the agreement to make sure it is suitable and working. This important step helps to develop and maintain what Hansberry (2016) terms 'the 3 Es' of *engagement*, *explanation* and *expectation*. These ensure that pupils are actively involved in the process and understand what they need to do, as well as being clear on any new expectations for their behaviour.

To summarise, RA is a whole-school approach based on respect, responsibility, repair and reintegration. Research (Kokotsaki, 2013) shows that the approach has advantages, specifically:

- pupils feel their teachers are fair, show care and respect;

- pupils feel safer and more comfortable at school;

- attendance improves;

- reduction in low-level disruption;

- particular benefits for vulnerable children and those with social, emotional and behavioural difficulties (SEBD);

- higher levels of participation and engagement in lessons;

- improved attainment.

However, like all approaches, research (Howard, 2009) suggests that there are also some issues which include:

- Senior Leadership Team (SLT) support is crucial;

- remaining neutral can be an issue for some teachers;

- restorative approaches need to be embedded in the school's ethos and values;

- it is not a 'quick fix';

- restorative interventions are voluntary for all those involved (both an advantage and a disadvantage).

Reflection and discussion activity

Reflection

Trainee, what do you think the advantages of RA might be? Are there any aspects which you could implement in your classroom?

Mentor, have you used RA in the past? Do you foresee any other issues with this approach, or any other advantages?

Discussion

Look at the list of issues with RA. How could they be addressed? Consider specifically the voluntary aspect of RA. How could this be both an advantage and disadvantage?

Find out more from . . . websites and books

A very brief overview of RA in school – a great beginner's guide: **www.educ.cam.ac.uk/research/projects/restorativeapproaches/RA-in-the-UK.pdf**

Detailed websites, both with a section of free downloadable resources:

www.restorativejustice4schools.co.uk/wp/?page_id=45

www.transformingconflict.org/content/restorative-approaches-0

All accessed January 30, 2017

A very comprehensive book: Hansberry, B (2016) *A Practical Introduction to Restorative Practice in Schools: Theory, skills and guidance.* London: Jessica Kingsley Publishers.

Solution-focused approaches

Another strategy to positively manage behaviour which also contrasts with the traditional rewards and sanctions approach is that of solution-focused approaches (SFA). SFA has its roots in counselling and therapeutic approaches, and unlike the traditional view of managing behaviour, or the notion of 'harm' which exists in RA, SFA is a purely positive forward-thinking strategy. SFA can be used to work with individual pupils or the whole class. Unlike other strategies for managing behaviour where the 'problem' is 'within the child' which can lead to labelling, SFA is predicated on the notion that pupils have their own ideas and strengths, and are able to decide what best works for them, which removes the need for some form of 'treatment' or intervention from outside adults. Within SFA teachers work alongside pupils and, like aspects of RA, is 'done with' rather than 'done to' pupils.

 Reflection and discussion activity

Reflection

Trainee, how many labels or categorisations have you seen or heard so far in schools? What are the advantages of 'categorising' or labelling pupils? Are there any disadvantages?

Mentor, consider some of the labels which you use in your class or school. How are they helpful for teachers? Do they place any limits on teachers or pupils? How are these overcome?

Discussion

Share your thoughts from the reflection activity.

Try to be mindful of the labels you use in your own practice. What would happen if we stopped labelling pupils?

A key difference between SFA, and other classroom practices, which may sound surprising, is that the problem is not important. Here, you are *too busy helping pupils find solutions to difficulties* to be investigating the problem itself (Milner and Bateman, 2011, p.17). That is quite a switch in thinking for many teachers. Milner and Bateman (2011, p.17) found that children *may not wish to, or feel unable to explore the reasons why they are struggling*. They suggest that 'digging into the problem' even when our intentions are to help can be 'disrespectful and possibly painful' for the pupil. However, if a pupil wanted to share a problem, you would obviously be available and listen. The idea of not forcing the pupil to discuss the 'problem' also links to the bigger view in SFA that you as the teacher are neither the expert in, nor responsible for, finding a solution to the problem. Again, both of these are radical shifts in most teacher's practice, particularly the traditional methods of managing behaviour where teachers often tell pupils what their 'problem' is – i.e. 'you can't sit still', 'you can't concentrate', 'you can't stop talking' and then make themselves the holder of the solution 'you need to move seats', 'stand up', 'stay in at playtime' and so on.

With SFA, the solutions to the 'problem' and the best way forward are all the responsibility of the pupil, your job is to support them in finding a solution. Here the pupil (rather than teacher, educational psychologist, doctor etc.) is the 'expert' in their own lives and possesses all the skills and knowledge they need to arrive at the solution. Your job is to develop supportive conversations which allow pupils to use their own knowledge, strengths, skills and abilities to work towards a solution.

The philosophy underpinning SFA includes an unwavering belief in children's capacities to find their own solutions – the guiding principle is if it works, do more of it. If it doesn't work, do something different.

(Milner and Bateman, 2011, p.25)

Reflection and discussion activity

Reflection

Trainee, what skills might you need to facilitate these types of conversations? Can you see any advantages or disadvantages to this type of approach?

Mentor, reflect upon your own experiences of being an 'expert' in the pupil's problem and providing solutions. Are there times when this hasn't worked well?

Discussion

Before you continue reading, how does this approach make you feel? How and why is it different to a traditional 'authoritarian' approach?

Like RA, SFA is a very structured approach which provides you with a 'security blanket' when using strategies that are new. SFA can be used with both children and adults, focusing on the 'light at the end of the tunnel' rather than on the oncoming train. The process is very easy to do and requires no expensive or specific resources, only a pen, paper and time. The first step is to consider the pupils' long-term goals by asking them structured questions, sometimes, referred to as the 'miracle question'. James's (2016, p.151) version of this is simply: *Suppose things are going to get better, what would you notice that's different?*

The more comprehensive 'miracle question' is: *Suppose that while you are sleeping tonight, a miracle happened. The miracle is that the problem you have is solved. However, because you are sleeping, you don't know the miracle has happened. So when you wake up tomorrow morning what will be different that will tell you that the miracle has happened and the problem is solved?*

(Milner and Bateman, 2011, p.51)

You can see that both of these questions focus on the solution rather than the problem. Simply asking a pupil to envisage a time when things are better immediately has a positive effect. It might then be necessary to narrow down their answer a little, possibly by asking questions that focus on what they will be doing. For example, if, after giving the pupil time to think and absorb the question, they say 'I'll be happy', you might need to make it more specific by asking them, as Milner and Bateman (2011, p.52) suggest, 'What are you doing when you're happy?', 'How do other people know when you're happy?'. Focus on what the pupil will 'see' and 'do', which helps make the goal more concrete and less abstract. Again, simply picturing themselves doing these things will positively affect a pupil. These types of questions can be used with individuals, groups and even a whole class.

As part of this process, you can ask pupils an 'exception' question. For example, if the pupil suggests when things are going well they will not be 'shouting out', ask them if they can think of a time they were about to, or could have shouted out but did not. Pupils often find this tricky, so you can support them by reinforcing that it is a really difficult question, and that 'I don't know' is an acceptable first answer, but don't settle for this. Keep encouraging the pupil to think of one occasion where they did not shout out etc. This 'exception' then shows pupils that they are actually already making progress towards their goal.

The next step in the process is 'scaling', where the pupil, group or class will scale themselves between 1 and 10. This is very helpful as it provides a visual reminder to pupils about how much progress they are making and it can be done as often as necessary (at the end of every lesson, morning, day, week or whatever is required). Once explained, it only takes moments to do, so is easy to fit into a busy school day. On the scale, 1 represents no achievement towards their goal and 10 represents meeting their goal. This strategy is for the pupil – the teacher cannot impose their views. For example, if the pupil feels they are a 5 the teacher cannot step in and say 'but you're shouting out, you're only a 2!' As the pupils rate themselves, you can continue to support them by asking further questions, for example, 'I see you are a 3 now, what will you be doing at 4? What will that look like?' A great way to end an SFA conversation is with a compliment: this might be related to some changes in the pupil's behaviour, about progress they have made, or the way they are engaging with the process. As the pupil develops, you could even see if they can give themselves a compliment.

It can be seen that the whole emphasis on SFA is about positively moving forward, focusing on progress, what has worked, and future developments. This can often start a virtuous cycle, rather than the vicious cycle of sanctions, and make the classroom a much happier and brighter place to be.

 Reflection and discussion activity

Reflection

Trainee, use the miracle question to consider an aspect of teaching you are currently anxious about. For example, if managing behaviour is an issue that concerns you (as it is for the majority of new and trainee teachers) ask yourself some of these 'miracle question prompts' from Milner and Bateman (2011).

When you are meeting your specific goal in managing behaviour:

- *What will you notice?*

- *What will you see?*

- *What will be different?*

- *What will other people and your class notice about you?*

- *What sort of things are you saying to yourself at the end of the day?*

Has this already made you feel a bit more hopeful and positive? Try scaling now: mark 1–10 on a piece of paper. Think about your best possible hope for managing behaviour. Where are you now? Mark it and date it. Follow this up as regularly as necessary, at least daily for a couple of weeks to track the progress you are making.

(Continued)

(Continued)

Mentor, think about how you can engage in a solution-focused conversation with the trainee about their scaling chart. Encourage them to articulate what the next step on the scale would look like. Can you give them a compliment and encourage them to compliment themselves?

Discussion

Have the solution-focused conversation together in a mentor meeting.

How does this approach make you feel? Which aspects do you feel you could use now? What aspects would you like to find out more about?

 Find out more from . . . books and websites

A very readable and practical text.

James, G (2016) *Transforming Behaviour in the Classroom: A solution- focused guide for new teachers.* London: SAGE.

A very accessible and comprehensive text with lots of case studies.

Milner, J and Bateman, J (2011) *Working with Children and Teenagers Using Solution Focused Approaches: Enabling children to overcome challenges and achieve their potential.* London: Jessica Kingsley Publishers.

A good introductory website with free downloadable resources:

www.behaviourwall.com/resources/solution-focused.php

Accessed January 30, 2017

 Chapter summary

Hopefully, through this chapter you will have seen that there are a wide range of strategies for managing behaviour. Often, many aspiring and new teachers are specifically concerned with issues in relation to managing behaviour. However, careful and considered proactive management of behaviour can do a lot to ameliorate those worries. It is also very important to remember that behaviour does not occur in a vacuum and a myriad of factors, including how well-planned, resourced and engaging your teaching is, will all impact on the behaviour your pupils display.

Although the strategies you use to manage behaviour will be informed by your own values, beliefs, experience and the school's own behaviour policy, Visser (2005) devised a list of *eternal verities* based on his time supporting pupils with challenging behaviour. These 'eternal verities' he believed were features of good practice in classroom management. They included:

- a shared understanding of labels;

- inclusive practice;

- a belief that behaviour can change;

- prevention is better than intervention;

- acceptable behaviour needs explicit modelling;

- communication;

- empathy;

- boundaries and challenges are set;

- relationships are positive;

and finally,

- humour.

(Visser, J (2005) Key factors that enable the successful management of difficult behaviour in schools and classrooms. *Education 3-13*, 33(1), 26–31)

 Reflection and discussion activity

Trainee, how might these 'verities' look in practice? Can you try to and illustrate what your mentor might see if s/he walked into the classroom and these were enacted? How many of these have you seen in action? Are there any that you think are more important than the rest? How many exist in your current practice and the practice you have observed?

Discussion

What strategies discussed in this chapter can help foster these 'eternal verities' in classrooms?

References

Bennett, T (2016) Challenging Behaviour. In Association of Teachers and Lecturers Changing Behaviour. *Report Magazine*, January.

Canter, L and Canter, M (1976) *Assertive Discipline: A take-charge approach for today's educator.* Santa Monica, CA: Lee Canter & Associates.

Canter, L and Canter, M (1992) *Assertive Discipline: Positive behavior management for today's classroom* (2nd edn). Santa Monica, CA: Lee Canter & Associates.

Cowley, S (2014) *Getting the Buggers to Behave* (2nd edn). London: Bloomsbury.

Department for Education (2012) *The Teachers' Standards*. London: HMSO.

Floress, M and Jenkins, L (2015) A preliminary investigation of kindergarten teachers' use of praise in general education classrooms. *Preventing School Failure*, 59: 253–62.

Hansberry, B (2016) *A Practical Introduction to Restorative Practice in Schools: Theory, skills and guidance*. London: Jessica Kingsley Publishers.

Hendry, R, Hopkins, B and Steele, B (2011) *Restorative Approaches in Schools in the UK*. Swindon: ESRC.

Howard, P (2009) *Restorative Practice in Schools*. Available at: www.cfbt.com/en-GB/Research/.../r-restorative-practice-in-schools-2009

Kokotsaki, D (2013) *A Review of the Implementation of Restorative Approaches and its Outcomes within Durham Local Authority*. Durham: CEM.

James, G (2016) *Transforming Behaviour in the Classroom: A solution-focused guide for new teachers*. London: SAGE.

Milner, J and Bateman, J (2011) *Working with Children and Teenagers Using Solution Focused Approaches: Enabling children to overcome challenges and achieve their potential*. London: Jessica Kingsley Publishers.

Payne, R (2014) Using rewards and sanctions in the classroom: pupils' perceptions of their own responses to current behaviour management strategies. *Educational Review*, 67: 483–504.

Porter, L (2014) *Behaviour in Schools: Theory and practice for teachers* (4th edn). Maidenhead: Open University Press.

Rogers, WA (2012) *You Know the Fair Rule: Effective behaviour management in schools* (3rd edn). London: Pearson Education.

Shreeve, A, Boddington, D, Bernard, B, Brown, K, Clarke, K, Dean, L, Elkins, T, Kemp, S, Lees, J, Millar, D, Oakley, J and Shiret, D (2002) Student perceptions of rewards and sanctions. *Pedagogy, Culture & Society*, 10: 239–56.

Sproson, B (2004) Some do and don't: teacher effectiveness in managing behavior. In Wearmouth, J, Glynn, T, Richmond, R and Berryman, M (eds) *Inclusion and Behaviour Management in Schools: Issues and challenges*. London: David Fulton Publishers, pp.311–21.

Visser, J (2005). Key factors that enable the successful management of difficult behaviour in schools and classrooms. *Education 3-13*, 33(1): 26–31.

10
Vulnerable groups
Shaun Thompson

This chapter will

- develop your understanding of different vulnerable groups and begin to identify the barriers to learning, which may impact upon progress of these pupils;

- consider distinctive approaches to planning, teaching and learning in order to engage and support vulnerable pupils;

- develop your understanding of a range of support and interventions for vulnerable learners and consider how to maximise progress for these pupils;

- engage with monitoring and tracking the progress of vulnerable groups in order to evaluate the impact of your practice;

- reflect upon the needs of vulnerable learners within your class and consider a variety of approaches to enhance your practice.

Introduction

The DfE (2008, p.8) define 'vulnerable groups' as 'disadvantaged groups'. In Ofsted (2013) terms, vulnerable children are among those groups that may need additional support or intervention in order to make optimum progress.

Many children, at some point, may be described as 'vulnerable' due to their exposure to social or personal factors. However, certain groups of children are more likely to be at a greater risk of requiring targeted support, due to factors which may impact upon their learning and progress, such as specific learning needs, behavioural difficulties, issues surrounding attendance at school, family circumstances and poverty. While care must be taken not to automatically apply labels to children and make assumptions about their ability based on their specific needs or circumstances, it is essential that you have an understanding of the potential barriers to learning, which may be a consequence of such factors.

It is also important to remember that when considering vulnerable children, it may not only be related to those individuals who find learning challenging. Those pupils who are very able or the higher attainers may also be considered as 'vulnerable'. If sufficient challenge and strategies to enable these individuals to enhance their knowledge and skills further is not considered carefully in planning, teaching and assessment by the teacher, the impact upon progress may well be substantial.

It is often much simpler to identify those individuals who are already presenting difficulties or who have by now been 'labelled' or become known to other agencies. However, as a teacher, it is also of great importance to be aware of those pupils who may be 'at risk' of doing so, in order to ensure that support and intervention may be put in place early. You may begin to notice small behavioural changes, be aware of a change in circumstance at home, or simply notice specific areas of difficulty or anxiety among individuals. Identifying and targeting such individuals early on may enable prevention of difficulties later on.

 Reflection and discussion activity

Reflection

Trainee:

- Consider any individuals within your class who have specific learning needs already identified. Discuss with your mentor how this may impact upon their learning.

- Are there other individuals within your class who may be considered as 'vulnerable'? Use one of your mentor meetings to share this discussion with your mentor and to explore the impact this may have upon your own classroom practice.

- Discuss with your mentor any individuals who you may consider to be 'at risk' within your class. What is your evidence for this? Reflect upon your observations of these individuals and how this may impact upon your practice.

Mentor:

- Consider your trainee's understanding or awareness of any 'vulnerable' individuals within the class.

- Encourage your trainee to reflect upon the individual learning needs and circumstances surrounding specific pupils within the class, which may impact upon their teaching.

- Discuss with your trainee any specific barriers to learning, which may be present for individuals within the class and support them in reflecting on these implications for their planning and teaching.

- Discuss with your trainee those pupils who are making less than or at risk of making less than expected progress within the class. Support your trainee with identifying these individuals and how this may impact upon their planning and teaching.

Special Educational Needs and Disabilities (SEND) and Inclusion

According to DfE guidance, a child or young person has SEN if they have a learning difficulty or disability which:

- calls for special educational needs provision to be made for him or her;

- has a significantly greater difficulty in learning than the majority of others of the same age;

- has a disability which prevents or hinders him or her from making use of facilities of a kind generally provided for others of the same age in mainstream schools or mainstream post 16 institutions.

Many children and young people who have SEN may have a disability under the Equality Act 2010 that is:

> *a physical or mental impairment which is long term and (has) substantial adverse effect on their ability to carry out normal day-today activities. The definition includes sensory impairments, such as those affecting sight or hearing, and long term health conditions such as asthma, diabetes, epilepsy, and cancer.*

(DfE, 2015)

With this definition in mind, teachers' focus should be on *inclusion* for these individuals. According to Booth *et al.* (2000, p.13), 'Inclusion is seen to involve the identification and minimising of barriers to learning and participation and the maximising of resources to support learning and participation' and as Slee (2001) points out, 'Inclusion starts with ourselves [as teachers]'. Teacher expectations can play a significant role here: low expectations can breed low aspirations. The focus should not be on what pupils cannot do, but what the barriers are, which are preventing them from accessing the learning.

There will most likely be individuals within your class who have been identified as having specific learning needs or disabilities. With regard to these pupils, consider what the barriers to learning may be. Typical barriers to learning may include:

- difficulty in concentrating;

- organisational difficulties;

- behavioural difficulties;

- difficulties in accessing learning materials;

- challenges with expressive or receptive language;

- anxiety or frustration when faced with tasks.

Find out more from ... government documents

www.gov.uk/government/uploads/system/uploads/attachment_data/file/398815/SEND_Code_of_Practice_January_2015.pdf

Accessed January 30, 2017

Implications for planning

Being aware of the potential barriers faced by individuals within the class will enable you to plan appropriately so as to minimise or remove these barriers to learning. As Black-Hawkins *et al.* (2007, p.31) state, 'if feelings such as fear, humiliation, failure, intolerance and anger are ignored then barriers to inclusion and achievement are strengthened'. In order to reduce or remove these barriers to learning, when planning your lessons, consider the following:

- Have you provided opportunities for these pupils to succeed?

- Is the task structured into manageable 'chunks'?

- Are there resources available, which may support the learning for these pupils, e.g. concrete apparatus, visual cues, word banks, key vocabulary, etc.?

- Are your expectations high, yet achievable?

- Could you make use of peer support or additional adult support (if available)?

- What is your role in supporting these learners?

- Do you need additional resources/items to overcome any organisational issues?

- Have you planned for key questions, which you know these individuals will be able to answer, in order to increase their confidence?

- Have you considered the likely misconceptions or difficulties based on previous assessment/lessons, which may impede the learning of these individuals?

Some pupils within your classroom may have a support plan in place (sometimes this may be an Individual Education Plan (IEP) or an Education Health Care Plan (EHCP). If this is the case, ensure that you consider this when planning your lessons – you may find that specific resources and strategies for teaching and learning are referred to within the plan.

Application to practice

By focusing on removing the barriers to pupils' learning, along with careful planning, you may also wish to consider the physical environment of your classroom.

Reflection and discussion activity

Think about the individual needs of learners within your class and consider the physical environment of the classroom.

Mentor and trainee, think about the questions below and reflect on how you are meeting the needs of all the children.

- How do the displays support learning?
- Are there visual cues to support learning?
- Is a range of children's work displayed to ensure they feel valued?
- Do the seating arrangements take into account individual pupils' needs (e.g. distractions, peer groups, etc.)?
- Do individuals need to be positioned nearer the front/back of the classroom? If so, are they?
- Can all learners clearly see you and your modelling?

During your teaching, it is important to remember the aspects within your planning to removing barriers. For example, if resources are useful to supporting individuals, ensure that you model how to use these resources effectively.

If you have additional adult support within your lesson, consider carefully their role during your teaching. How can they be best utilised during this time to support learning? Trainees sometimes fall into the trap of utilising adult support effectively when the children are working independently, but often fail to consider their support during the teaching input. Additional adults may be used to support learning in a variety of ways, for example, managing behavioural issues, reinforcing learning through additional modelling or questioning, supporting teaching with additional resources and so on. The key here is effective communication with your additional adults – do they know what is expected of them?

Case study

Anna has a poor attention span and often struggles to understand concepts demonstrated by the teacher when she is on the carpet. She becomes easily distracted and disengaged from learning. The teaching assistant often sits with her to try to maintain her focus. When she returns to her table to carry out her work, the teaching assistant usually begins by remodelling the tasks with her and then supporting her with her work. While Anna has the teaching assistant with her, she is usually able to complete her tasks well. However, as soon as she is left alone, she goes off task and usually explains to the teacher that she does not understand, and that the work is too hard.

Reflection and discussion activity

Mentor and trainee, think about this case study. Before reading on, discuss whether you think this support is actually promoting the best opportunities for Anna's learning throughout the whole lesson?

In the case study above, Anna has been receiving support within lessons to help her with her concentration and understanding. It has become usual practice for the teaching assistant to follow this routine the majority of the time. By sitting with her on the carpet and maintaining her concentration, the teaching assistant may be managing her behaviour more than supporting her learning. Also, Anna may well be used to the teaching assistant working with her on her tasks and continually modelling and reassuring her, whereas in reality, it may be that Anna's independent skills are being hindered as a result of over-reliance on this support.

The teacher may wish to reconsider how the teaching assistant could be successfully deployed to support Anna's learning throughout the whole lesson. Rather than sitting with her on the carpet to maintain her attention, perhaps she could reinforce the learning through small group modelling with Anna (and other children if appropriate) in parallel with the teacher, enabling her to engage with learning right from the start.

By doing this, it may be that Anna is then confident to tackle one or two questions or examples independently, before the teaching assistant or teacher then returns to check on her understanding and move her learning on to the next step.

Children such as Anna can easily become dependent on additional support, especially if that is what they are used to. By the teacher effectively communicating with the teaching assistant beforehand to enable her to mirror the teaching input with Anna and therefore support her learning from the start, hopefully Anna will gradually begin to apply her learning independently. This can then be gradually increased over a period of time, enabling Anna to develop her independent learning skills.

Support from other professionals

Working with pupils with SEND can be both rewarding and challenging. A key part of your professional role is to work alongside other professionals in order to achieve the best outcomes for pupils. There may be a wide variety of professionals, both internally and externally, who are involved with specific pupils within the class. These may involve: the Special Educational Needs and Disabilities Coordinator (SENDCo); learning mentors; behavioural support staff; speech and language therapists (SALT); educational psychologists; physiotherapists; school nurse, and so on. These professionals are experts: remember they are there to support you as well as the individual pupil.

Parents and carers play an integral role in all pupils' learning. However, for pupils with SEND, it is essential that they are also involved at all stages with their child's education. Effective communication with parents and carers can often alleviate anxiety and concerns and can prove beneficial in terms of sharing successful strategies or triggers for certain behaviours for their children.

 Reflection and discussion activity

Reflection

Trainee:

- Are you familiar with any IEPs/EHCPs for individual pupils within your class? How will these impact upon your planning and teaching?

- What are the specific barriers to learning for individual pupils within your class? What strategies may be effective in reducing or minimising these barriers?

- Reflect on your expectations for all pupils within the class and consider whether your expectations are high for all pupils, including those with SEND. Consider how you demonstrate this within your planning and teaching.

- Consider how can you best utilise any additional adult support you may have within your lessons and what the desired impact upon pupils' learning is.

- Arrange to meet with the SENDCo to discuss their role and the support they can offer. Discuss with them how they support individual pupils and colleagues throughout the school and how they coordinate support from external agencies and parents and carers.

Discussion

Mentor:

- Discuss with your trainee how they are considering inclusive approaches within their planning.

- Encourage and help your trainee to explore available support and resources throughout the school to support the learning of pupils with SEND as part of their professional development.

- Consider the trainee's planning and observations you have carried out to encourage them to reflect upon their deployment of additional adults within all parts of their lessons. Encourage your trainee to consider whether additional adults are supporting learning at all points of the lesson.

Higher attaining pupils and inclusion

The terms 'gifted' and 'talented' are sometimes still used within classrooms today – 'gifted' referring to the most-able pupils academically and 'talented' to those most-able pupils creatively or artistically. For the purposes of this book, we will consider those pupils who are deemed 'more' or 'most-able' or those who are identified as the higher attainers. So who are they? According to work by Koshy *et al.* (2012) and much of the DfE guidance, these pupils form the top 5–10 per cent of the pupils within the class or school.

In terms of identification of these pupils, it is those pupils who are consistently working significantly above their age-related expectation, within a particular subject. This is not always easy to identify. Again, you must proceed with caution here, as your responsibility as a classroom practitioner is to set high expectations for all pupils and provide an environment which will enable all children to thrive. You must ensure that you do not get caught up too much with labels. Nevertheless, those higher attaining pupils within classrooms are all too often overlooked in terms of their development and thus their progress.

Monitoring the progress of these pupils is essential in order to ensure that they continue to make expected or better progress over time and not simply 'coast' along. A common mistake, often made by trainee teachers (and some experienced teachers), is to simply provide more of the same for these pupils as an extension task or to simply move them on to the objectives of the following year group. The National Curriculum (2013) does not endorse this. It states: *[teachers] should plan stretching work for pupils whose attainment is significantly above the expected standard*. With such pupils in mind, as a teacher, you need consider developing the depth and breadth of pupils' learning and understanding, rather than simply continuing on to the next year's objectives. This links in closely with teaching for mastery, discussed further in Chapter 7. Consideration should be given to the pupils' application of the knowledge and skills taught to a wide variety of contexts such as problem solving and investigation in mathematics.

 Reflection and discussion activity

Reflection

Mentor and trainee, using the school's tracking system, look at the pupils within your class. Who appear to be working consistently above their age-related expectations in reading, writing and/or maths?

Discussion

Are they the same pupils or are there differences between subjects? How is this taken account of when planning for differentiation within these lessons or grouping of these children in certain lessons?

Barriers to learning

While some pupils will quite happily plough on through pages of calculations in maths, or produce lengthy, well-structured pieces of writing in literacy with ease, for many, this simplistic approach to their work can cause boredom. This in itself may well lead to other unwanted behaviours such as distractions to others, lack of effort or interest, production of poor quality work, and perhaps even very little, or no progress whatsoever. Who could blame them? Your responsibility for teaching these pupils needs to ensure that you have high expectations for them which may be further challenge once they have achieved the objective of the lesson.

Implications for planning and teaching

As previously discussed, knowing who these higher attaining pupils are within different subjects is essential. You need to be responsive to their needs.

Reflection and discussion activity

Reflection

Trainee, in terms of lesson planning, consider the following questions:

- What do the higher attaining pupils already know?
- What do you want them to achieve by the end of the lesson?
- How will you move their learning on?
- Will they work independently or be guided by an adult?
- How can you embed the objective in order to deepen and broaden their knowledge and skills?

Discussion

Mentor, can you share some useful examples with the trainee about how you support the higher attaining children in different areas of the curriculum.

Adult support should not just be limited to those pupils who find learning more challenging: higher attaining pupils need to be taught how to apply their knowledge and skills and to deepen their understanding through accurate and clear modelling. Consideration should also be given to vocabulary development. Can these pupils explain their mathematical reasoning clearly or explain why a particular approach is more beneficial than others? Can they further develop the vocabulary they are using within their written work? Do they understand this vocabulary? It is not enough for them simply to include subordinate clauses within their writing, because that is what you have taught them, but can they understand why and when they are used? Can they use them effectively to modify their writing?

You may also want to consider the questions you are asking during the lesson to these pupils. Can they explain why a particular concept works or how improvements can be made? It is not about trying to catch these individuals out or to give them unachievable goals, but to teach them how to reflect upon their work, how to improve, how to challenge and be critical and deepen their understanding. Chapter 8 about questioning and dialogue will help you to think about the different questions you might want to ask to challenge and encourage higher order thinking.

Reflection and discussion activity

Reflection

Trainee, look through one of your lesson plans from earlier in the week and consider, through discussion with your mentor, how you have catered for those highest attaining pupils within the class. You may wish to choose a focus child or a group to reflect upon when discussing these questions.

(Continued)

(Continued)

- Are these pupils identified within your planning?

- Did you use questioning as a tool for extending their learning?

- Did you use adult support to extend and challenge these pupils or did they learn independently?

- Did you provide a clear model to enable these pupils to apply or develop their skills?

- What could they do by the end of the lesson that they couldn't at the start?

- Did they make progress? How do you know?

Free school meals/pupil premium grant

Free school meals (FSM) were first introduced under the 1944 Education Act in order to ensure that children from the lowest income working families would have access to at least one good meal a day. This scheme continues to be in place for children from families meeting certain criteria today, namely those in receipt of:

- Income Support;

- income-based Jobseeker's Allowance;

- income-related Employment and Support Allowance;

- support under Part VI of the Immigration and Asylum Act 1999;

- the guaranteed element of Pension Credit;

- Child Tax Credit (provided you're not also entitled to Working Tax Credit and have an annual gross income of no more than £16,190);

- Working Tax Credit run-on – paid for 4 weeks after you stop qualifying for Working Tax Credit;

- Universal Credit.

(DfE, 2016)

Children who are eligible for FSM enable the school to qualify for additional funding to support these learners, known as the pupil premium grant (PPG). In addition to those children currently in receipt of FSM, eligibility for the school to receive PPG funding also includes those pupils:

- recorded in the January 2016 school census who are known to have been eligible for free school meals since May 2010, as well as those first known to be eligible at January 2016 (known as 'Ever FSM 6);

- who are or have previously been looked after in care (LAC);

- who are from families where one or more parents are serving in the armed forces (known as service children).

Allocation of these funds to mainstream schools is generated from data collected in the January school census. Those schools, which are academies, will receive their funding directly from the Education Funding Agency (EFA).

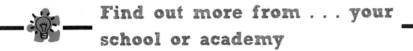

Find out more from ... your school or academy

Your institution will hold a central record of all pupils who are currently eligible for PPG.

Barriers to learning

According to Field (2010), a young person living in poverty at 16 has an increased risk of still living in poverty in their thirties and older. The socioeconomic status of the family may significantly impact upon a child's educational achievements. Various researchers (Sylva *et al.*, 2010) have identified how parental aspirations and engagement with their children's learning may give rise to what Bourdieu (1976) described as a 'cumulative effect' for pupils who are overall lower attainers, as he suggests that they must be even more successful than some of their peers, in order for their families or teachers to recognise this success and encourage further study. Bourdieu (1976) goes on to discuss how influences from family life and backgrounds, particularly with respect to success or failure at school, may give rise to a self-perpetuating notion of low aspirations as they may have witnessed first-hand the objective chances of social mobility through education.

Implications for planning: planning for inclusion

Within their revised National curriculum documentation, the DfE (2013) place great emphasis on the requirement of teachers to 'set high expectations for every pupil' (p.8). As discussed earlier in the chapter, caution must be applied to ensure that assumptions or labels are not used to create stereotypes, however, it is important that you are aware of these individuals within your class and ensure that you plan your lessons carefully to overcome any barriers to learning. By considering Bourdieu's (1976) theory, you must ensure that you do not contribute to the 'cumulative effect' of underachievement for these pupils, by disregarding the need for high expectations. According to Ofsted (2013), high-quality teaching is seen to be the most effective element in the redistribution of equality. Careful planning, along with the school's strategic approach for spending the PPG funding to support learning, may involve activities such as:

- additional classroom resources to aid learning;

- additional adult support to enhance teaching and learning within the classroom;

- the use of additional adult support to provide teaching and learning support outside of the classroom (interventions);

- financial support for families to enable their children to engage in educational visits of enrichment opportunities.

 Reflection and discussion activity

Reflection

Consider the children within your class who are eligible for the PPG. Reflect upon the following questions and then discuss them with your mentor:

- Are there any specific barriers to learning that you can identify for these children?

- What is the impact of these barriers upon their learning?

- What can you do to overcome these barriers?

- Are your expectations high for *all* learners within your lessons?

- Is it clear in your planning and teaching how you are supporting these learners to overcome their barriers to learning?

Discussion

What else could you do to enhance their educational achievement?

Many of the strategies discussed earlier, relating to supporting children with additional needs is still relevant for these pupils. You may wish to consider the following:

- Is the learning environment within your classroom conducive to promoting high self-esteem and high expectations?

- Do you promote inclusive attitudes within your classroom through activities such as circle time, supporting the development of relationships and peer working?

- Do you help to ensure positive relationships with parents and carers through effective communication and contact?

Some schools may have a designated member of staff to support with pupils who are eligible for PPG. This may be a specific role assigned to them or may be part of the role of the SENDCo. Who is this in your school?

Other vulnerable groups

In addition to the specific groups already discussed within this chapter, there may be other factors that can contribute to children becoming vulnerable. These may be related to attendance, both long- and short-term. Children who have poor attendance at school are likely to be vulnerable to low educational achievement due to gaps in their knowledge. Poor attendance may be due to a variety of reasons: frequent need for medical appointments, family issues, cultural factors (e.g. children from traveller families). It is important that you are aware of any children with issues surrounding attendance and to attempt to understand why this may be.

Find out more from . . . your local authority or academy chain

They will have information and specific formats for recording targeted support through the 'Team Around the Child' (TAC).

Reflection and discussion activity

Are there any children within your class who have (or are known to have) poor attendance? If so, find out what the reasons for this may be. Arrange to discuss with your class teacher/mentor or other members of staff (SENDCo, PPG Co-ordinator, family liaison worker) about issues surrounding attendance. How does the school support families and individuals where attendance may be an issue?

There may, of course, be other reasons why individuals may be considered 'vulnerable'. It could be that there are concerns surrounding safeguarding or specific child protection issues relating to a child in your class. If this is the case, it is important that you are aware of these, but remain sensitive to the needs of the child and family concerned. Remember, confidentiality is a key professional attribute.

Support and intervention

When considering any of the vulnerable groups discussed in this chapter, your role as a teacher is to ensure the best access to high-quality teaching and learning for these children through applying your knowledge and understanding of the barriers to learning within your own practice. Many strategies have already been discussed, but you may wish to consider the following questions when reflecting on your classroom practice:

- Do you provide opportunities for peer support/mentors within your lessons to enhance peer relationships and promote high expectations?

- Are there any external agencies involved with individual pupils within your class? If so, have you liaised with them and followed their guidance?

- Have you drawn on the expertise of other members of staff within the school to support you in your own practice? e.g. Perhaps there is a teacher who demonstrates excellent behaviour management – have you arranged to observe them?

Find out more from . . . online documents

Department for Education (2010) *Intervening to improve outcomes for vulnerable young people: A review of the evidence*. Available at: **www.gov.uk/government/uploads/system/uploads/attachment_data/file/182255/DFE-RR078.pdf**

Accessed January 30, 2017

When considering interventions to support individuals or groups of pupils, ensure that the intervention is appropriate. It is important that you match up the needs of the individuals with the specific interventions being delivered. This may well link in to your formative and summative assessment in the classroom – if there are specific gaps in pupils' knowledge or understanding, ensure that the intervention is matched to address these. A common method of delivering interventions is after a sequence of teaching. While this can be very effective, consider alternatives – would it be beneficial to provide intervention or support before teaching a particular sequence or aspect? Read the case study about Mark, below, and consider how you might provide support before your lesson.

Case study

Mark has specific difficulties with expressive and receptive language. He struggles with recalling specific facts and grasping new vocabulary when it is first introduced to him. As a result, he has become very quiet and lacks confidence in many lessons, particularly when new concepts or vocabulary are introduced. He will frequently become upset and frustrated when faced with work, which requires him to apply new concepts or use vocabulary which is new to him.

Mark's mother frequently visits the school to discuss her concerns with his difficulties. She has a good relationship with the class teacher and support staff, and is always wanting to know how she can help him at home.

Reflection and discussion activity

Think about a topic you know is coming up soon, in science or history, for example. Considering Mark in the case study above, what support might you be able to provide before you begin to teach the new topic? What key vocabulary will you be introducing in this topic? Discuss how you might provide some support to Mark in becoming familiar with this key vocabulary before you introduce the topic. What activities could you advise his mother to do with him in order to support him before you introduce the new topic?

 Chapter summary

Within this chapter, some examples of vulnerable groups have been discussed, along with some of the barriers to learning which may present themselves. Caution around labelling and stereotyping 'vulnerable groups' has also been discussed throughout the chapter. A range of strategies have been explored in order to support your own classroom and professional practice when considering 'vulnerable groups'. An emphasis on identifying and reflecting upon the barriers faced by these children has been identified as crucial in terms of planning and teaching to effectively support these pupils. By reflecting on your own practice and discussing with your mentor and other key members of staff within the school, you will continue to develop and enhance your own practice. Maintaining high expectations for all pupils and supporting them through specific interventions, both prior to and following your lessons, is an effective technique in helping them overcome their barriers to learning. By having a clear understanding of the steps needed to succeed, and the next steps in developing pupils' knowledge and understanding, you will contribute to ensuring expected or better progress for these pupils. This chapter has also highlighted the importance of effective planning of lessons in order to consider the resources or teaching strategies required to ensure the best outcomes for all children. Chapters 3, 4 and 5 will also be helpful for reflecting about planning and teaching for vulnerable groups.

References

Black-Hawkins, K, Florian, L and Rouse, M (2007) *Achievement and Inclusion in Schools.* Oxford: Routledge.

Booth, T, Ainscow, M, Black-Hawkins, K, Vaughan, M and Shaw, L (2000) *Index for Inclusion.* Bristol: Centre for Inclusive Studies in Education.

Bourdieu, Pierre (1976) The school as a conservative force: scholastic and cultural inequalities. In Dale, R, Esland, G and MacDonald, M (eds) *Schooling and Capitalism.* London: Routledge & Kegan Paul, pp.110–17.

Department for Education (2013) *Key Stages 1 and 2: Framework Document* (DFE-00178-2013). Available at: **www.gov.uk/government/uploads/system/uploads/attachment_data/file/425601/PRIMARY_national_curriculum.pdf** (accessed January 30, 2017)

Department for Education (2015) *Special Educational Needs and Disability Code of Practice: 0 to 25 years. Statutory guidance for organisations which work with and support children and young people who have special educational needs or disabilities.* Available at: **www.gov.uk/government/publications/send-code-of-practice-0-to-25** (accessed January 30, 2017).

Department for Education (2016) *Pupil Premium 2016 to 2017: Conditions of grant.* Available at: **www.gov.uk/ government/publications/pupil-premium-conditions-of-grant-2016-to-2017** (accessed January 30, 2017).

Education England, (1944) Education Act, 1944. Available at: **www.educationengland.org.uk/documents/ acts/1944-education-act.pdf** (accessed January 30, 2017).

Field, F (2010) *The Foundation Years: Preventing poor children becoming poor adults.* Report of the Independent Review on Poverty and Life Chances. London: Cabinet Office.

Koshy, V, Pinheiro-Torres, C and Portman-Smith, C (2012) The landscape of gifted and talented education in England and Wales: how are teachers implementing policy? *Research Papers in Education*, 27(2): 167–86.

Ofsted (2013) *Unseen Children: Access and Achievement 20 Years On.* Report ref: 130155. Available at: **www.ofsted. gov.uk/resources/unseen-children-access-and-achievement-20-years** (accessed January 30, 2017).

Slee, R (2001) Inclusion in practice: does practice make perfect? *Educational Review*, 53(2): 113–23.

Sylva, K, Melhuish, E, Sammons, P, Siraj-Blatchford, I and Taggart, B (2010) *Early Childhood Matters: Evidence from the effective pre-school and primary education project.* London: Routledge.

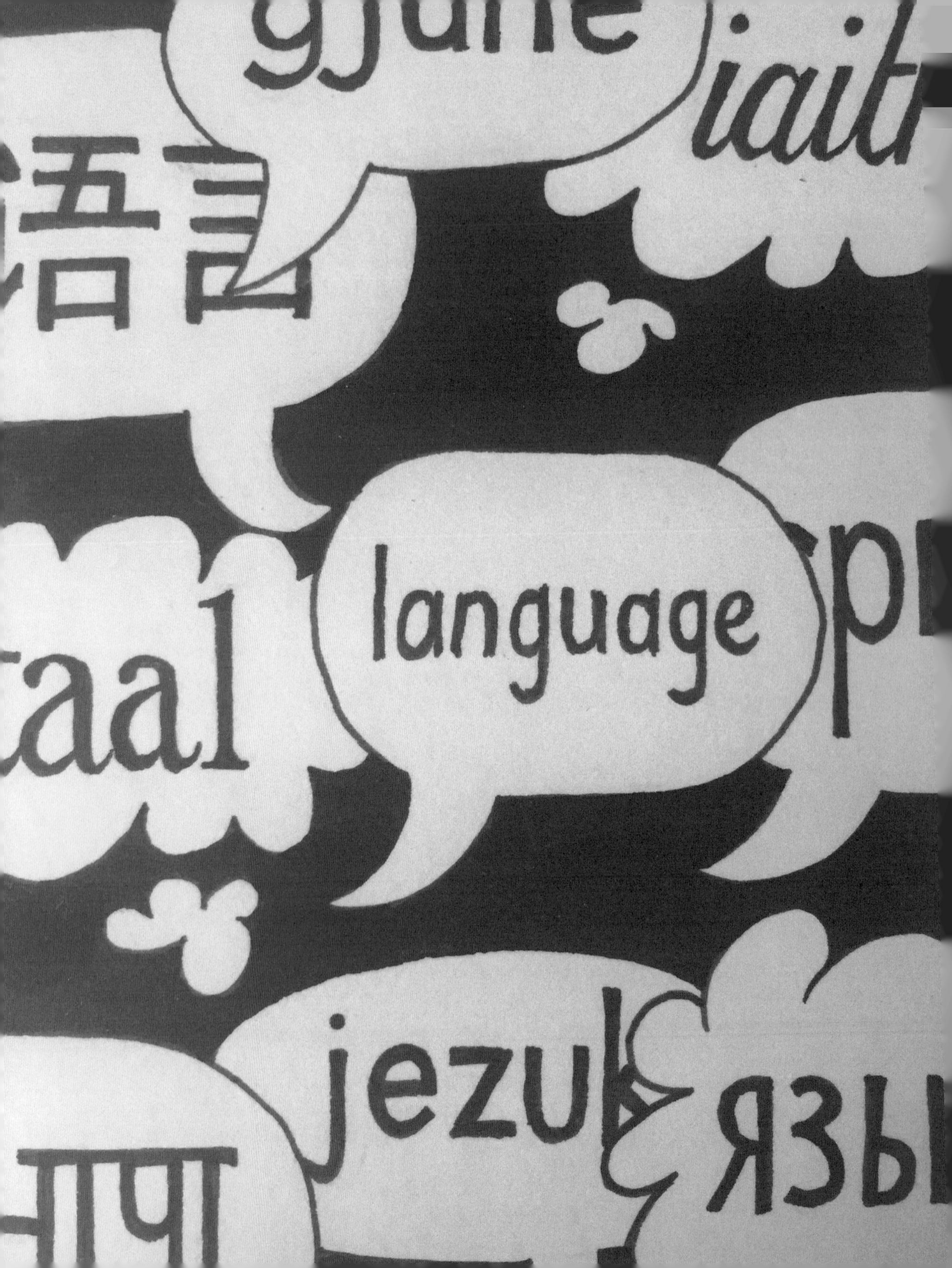
language

11

Supporting learners with English as an Additional Language (EAL)

Ami Montgomery

This chapter will

- support you in reflecting upon how teachers can:

  o support bilingual learners;

  o support language development for all EAL learners including learners at various stages of second language acquisition (SLA);

  o support all learners for life in a multilingual world;

- provide you with the opportunity for discussion around issues relevant to EAL and diversity in the primary classroom;

- introduce you to practical and accessible resources and a range of strategies for developing language proficiency for learners of EAL;

- provide theoretical explanations for English language support and provision.

Introduction: language diversity and understanding EAL

In this chapter, the term a learner of English as an additional language (EAL) will be used to refer to pupils whose first language is other than English: *First language is the language to which the child was initially exposed during early development and continue to use in the home and community* (DfES, 2007).

Throughout this chapter I will argue that for effective EAL provision to be in place in your primary classroom, you need to connect the issues of language, literacy and culture in a more practical way (explored later in the chapter). Up until now, these issues have generally been considered to exist largely detached from one another, both in research and in practice. Traditionally, educators would consider culture as distinct from language, except in the most superficial of ways. By this I mean that learning the English language for a child with English as an Additional Language (EAL) would appear *divorced from the influence of native culture on learning* (Nieto, 2010, p.1). However, it is now evident that language, literacy and culture are connected in many ways and you should hold an awareness of how these aspects will affect your pupils' education. A deeper understanding of race, culture and ethnicity is vital to effective EAL provision and practice.

The number of learners of EAL entering English-speaking education systems is globally increasing. Current statistics in UK mainstream classrooms alone indicate a considerable growth in children learning English as a second, third or even fourth language, with increasing numbers of children entering the primary classroom with little or no English. Most teachers now have experience of working with children at varying levels of EAL, whether newly arrived or from resident families that are bilingual. This may be something you have experienced yourself when out on placement or during work experience in the primary classroom. To prepare yourself for this in the future, it is important for you to have secure awareness of the English language, to understand the different stages of language development and to acknowledge the benefits and barriers of bilingualism/multilingualism.

 Reflection and discussion activity

Reflection: benefits of bilingualism and multilingualism

Trainee, before reading the next part of the chapter, reflect upon the following:

Either think about someone you know who is bilingual or multilingual or watch this clip of learners in a multilingual classroom.

Case Study: The Bilingual Stream - preparing the children for the world of tomorrow.

www.youtube.com/watch?v=xO2dg8KLYJY

Accessed January 30, 2017

Think about what pupils benefit from if there is a range of languages in the classroom.

- What do you notice about what encourages positive attitudes towards community languages? This can be based from what you have seen from around school, talking with other colleagues, or from the clip above.

- What barriers could you face in a bilingual/multilingual classroom?

Mentor, reflect on your own experiences of working with bilingual and multilingual pupils.

Think about some of the possible barriers to meeting the pupils' diverse needs. How do you promote positive attitudes towards other languages within the classroom?

Discussion

Mentor and trainee, share your ideas from the reflection. Are there similarities and differences?

Find out more from . . . internet clips

Further information can be found from 'The benefits of a bilingual brain' – Nacmulli, M (2015).

www.youtube.com/watch?v=MMmOLN5zBLY&t=202s

Accessed January 30, 2017

What does it mean to be a learner of EAL?

When considering this question, it is helpful to acknowledge a few initial assertions. First, a large and growing number of EAL learners who attend UK primary schools face the dual challenge of reaching proficiency in spoken English while grasping the curriculum and developing their written language skills in English simultaneously.

Second, within the literature, the current definition of EAL covers a wide range of pupils with varying needs and outcomes, learners who do not have English as their first language including bilingual children who are fluent English speakers and new migrants who may not speak any English. This challenges the misconception of EAL being only those children newly arrived in schools. Hayden (2006) highlights that there are approximately 1.5 billion users of English in the world and predicted *by 2015 half of the world's population (approximately 3.5 billion) will be speaking or learning English* (Hayden, 2006, p.163).

EAL Learners' Umbrella

All EAL learners possess diverse experiences and a breadth of knowledge of languages, literacies, cultures and schooling which they bring to their new classroom, and similarly require different approaches and provision. Irrespective of their level of English, a learner of EAL will require ongoing and long-term support. As

Table 11.1 Definitions of EAL

Advanced bilingual learners	2nd and 3rd generations of settled ethnic minority
New to English learners	Recent arrivals new to English, little or no experience of schooling and others who are literate in first language
Refugee and asylum-seekers EAL learners	Education has been disrupted because of war/other traumatic experiences
Isolated EAL learners	In school settings with little prior experience of bilingual pupils
Sojourner EAL learners	Parents are working and studying and in England for short period of time

highlighted in the work of Cummins and Nakajima (1987), it often takes on average five to seven years to become fully competent in a second language. This can vary from one individual to another. However, some non-native speakers of the English language can develop conversational competency and often native-like fluency within only two years. You need to be aware that although their spoken English may be very good, the learner will still need language support, possibly for several years. Teachers have the initial responsibility of creating a safe environment for new arrivals and for ensuring that all are accepted and included. Newly arrived learners of EAL face many barriers: being unable to speak any English at all results in the learner of EAL feeling particularly shy and worried about how to communicate with others. They often want to be on their own with limited interaction with peers and teachers. After all, one of the most difficult and frustrating things is the inability to communicate with others and to tell them how you feel or what you want.

 **Case study**

Isabel is the youngest of three siblings. They were all born in the UK. However, their family only speak Portuguese at home, despite the fact that they all speak English fluently. Isabel's grandparents moved to the UK for work. Isabel attends a local Portuguese Supplementary School at the weekends in addition to studying at her local primary school Monday to Friday.

Asad was born in Somalia but he left with his family when he was a young child. For many years, Asad lived in Saudi Arabia until his family came to England when he was seven. They lived in temporary accommodation at first and Asad did not immediately find a school place.

Nadia is a Year 5 pupil who attends a small primary school in a small village in England. She has been living in the UK for three years. However, she hasn't always been at her current primary school. Previously, Nadia attended a large multicultural school in the south of England, where there were other native speakers of Arabic who Nadia spent time with in and outside of school. However, due to work commitments, Nadia's family have relocated to an area where they are isolated.

Reflection activity

Trainee, read the case studies above and use the definitions on Table 11.1 (see p.185) to try to identify which group of EAL learners these children belong to.

In the case studies above you were introduced to three EAL learners and asked to use Table 11.1 to identify which group they would belong to. Each of these children (Isabel – an advanced bilingual learner; Asad – a refugee learner new to English; and Nadia – an isolated learner), have particular experiences and knowledge which can be seen as strengths and benefits to the primary classroom, or weaknesses and barriers to learning.

Being aware of these different categories of EAL is especially important for preparing and providing for those more vulnerable learners of EAL, who are experiencing emotional difficulties due to experiences of war, loss or trauma. It is the educational rebuilding of worlds, along with economic and sociocultural support, which above all will determine the long-term well-being of millions of child survivors of war. Conteh (2015) identifies refugee and asylum seekers as an additional group who require further consideration and thought due to their diverse backgrounds, and the fact that their previous education may have been disputed. This group of EAL learners is a particularly diverse group. While some children may arrive in the UK with both parents or being cared for by only one parent, others may live with older siblings, relatives or friends, or even arrive alone and unaccompanied. Schools and teachers play a vital role in promoting the well-being of refugee children, helping them to rebuild their self-esteem and friendships, and to fully achieve their full potential.

 Discussion activity

Mentor, talk to your trainee about pupils you have taught who might fit into any of the following categories

Learners who are:

- second and third generation members of settled ethnic minority communities (advanced bilingual learners);

- recent arrivals and new to English with little prior schooling;

- recent arrivals and new to English who are literate in their first languages;

- asylum seekers or refugees whose education has been disrupted due to war or other traumatic experiences;

- isolated learners in school settings with little prior experience of bilingual learners;

- Roma and Gypsy pupils;

- children of parents who are studying or working for a short period of time.

(Conteh, 2015).

From your experience, what may be the strengths and possible needs of these children?

Any new arrival entering the English mainstream classroom will require access to the English language as quickly as possible, referred to by Cummins (1979) as Basic Interpersonal Communication Skills (BICS). These are the skills required for developing the appropriate language for the given social context and for oral fluency. This level of linguistic competence is required before they can access cognitive/academic language proficiency (CALP), which is the linguistic knowledge and literacy skills required for full academic proficiency. This means that before pupils can access more complex language, including academic language used in learning, they need to be competent in basic language (BICS).

How do learners of EAL acquire the English language?

Second language acquisition

There are many factors which need careful consideration when exploring second language acquisition for learners of EAL. First, the stages in which a language is learned for a bilingual learner. As set out by Tabors (1997, p.39), the first of the four stages of acquisition includes a period of time where the learner of EAL will continue to use their home language in the second-language learning environment, or may even enter a 'silent period'. It is important that the learner of EAL feels able to do this and that their home culture is recognised and celebrated.

During the second stage of early acquisition, a learner of EAL may also enter a non-verbal period, as they start to collect information about the linguistic characteristics of the new language and experiment with new sounds. For the duration of the 'silent period', EAL learners will familiarise themselves with the similarities and differences in the sounds of their native language and the English language. Throughout this early stage of acquisition, it is important to ensure learners of EAL have access to good models of the English language and also survival language. Survival language is that key vocabulary your EAL learner will need on a daily basis: this includes key classroom vocabulary, language to assist with communicating with friends in and out of the classroom and language for daily routines.

 Reflection and discussion activity

Reflection

Mentor and trainee, consider some of the suggested strategies below for assisting EAL learners when in a non-verbal phase of second language acquisition (SLA).

- Continue to talk - even when the learner does not respond.

- Continue to include the learner in small groups with other children.

- Use a variety of question types to draw answers and contributions.

- Include other children as the focus in the conversation.

- Promote the use of their first language (L1).

- Accept non-verbal responses from the learner.

- Praise the learner for limited or minimal contribution.

- Set clear expectations which include the need for the learner to respond with repeated words and/or counting.

- Structure lessons and activities which encourage child-to-child interaction.

- Provide activities which reinforce language practice through role play.

(Clarke, 1992, pp.17-18)

Discussion

Mentor and trainee, discuss these ideas. Would they all work well? How might these vary depending on the situation? Why might having a variety of approaches be useful?

Subsequent to the experimentation of sounds phase, where your EAL learners will be familiarising themselves with the similarities and differences in sounds of their new additional language, your EAL learners will start to use individual words and phrases in the new language. This is often in the form of *repetition and language play, use of formulae, routine and single words* (Drury, 2007, p.37). They use formulae and language chunks as ready-made phrases for specific routine situations which allows the EAL learners to interact with others. These language chunks often include memorised sequences of routine language used within the setting which include answering the register, asking to go to the toilet or language in rhymes and stories. It is essential during this time that your EAL learner is immersed in a language-rich environment with good models of the English language.

Eventually, EAL learners begin to develop a more productive use of the second language which marks the beginning of developing more efficient and complex uses of the English language. They may combine some of the language chunks they have acquired in earlier stages and begin to produce longer and more complex sentences which approximate more closely to the intended meaning.

Many theoretical frameworks attempt to understand which method would be most effective when approaching teaching English, and place different values on the role of interaction in second language acquisition (SLA).

Krashen's (1985) theory, which became a predominant influence in both second language teaching practice and later theories, proposes that SLA is determined by the amount of understandable and comprehensible input, at a level just beyond the current linguistic competence of the learner. Similar to Vygotsky's *zone of proximal development* (1962) – the difference between what a learner can do without help and what he or she can do with help – Krashen's scaffolding theory maintains that a second language is acquired unconsciously

Table 11.2 Theoretical frameworks for second language acquisition

Pre-20th century	Early 1900s	1940s, 1950s	1960s, 1970s	1980s, 1990s	1990s-present
Grammar, translation	Audiolingual, Direct Method	Behaviourist, S-R-R	Universal Grammar, LAD	Information Processing Models	Social Interactionism
	Bloomfield, Fries	*Skinner*	*Chomsky, Krashen*	*Anderson, MaLaughlin*	*Vygotsky, Snow*

in a manner similar to the acquisition of a first language. He further highlights how acquiring language is predicated upon the concept of receiving messages learners can understand. Teachers can make language input comprehensible through a variety of strategies, such as linguistic simplification, and the use of visuals, pictures, graphic organizers, and other strategies used with learners with EAL.

Other theoretical frameworks take an interactionist position and acknowledge the role of two-way communication. Pica (1994), Long (1985), and others emphasise that conversational interaction facilitates SLA under certain conditions, *in meaningful activities learners are compelled to negotiate for meaning . . . to express and clarify their intentions, thoughts, opinions . . . which permits them to arrive at a mutual understanding* (Lightbrown and Spada, 1999, p.122).

 Reflective activity

As you continue to work through the activities in this chapter, refer back to the following statements and think about whether you agree or disagree with them.

1. Learning a second language is just like learning a first language.

2. Parents should be told to promote the use of English at home to ensure their child acquires the English language sooner.

3. EAL learners born in England will acquire the English language before starting school.

4. A child's first language gets in the way of their learning of English.

5. It is not important for teachers to concern themselves with the EAL learner's first language and culture, just to ensure they deliver the curriculum.

6. Younger EAL learners will acquire the English language quicker than older EAL learners.

7. EAL learners need to learn the basics and simple English language structures first before they can be immersed in the mainstream classrooms and curriculum.

8. EAL learners speak English just like monolingual native English children.

9. Learners of EAL have an adverse impact on attainment and depress standards in schools.

Practical approaches for promoting language learning for learners of EAL

Preparing for New Arrivals: essential conditions for learning and emotional well-being

When preparing for the arrival of an EAL learner, it is important to consider essential conditions for learning. Children need to feel safe, settled, valued and secure, and have a sense of belonging, where learning builds on what the learner knows and what they can do. Schools should recognise the positive contribution that new arrivals can make to the school and it is important for new arrivals to see their language and culture positively reflected in school, *young children need to have their languages valued and their home experiences affirmed in order to feel secure enough to venture into the language and culture of their early years setting* (Siraj-Blatchford *et al.* 2003). No child should be expected to cast off the language and culture of home as s/he crosses the school threshold.

There are numerous external and internal factors which influence the rate at which a learner of EAL acquires English. External factors include a learner's attitude, gender, age, social class, ethnic identity and language input, influenced by their new learning environment (Ellis, 1994). It is essential that you understand the importance of getting to know your EAL learner and their background, to promote their emotional well-being and to successfully prepare the essential conditions for learning.

To do this, you need to consider the new arrivals' cultural and language background. Consider if they:

- have had schooling in the UK or other country – full, interrupted or none;

- have specific cultural, religious, national and linguistic backgrounds which need catering for;

- are literate in one or more languages;

- are highly motivated to learn;

- are higher attaining pupils;

- have learning difficulties;

- are living with adults who are experiencing emotional difficulties or withdrawal themselves;

- are experiencing cultural disorientation as well as feelings of loss, grief and isolation.

 Find out more from . . . websites

Here is a handbook to give support in preparing for EAL learners from backgrounds of war. Read Nonchev and Tagarov's (2012) work on integrating refugee and asylum-seeking children in educational systems.

www.csd.bg/fileadmin/user_upload/INTEGRACE_handbook.pdf

Accessed January 30, 2017

The multicultural classroom and multicultural education

Multicultural classrooms must thrive on the differences and uniqueness of their children and use them as an underpinning for development and growth. Diversity and differences command work, resolution, openness and understanding, and for those teachers who address and embed this into their practice, they will succeed in creating a learning environment that will advance the educational goals of all children.

As a teacher, you are required to identify, differentiate and understand what it means to teach in a classroom which is multicultural and to understand that this includes, but is much more than, content integration. Content integration deals with the extent to which you use examples and content from a variety of cultures and groups to illustrate key concepts, principles, generalisations and theories. This is often seen as only benefiting learners who are of ethnic minority. However, it becomes clear with practice that this has benefits for all.

A range of nationalities in a primary classroom is an asset: children bring with them different backgrounds, cultures, faiths and language. This is something we should celebrate. Differing cultural perspectives provide a dynamic and vivid opportunity for debate and the need for mutual respect adds to the general dignity of the environment.

The immersive language classroom

Many theoretical frameworks attempt to understand which method would be most effective when approaching teaching English as a second language. However the communicative approach has been identified as key in SLA (Pica, 1998; Canale and Swain, 1980). Oral communication becomes the most important component because it allows the learner to possess the basic knowledge of the second language that is necessary before grammatical rules can be applied. An inclusive setting, where the learner is fully immersed in the native language, is seen to be most beneficial, because it allows the learner with second language difficulty to practise with their native peers and those who are fluent in the English language. Within this context, both first and second languages are used and are a source of inspiration for any activity. An example of this is when learners are asked to engage in a writing activity and are given the opportunity to complete part of the activity in their first language. The main ideas that the learner wishes to convey are in their first language and then the written account is produced in their second language, which can be with the assistance of what Vygotsky would call a *more knowledgeable other.*

The communicative approach additionally allows for collaborative learning which is extremely important for language teaching and learning as it is language-focused and EAL friendly. With three main areas of focus – empowerment, access and exploratory talk – collaborative learning is a situation in which two or more people learn or attempt to learn something together, where they capitalise on one another's resources and skills.

- Empowerment – Building on and valuing a child's prior knowledge and understanding and encouraging children to share ideas confidently.

- Access – Ensuring that children have access to difficult concepts/areas of learning. This is often done through the use of visuals and tries to move the learners from the concrete concept to abstract ideas.

- Exploratory talk – Encouraging peer talk to aid and assist learning as opposed to the increased use of teacher talk.

Teaching communicative competencies across the curriculum can benefit all children in a group of learners, not just those who are bilingual.

Find out more from .... websites

Here there is information about collaborative learning and access further learning resources:

www.collaborativelearning.org/

Accessed January 30, 2017

How to assess and monitor learners of EAL?

Differences in educational, social and linguistic experience will mean that EAL learners of the same age and same length of time in the UK might be at very different stages of EAL development with regard to the four skills and in the various areas of language. A useful EAL assessment system should: measure development in speaking, listening, reading and writing; link to the language needed in the curriculum; be age-related; and support teachers to plan for effective teaching and learning. To successfully map the development of your learners of EAL, especially in the early stages of acquiring English, it is essential that formative assessments are implemented effectively. However, initial formal assessments have been judged negatively as they can often lead to false conclusions which may be highly damaging to the progress of the child, particularly if results place the pupil in a lower-ability group. The need for early monitoring and careful tracking of your EAL learner's development is highlighted in recent school performance tables and statistics which show that by the end of the Early Years and Foundation Stage (EYFS) only 44 per cent of learners of EAL are at a good level of development (GLD).

A Language in Common (2000), produced by the Quality and Curriculum Authority (QCA), is a document which provides an overview of some of the language focuses for formative assessment for EAL learners and offers some helpful guidance on how to record language development and progress. A further example of early formative assessments which can be incorporated to map the progression of your EAL learners is NASSEA's EAL Assessment Framework. This framework provides an overview of the stages and steps in language progression, outlines key descriptors for each of the four language skills, and provides case studies to assist with identifying these descriptors for your EAL learners and planning for progression templates.

Reflection and discussion activity

Reflection

Prior to undertaking this task, you will need to be familiar with QCA's *A Language in Common* (2000) and/or NASSEA's EAL Assessment Framework (2016) and other possible assessment methods used in the school.

Trainee, identify two EAL learners in the school: one new to English and the other an advanced EAL learner.

Observe both EAL learners, in a wide range of settings if possible, to find out the following information:

(Continued)

(Continued)

- What language(s) do the two children understand, speak, read and write in?

- Do they attend supplementary or community language classes? If possible, try to find out which language(s) are used when and for what purposes.

- Were they born in England or abroad? If they were born abroad, how long have they been in England and what their pattern of migration was?

- How long have they been in this school?

- Do they have the opportunity to use their first language(s) with other pupils in the school or with staff? If so, how often and when? How do they feel about this?

- Use the 'NASSEA EAL Assessment Framework' (2016) system to identify their stages of EAL acquisition for speaking, listening, reading and writing. Then identify specific areas for development for each child in each of the four skills.

Discussion

Trainee and mentor, compare your findings with regard to the assessment stages for each of the four language skills: speaking, listening, reading and writing. Discuss what their EAL needs are and how these are met in the context of the mainstream primary classroom.

How to plan for learners of EAL in your class

Planning for your learners of EAL can be a daunting task but it does not need to be. When planning for learners of EAL in the primary classroom, there are several principles which you need to keep in mind. First, it is essential that you develop a positive ethos for learners of EAL, which reflects the language and cultures of all children in your class, and that you provide the opportunity for learners to use their first language in everyday activities. This offers further opportunity for your multilingual learners to *affirm their indentity* (Conteh, 2015, p.70) and to learn in a safe and secure learning environment. Another vital principle you need to consider when planning for your EAL learners is the importance of talk, and the opportunity for them to be able to explore their ideas and concepts orally with others, in addition to extensive opportunities for more practical and hands-on activities which enhance language learning. These are especially important before extended writing activities.

To plan effectively for your EAL learners, you need to consider the balance between teaching the curriculum content in an interesting and challenging way while making sure that you are supporting their specific English language needs. When planning, you need to consider what you are expecting your EAL learners to do with the language they are learning and the 'kinds' of language they will require to access the learning (Conteh, 2015, p.75).

Reflection and discussion activity

Reflection

Read the following examples of classroom practice and consider the questions below.

In an RE lesson, the two newly arrived pupils are working together supported by a teaching assistant and are colouring in a picture of a mosque. The rest of the class are working on an activity to identify the names and function of each section of the mosque.

Leticia is a new arrival in Year 5 and a beginner in English. Her school reports from Colombia show that she has good literacy skills in Spanish. The class teacher gives her some English grammar worksheets to complete while the other pupils are doing extended writing.

Discussion

- Is there any good practice here?

- How could practice be improved?

Trainee and mentor, now compare your ideas and discuss the similarities and differences in your responses.

There are a number of approaches to engaging learners of EAL. Some of these are presented in the work of Nichiols (2010):

- A whole brain approach to learning that incorporates the theory that learners have different preferred ways of learning and acquiring information.

- Uses a variety of training techniques and activities that appeal to multiple intelligences and that of a wide variety of learners.

- Creates a stress-free environment for learners that promotes the idea of learning being powerful and fun.

- Reduces the time spent in the classroom as well as designing learning programs due to the activity-based nature of Accelerated Learning (see Figure 11.1).

(Nichiols, 2010, p.6)

The four-stage accelerated learning cycle is a proven, effective sequence for learning that is a fundamental part of accelerated learning, see Figure 11.1. The connect phase does exactly that: it connects learners with what has already been learned. It involves activating the learner's prior knowledge. This can be seen in the use of mental starters where learners have the opportunity to revisit prior learning which may include key vocabulary or

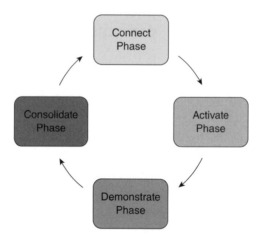

Figure 11.1 The Accelerated Learning Cycle (Smith, Lovatt and Wise, 2005, p.20, cited in Nichiols, 2010, p.8)

grammatical form. The activate phase involves obtaining the information required to solve the problem. This phase provides the opportunity to inspire learners through the use of VAK learning styles and multiple intelligences. The third phase is the demonstrate phase: this includes providing the learners with the chance to apply what has been taught and demonstrate their understanding. The consolidate phase includes the opportunity for reflection for the learner. They can reflect on their learning, which should then be linked back to the connection phase: what do I now know which I did not know before?

Activity

Below you will see a simple lesson plan for a KS1 EAL learner with a focus upon 'Drawing a story'.

Look over the lesson plan and consider how the sections of the plan relate to the four-stage accelerated learning cycle above.

Table 11.3 Sample lesson plan

Date	Year group: Lower KS1	Language level: Beginner
Lesson aims: • To encourage learners to use English in a creative way • To develop listening skills and visual skills		

Date	Year group: Lower KS1	Language level: Beginner
• To enjoy listening to a story • To create a picture book • To retell a story using visual prompts		
STARTER	Draw a picture of a story book on the board and ask *What's this?* Have a class discussion about stories. Use a few of these questions to generate ideas: What is your favourite story? What kind of stories do you like? What kind of characters appear in stories? Do you like (fairy) stories? Do you like looking at pictures in story books?	
INTRODUCTION	If necessary, pre-teach or revise some key vocabulary from the story using flashcards, simple drawings, miming, etc. e.g. *carpet, shop, magic, jungle, desert, ice, snow, mountains, foggy, forest, windy, island, thunder, lightning, storm.* Tell learners that they are going to listen to a story and they should try to imagine everything they hear. If they want to close their eyes to help concentrate, they can. Either play the audio of the story (without showing the images) at: **http://learnenglishkids.britishcouncil.org/ en/short-stories/ali-and-the-magic-carpet*** Or, read the story aloud (see the story text), pausing after each section for learners to assimilate the information. (*Accessed January 30, 2017)	
MAIN ACTIVITY	Elicit the main sections of the story and write them on the board with numbers, e.g. 1. Ali finds a carpet in his uncle's shop 2. The carpet starts moving and speaks 3. Ali flies to the jungle on the carpet 4. Ali flies to the desert on the carpet 5. Ali flies to the South Pole on the carpet 6. Ali flies to the mountains on the carpet 7. Ali flies to a forest on the carpet	

(Continued)

(Continued)

Date	Year group: Lower KS1	Language level: Beginner
	8. Ali flies to an island on the carpet 9. Ali flies back to the shop Put learners into groups and appoint numbers 1-9 - each child will have two numbers. Explain that the numbers correspond to the key moments in the story and they are going to illustrate these scenes to make a picture book. Play or read the story again to remind them of the details in their scenes. Learners draw and colour their illustrations.	
PLENARY	In groups, learners use the picture to retell the story of Ali and the magic carpet, with each child telling the part of the story that he or she has illustrated.	

For more information, follow the links below to listen to Cummins's talking about his five principles of supporting EAL learners.

1. Identify language and content objectives

2. Frontload the lesson

3. Provide input

4. Enable Language Production (oral and written)

5. Assess language and content objectives

www.youtube.com/watch?v=Zu-6V3N5RHI
www.youtube.com/watch?v=XjABYSrRGu8

What current teaching practice is taking place?

The Education Endowment Foundation (EEF) and The Bell Foundation have recently commissioned two reports to analyse the evidence on the achievement of pupils with English as an Additional Language (EAL). Together, these ground-breaking reports present a comprehensive overview of the issues relating to EAL facing schools today.

Find out more from . . . research

In Strand's report (Strand, 2015) there is a presentation of an in-depth analysis of the most recent England National Pupil Database (NPD) from 2013 addressing the question, 'Who are the most at-risk groups of EAL learners and what are the predictors of low attainment for these learners?'. Murphy's report is a systematic review of international research into interventions designed to improve their English language and literacy in order to identify the most promising programmes and interventions (Murphy, 2015).

You can find the reports here:

Strand, 2015:

https://v1.educationendowmentfoundation.org.uk/uploads/pdf/EAL_and_educational_achievement2.pdf

Murphy, 2015:

www.unboundphilanthropy.org/sites/default/files/EAL_Systematic_review1.pdf

Both accessed March 17, 2017

The current standards for teachers emphasise the provision required for learners of EAL in standard 5: *Teachers must take account of the needs of pupils whose first language is not English* and recognise *their ability to take part may be in advance of their communication skills in English* (DfE, 2012). This raises the question of how we effectively challenge curriculum learning while language development is still in the very early stages. The literacy skills that develop in primary school go on to serve as the foundation upon which further academic learning proceeds at secondary education.

Sometimes teachers are misguided by misconceptions of language learning and further myths when learning a new language.

Discussion activity

Look at the misconceptions below. Discuss together why teachers might have these misconceptions and how you can avoid this happening in your teaching.

1. *Languages should be kept separate or learners become confused - Interference.*

2. *Pupils will pick up English naturally in the classroom, they don't need teaching - Immersion.*

3. *Language diversity is a problem and better if pupils speak English at all times.*

4. *It is impossible, or very difficult, to learn a new language beyond a young age - the critical period.*

Focused language knowledge is required by all. Language is our tool for all learning, an *inextricable part of our personal and social lives, the cultures we live in, and who we are* (Conteh, 2015, p.33). Many primary school children with EAL struggle with the more passive and receptive language skills, listening and reading comprehension in particular (McKendry and Murphy, 2011). Therefore, it is critical that you have a thorough understanding of the development of language and literacy skills in order to be able to develop appropriate and effective pedagogical support. Every child is capable of learning, but in very different ways; you will need to understand how to mediate all other factors, social, cultural, emotional, affective and cognitive resources, political and historical, which contribute to or hinder their learning experience.

A further possible misunderstanding for teachers is the confusion between EAL and SEN. Language needs should not be perceived as learning needs and a learner with EAL must not be categorised as having special educational needs per se.

 ── **Find out more from . . . research** ───

Cummins (2001) argues that this misconception surrounding the crossover with EAL and SEN can have negative academic outcomes. It can lead to learners of EAL being assessed as having learning needs and placed within SEN groups when actually their needs are specifically language needs. They require specific language support to assist with developing across the four skills – speaking, listening, reading and writing – especially if they are to be able to cope with the demands of the primary curriculum. Cummins's theoretical models will help you develop an understanding of the different ways in which your EAL learners' experience language learning.

 ── **Chapter summary** ────────────

Within this chapter you have thought about the diversity in the range of experience and knowledge that multilingual and EAL learners bring to your classroom and strategies to help new arrivals embrace their new cultural experiences. You have also discussed the importance of recognising and reflecting on your experiences of language diversity and ethnicity for your own professional development.

You have looked at some research in the first part of the chapter which suggests some effective approaches to second language acquisition and how theoretical approaches can develop your own awareness and understanding of how language and learning are linked. Additionally, you have further considered practical approaches for EAL learners and promoting language learning through effective assessment and planning. Within this section I have introduced you to the importance of speaking and listening for learning, collaborative learning, and developed your understanding of how to plan and teach to promote language learning across the curriculum.

Finally, you have explored what current provision and teaching practice is taking place in our primary classrooms and offered practical suggestions which will assist with language learning for your EAL learners.

Throughout the chapter you were challenged to think about how primary classrooms must thrive on the uniqueness of all learners. Diversity and differences command work, resolution, openness and understanding. Through this you will be able to create a learning environment that will advance the educational goals of all children.

References

Canale, M and Swain, M (1980) Theoretical bases of communicative approaches to second language teaching and testing. *Applied Linguistics*, 1(1): 1–47.

Clarke, P (1992) *English as a 2nd Language in Early Childhood*. FKA Multicultural Resources Centre. Richmond: Victoria, Australia.

Conteh, J (2015) *The EAL Teaching Book*. London: SAGE.

Cummins, J (1979) Cognitive/academic language proficiency, linguistic interdependence, the optimum age question and some other matters. *Working Papers on Bilingualism*, 19: 121–29.

Cummins, J and Nakajima, K (1987) Age of arrival, length of residence, and interdependence of literacy skills among Japanese immigrant students. In Harley, B, Allen, P, Cummins, J and Swain, M (eds) *The Development of Bilingual Proficiency: Final report*. Toronto: Modern Language Centre, OISE.

Cummins, J (2001) *An Introductory Reader to the Writings of Jim Cummins*. Clevedon: Multilingual Matters.

Department for Education (2007) *Ensuring the Attainment of Pupils Learning English as an Additional Language: A management guide*. Ref: DfES 00011-2007. Available at: **www.naldic.org.uk/Resources/NALDIC/Teaching%20and%20Learning/ks3_ws_eal_mgmt_gd_sch_strat.pdf** (accessed March 17, 2017).

Department for Education (2007) *New Arrivals Excellence Programme Guidance*. Ref: 00650-2007BKT-EN

Department for Education (2011a) *Schools Pupils and their Characteristics*. Available at: **www.education.gov.uk/rsgateway/DB/SFR/s001012/index.shtml** (accessed January 30, 2017).

Department for Education (2011b) *Teachers' Standards*. Available at: **www.education.gov.uk/publications/standard/publicationDetail/Page1/DFE-00066-2011** (Accessed January 30, 2017).

Department for Education (2012) *Teachers' Standards*. DFE-00066-2011. Available at: **www.gov.uk/government/uploads/system/uploads/attachment_data/file/283566/Teachers_standard_information.pdf** (accessed January 30, 2017).

Drury, R (2007) *Young Bilingual Learners at Home and School*. Stoke-on-Trent: Trentham.

Ellis, R (1994) *The Study of Second Language Acquisition*. Oxford: Oxford University Press.

Hayden, M (2006) *Introduction to International Education: International schools and their communities*. London: SAGE Publications.

Krashen, S (1985) *The Input Hypothesis*. Beverly Hills, CA: Laredo Publishing Company.

Lightbrown, PM and Spada, N (1999) *How Languages are Learned*. Oxford: Oxford University Press.

Long, MH (1985) Input and second language acquisition theory. In Gass, S and Madden, C (eds) *Input in Second Language Acquisition*. Rowley, MA: Newbury House, pp.377–83.

McKendry, M and Murphy, VA (2011) A comparative study of listening comprehension measures in English as an additional language and native English-speaking primary school children. *Evaluation and Research in Education*, 24: 17–40.

Murphy, V (2015) A systematic review of intervention research examining English language and literacy development in children with English as an Additional Language (EAL). Oxford: Oxford University Press.

Nichiols, G (2010) Accelerated learning and elearning: an overview. IT6930, Internship in Information and Learning Technologies.

Nieto, S (2010) *Language, Culture, and Teaching: Critical perspectives*. New York: Routledge.

Nonchev, A and Tagarov, N (2012) Integrating refugee and asylum-seeking children in the educational systems of EU member states. Bulgaria: Center for the Study of Democracy.

The Northern Association of Support Services for Equality and Achievement (NASSEA) (2016) EAL assessment framework. Bury: NASSEA.

Pica, T (1994) Research on negotiation: what does it reveal about second language learning conditions, processes and outcomes? *Language Learning*, 44: 493–527.

Pica, T (1998) Second language learning through interaction: multiple perspectives. In Regan, V (ed.) *Contemporary Approaches to Second Language Acquisition in Social 13–14 Contexts: Crosslinguistic perspectives*. Dublin: University College Dublin Press, pp.9–31.

Quality and Curriculum Authority (QCA) (2000) *A Language in Common: Assessing English as an additional language*. London: QCA Publications.

Siraj-Blatchford, I, Sylva, K, Taggart, B, Melhuish, E, Sammons, P and Elliot, K (2003) *The Effective Provision of Pre-School Education (EPPE) Project: Technical Paper 10 'Intensive Case Studies of Practice Across the Foundation Stage'* (DfES Research Brief, RBX 16-03). Available at: **www.dcsf.gov.uk/research/data/uploadfiles/RBX16-03. pdf** (accessed January 30, 2017).

Smith, A, Lovatt, M and Wise, D (2005) *Accelerated Learning: A user's guide*. Stafford: Crown House Publishing.

Strand, S (2015) *English as an Additional Language (EAL) and Educational Achievement in England: An analysis of the National Pupil Database*. Oxford: Oxford University Press.

Tabors, P (1997) *One Child, Two Languages: A guide for Preschool Educators of Children Learning English as a Second Language*. Baltimore, MD: Paul Brookes Publishing.

Vygotsky, L (1962) *Thought and Language*. Cambridge, MA: MIT Press.

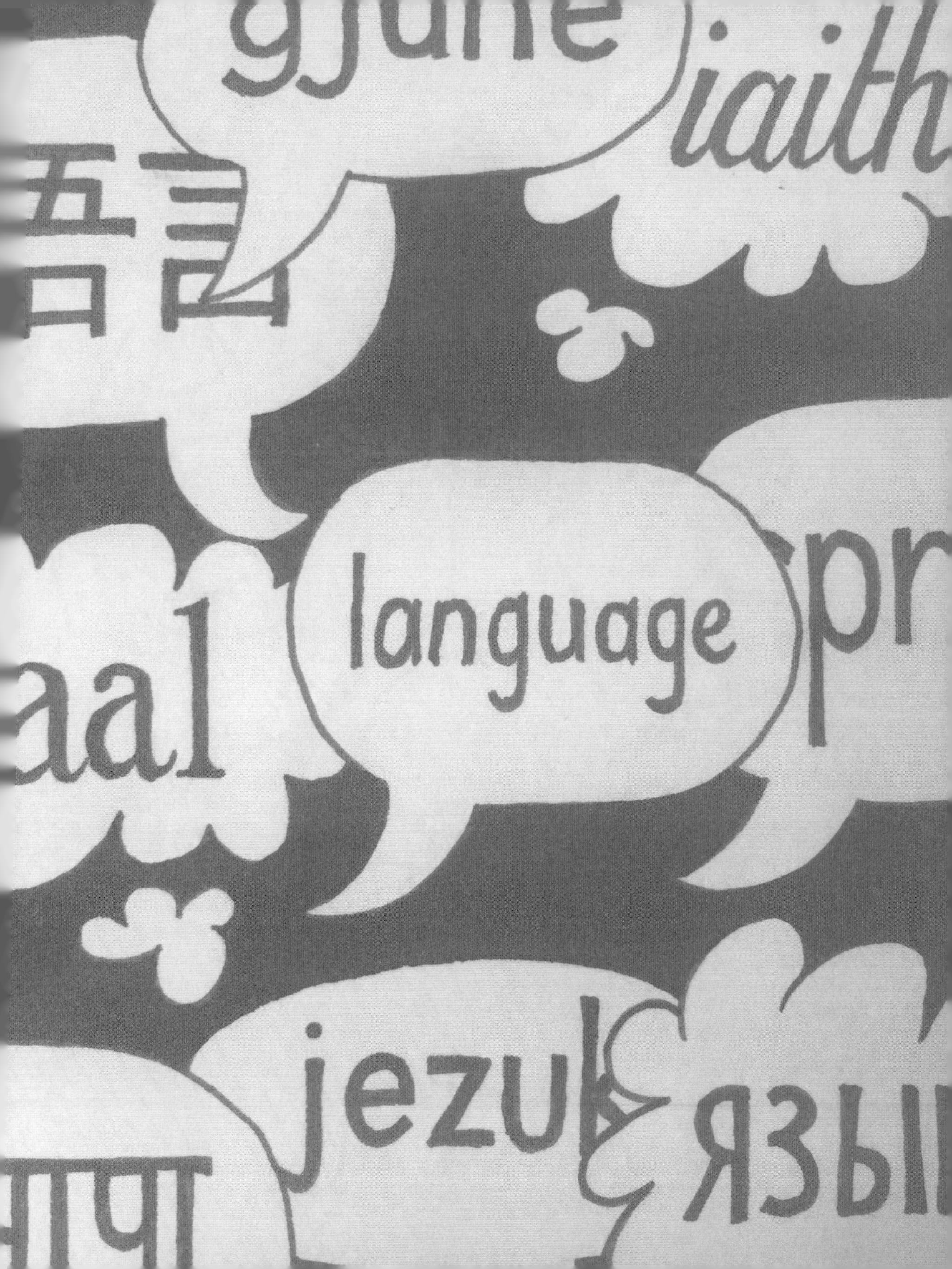
language

12
Working with Teaching Assistants
Emma Clarke

 **This chapter will**

- develop your understanding of how to work with other professionals in schools;
- consider how best to deploy Teaching Assistants (TAs);
- be aware of some recent research and guidance on deploying TAs;
- reflect on some of your own values and beliefs which will impact on the way you work with TAs.

Introduction

Deploying support staff effectively is a requirement within Standard 8 of the Teachers' Standards (DfE, 2011) and relates to fulfilling your wider responsibilities as a teacher. Working with other adults, specifically TAs, is a fact of life for most teachers now with the Education Endowment Foundation research (Sharples *et al.*, 2015) stating that there are now more TAs than teachers in primary schools. Your chances of working with a TA are therefore very high, and it is essential that you get this important relationship right. However, TAs are not the only group of adults working in schools: you may also encounter parent helpers, office staff, governors, administrators, faith leaders and many more. Although this chapter focuses specifically on working with TAs, many of the strategies, skills and key points discussed will also relate to other adults.

Reflection and discussion activity

Reflection

Trainee, think of all of the different adults you may encounter in school.

Mentor, share with the trainee some of the roles that other adults in you school undertake.

Discussion

Mentor and trainee, discuss together some of the advantages of other adults working in schools.

Different expectations and roles of TAs

A key issue which often arises when working with TAs is that their role is very varied, and different schools use TAs in different ways. Historically, TAs were viewed by some as a *mum's army* of *paint pot washers* (Bach *et al.*, 2006). This somewhat negative and belittling view has thankfully long since gone and TAs are now viewed by some as 'paraprofessionals', taking on many of the roles of qualified teachers. However, in research (Bland and Sleightholme, 2012) pupils still noted not TAs' pedagogical role, but that they were required to *fetch coffee and biscuits for the teacher*. This is clearly not an effective use of support staff.

The roles that TAs play in schools have changed significantly over the years. TA numbers first experienced a significant increase with the introduction of the 1981 Education Act which encouraged pupils with special educational needs to move from special into mainstream schools. TA numbers continued to rise with the advent of the National Curriculum in the late 1980s, when increasing TA numbers was seen as a way of easing the increasing bureaucratic demands on teachers. In 2003, with the publication of *Raising Standards and Tackling Workload: A National Agreement* (DfES, 2003), the role of Higher Level TA (HLTA) was created, and later when the requirement for teachers to be freed up for planning, preparation and assessment (PPA) time was brought in, the role that TAs undertook expanded. Many HLTAs were used by schools to cover PPA times where teachers were not in classrooms. This raised some concerns for both HLTAs and teachers.

It is the expectation that TAs play an increasingly pedagogical role in schools that has been the most controversial and caused apprehension for teachers and TAs alike. Some changes were welcomed, with suggestions that being a TA was now a *profession* rather than being a *second class citizen* (Galton and MacBeath, 2008). The evolving TA role was also described as increasingly *interesting and professional*, and was shifting away from the perception that a TA is someone who only *staples something to a board for eight hours a day* (Cockroft and Atkinson, 2015). Nevertheless, the blurring of roles between the teacher and the TA was seen by some as producing a decline in teacher's professional status (Blatchford *et al.*, 2007) and *role creep* was viewed as a threat to teachers. This *role creep* was seen as a concern for both teachers and TAs, where

TAs felt to some extent coerced into responsibilities they were not trained or qualified for (Anderson and Finney, 2008), while some teachers viewed TAs' encroaching role as a threat to their autonomy and professionalism.

TAs' roles have now changed beyond recognition since the days where the job was viewed by some as *a bit of money for housewives* (Smith *et al.*, 2004), and research (Blatchford *et al.*, 2007) has shown that TAs 'direct pedagogical role' is now greater than time spent helping either the teacher or the school. However, this has resulted in many schools having a lack of a shared clear and cohesive understanding of TA expectations. This can make working with TAs in the classroom difficult as it can leave you in a position where you are unsure of what you can and cannot reasonably ask them to do. Schools will have job descriptions for TAs, but teachers often do not get to see these.

 Reflection and discussion activity

Reflection

Trainee, think about the range of tasks that a TA may be asked to undertake. Rehearse having a discussion with a TA about some of these specific tasks you would like them to do.

Discussion

Mentor, briefly explain how TAs are deployed in your school and the range of responsibilities they have.

Mentor and trainee, consider how the wide variety of ways in which TAs are deployed may be beneficial or problematic for teachers.

It might be beneficial when you sit down to meet with your TA to ask them what types of work they usually do in the classroom, what they would like to do, and possibly what they would not like to do. It is also important to know about any specific skills or strengths that TAs working with you possess, and if they are willing to share them. For example, if you have a TA who is highly skilled in art or music, this could enhance the teaching you provide; if your TA is bilingual, they could support your languages provision, and so on.

Different schools and teachers use TAs differently, with some TAs having largely pedagogical roles while others are deployed to support teachers, and it is important you find out how your class teacher or school deploys certain TAs. For example, some TAs might work one-to-one with a pupil with specific difficulties, others may carry out administration tasks, some (often higher level teaching assistants, HLTAs) may cover whole classes, while others might teach specific interventions. TAs are employed under different contracts at differing grades and some, specifically HLTAs, may have greater responsibilities than others and, therefore, you might deploy them in different ways and expect different things from them.

This chapter will look specifically at TAs who are allocated either to you as a class teacher or to your class more generally and are working under your direction.

How to develop professional working relationships with adults in the classroom: research

Mackenzie (2011) found in her research that teacher–TA relationships were exemplified by *tensions, misunderstandings and even antagonism*. Almost 20 years before that, Thomas (1992) noted that *good teamwork is notoriously difficult to achieve*, and he raised concerns over issues of cooperation between professionals who may hold radically different ideas on what should be done in the classroom as well as 'on what education is all about'.

This all clearly contradicts the *close partnership* between teachers and TAs which was cited as providing *a marked improvement in the quality of teaching* (HMI, 2002). Yet research (Blatchford *et al.*, 2007) showed that teachers believed that TAs had a positive impact on pupils' *motivation, social skills and behaviour*. Teachers reported that working with TAs also had advantages in improving pupils' learning outcomes, providing increased support for learning and teaching, and improved classroom management (Blatchford et al., 2004). This was echoed in later research by Galton and MacBeath (2008) who found that teachers particularly valued TAs' contributions when working with small groups, or specified pupils. Recent research by the Education Endowment Foundation (Sharples *et al.*, 2015) confirmed the benefits of teachers working with TAs, which included freeing up the teachers so that they were able to spend more time 'on the core functions of teaching'. Advantages were also seen in a reduction of teacher workload, and as echoed in other research an improvement in *teachers' perceptions of stress and job satisfaction*. Importantly, teachers stated that having a TA present also increased their confidence and ability *to cope* (Galton and MacBeath, 2008).

 Reflection and discussion activity

Reflection

Trainee, have you seen or heard about any of the advantages or pitfalls of working with other adults in the classroom? Were there any that have not been mentioned above? How might you manage some of the issues mentioned?

Mentor, share your experiences of working with adults in the classroom, both positive and negative. How did you manage the negative and foster the positive aspects of the relationship?

Discussion

Mentor and trainee, research stated that TAs improved the teacher's ability to 'cope'. What do you think is meant by this? How might TAs do this?

As a result of TAs' changing and evolving role, it is often rather difficult to clarify expectations. Research showed that where there was no clear definition of the TA role, the gap was often filled by an unsatisfactory reliance on the teacher and TA 'getting on' with each other. It could be seen that that this is not a professional way to conduct the teacher–TA relationship. It is important to ensure that you can have both a professional and friendly relationship with your TA. This will support you in getting the best out of the working relationship for you, the TA – and most importantly the pupils in your class. It will be key to understand some of the main issues emerging from research these include:

- *Time*: this is probably one of the most important issues to consider in developing a professional relationship with your TA or TAs.

  Webster *et al.* (2011) found that three-quarters of teachers questioned had no formal time to plan and talk over sessions with TAs, which resulted in *brief and ad hoc* discussions. This supported earlier research (Marr *et al.*, 2001), which found similar issues, but also reported that where joint planning and feedback took place, only one in five TAs were paid for the additional time. Gerschel's (2005) research showed that the *lack of prior notice* and necessity to *interpret teaching in the lesson* was a source of frequent complaints from TAs. Similarly, (Blatchford *et al.*, 2012) reported that two-thirds of teachers and three-quarters of TAs rated preparation and feedback time as *less effective*, reiterating reliance on TAs *goodwill*. These themes also recurred in Sharples *et al.*'s (2015) research, with TAs stating they often *went into lessons blind*, and that communication, as previously stated, often relied on TAs generosity meeting during unpaid hours.

  It can be seen, then, that it is imperative that you liaise carefully with any TAs you work with, and ensure (unless already done on a whole-school level) that you have time to discuss with your TAs the content of your lesson, and what you expect them to do, as well as ideally providing some forum for feedback at the end of the session. In some schools, this can take place in assembly time; others, where time is short, rely on 'communication books'. However, if you depend on writing rather than talking, ensure that at some point in the day or week you make time to chat with your TA. Be mindful, though, that playtimes and lunchtimes are not always convenient, and many TAs do not get paid for time before or after school. Several of the practical ideas later in this chapter rely on the assumption that you will have spent time discussing these with your TA, rather than simply surprising them in the middle of a session.

- *Training*: this is a key aspect to be aware of.

  Much research (including, but not only: Tucker, 2009; Symes and Humphrey, 2011; Sharples *et al.*, 2015) has shown a *mismatch* between the level of training that TAs receive and their increasingly demanding role. The DfEE (1997) cautioned that many *TAs had little or no training for the work they do* and Ofsted (2008) conceded that *weaknesses remained* in training and deployment. The same point was highlighted later (Webster *et al.*, 2011; Sharples *et al.*, 2015) with concerns continuing to be raised about the level of training that TAs had. It is important, therefore, that you take some time to discuss with your TA(s) whether they have had any specific training, and in what. If your TA has not received any recent training, bear in mind that they may need support and guidance if you have asked them to carry out specific focused intervention tasks, for example.

Case study

Pippa, an experienced teacher, and Jo, her TA, invested time in meeting together before the start of the year. They used this time to discuss the strengths and skills that each could bring to the classroom. Pippa discovered that Jo was a talented artist and they discussed how these skills could be shared with the pupils. They also considered how to keep each other informed about planning and progress for specific pupils, and decided a shared book would be useful. Pippa added the weekly plans when they were completed, and Jo added notes about specific pupils and more general feedback on progress. They also agreed to have an informal chat about the week when they were on playground duty together. This ensured there was a range of strategies to keep communication open between them and they were clear about the specific strengths each other had.

Reflection and discussion activity

Reflection

Trainee, how does the school you are in or other schools you have worked in manage some of these challenges? What have you seen that works well?

Discussion

Mentor, discuss what your school does or is planning to do to manage some of these challenges.

Trainee, what do you feel is 'best practice' here? How will you cope with these issues?

How to deploy TAs effectively: what research has shown

There has been a steady increase in the guidance on how schools should work with TAs, but some of the proposed strategies rely on whole-school negotiation and cannot always be implemented by individual teachers. However, some of the key ideas from research which you can implement will now be discussed.

- *Working with low-attaining pupils or pupils with SEND*: historically, TAs usually worked with these pupils, either in the classroom or in withdrawal groups which worked outside the classroom.

  Evidence from research (Webster *et al.*, 2012; Webster, 2014) has highlighted the continuing beliefs of some schools and parents that TAs were 'hardwired' to support pupils with SEND. Yet, findings (Blatchford *et al.*, 2012) demonstrated that when TAs worked with lower-attaining or SEN pupils, they actually had a negative impact on their achievement.

However, there are ways to deploy TAs with pupils who need the most support which positively impacts on their progress, which is through structured interventions for short periods. Sharples *et al.* (2015) highlighted that *positive effects are only observed when TAs work in structured settings with high-quality support and training*. These elements are, therefore, essential to keep in mind when planning interventions and deploying TAs to work with specific groups.

- *Supporting not replacing the teacher*: it is important that you do not expect the TA to take on your teaching role.

   Think carefully about where your skills and expertise are most needed, and how your TA can support you in freeing up time to work with those pupils in order to ensure that all pupils are making progress. When planning, make sure that you do not use your TA to support the same group of pupils for an extended period. Try to ensure that if you have asked your TA to work with a group outside the classroom on a specific planned intervention this is not for a prolonged period. Both the pupils and the TA should be included in whole-class activities; constantly working outside the classroom is not beneficial for either the pupils or for the TA.

 **Case study**

Lucy, an experienced TA, found that the teachers she now worked with asked her to undertake short-term interventions with a range of pupils usually outside the classroom. Lucy felt marginalised and was concerned that she was not seen as part of the class. She felt that being asked to work outside the classroom resulted in her not building relationships with the teacher or the pupils. As a result, she felt this hindered any specifically tailored work, as she did not know the pupils well and she found it difficult to understand what the teacher wanted because she did not know how the pupils achieved in class or the usual routines and expectations.

Developing pupils' independence

Research (Webster, 2014) showed that pupils who worked with TAs for extended periods, particularly those a one-to-one basis, had significantly less contact with the teacher and their peers, with the TA being their main source of interaction.

This model of the TA closely working with the same pupil or same small group of pupils also raises the issues of 'stereo teaching', where the TA simply repeats what the teacher says, and the 'velcro' model, where the TA works so closely with a pupil or pupils that they unintentionally reduce their interaction with others. These both promote reliance on the TA and reduce the pupil's, or pupils', independence, which is something that you as a teacher need to foster. Research (Russell *et al.*, 2013; Webster and Blatchford, 2013; Sharples *et al.*, 2015) has shown that TAs' interactions with pupils are different to teacher interactions. Task completion as opposed to a clear understanding of the objective is often prioritised by TAs, and closed, rather than open, questions are asked. There was also seen to be a difference in the amount of support versus 'spoon feeding' provided, with

TAs often not giving pupils long enough to answer questions. This effectively *closes-down* (Russell *et al.*, 2013) discussion and, coupled with the *vague explanations*, some TAs were observed to give constrained rather than enhanced learning. Nevertheless, with careful deployment, these issues can be minimised. Sharples *et al.* (2015) suggested encouraging your TA to focus on the following:

- *Providing the right amount of support at the right time*: this will help to develop pupils' independence and enquiry, rather than simply waiting for the TA to tell them the answer.

- Encouraging *pupils to be comfortable taking risks with their learning*: this links with the previous point. Encourage your TA to sit and wait, and to support the pupil in developing their own thoughts, ideas and understanding, rather than focusing on simply getting the task finished.

- *Giving the least amount first to help support pupils' ownership of the task*: again, this links closely with the above points. Support your TA in enhancing pupils' independence: this can be done by ensuring that your TA does not work with the same group or individual pupils all the time.

- *Use of open-ended questions*: The grid in Figure 12.1 was suggested to help TAs (and also teachers) develop open-ended, challenging questions.

Complexity ➡️

	Is …	Did …	Can …	Would …	Will …	Might …
Who						
What						
Where						
When						
Why						
How						

Complexity ⬇️

Figure 12.1 Use of open-ended questions, from Sharples et al. *(2015) Making Best Use of Teaching Assistants: Guidance report. London: Education Endowment Foundation*

Reflection and discussion activity

Reflection

Trainee, consider how questioning supports pupils' learning. Use the format in Figure 12.1 to ask some increasingly complex questions in the classroom.

Mentor, model for the trainee some questions using the grid in Figure 12.1. Taking a topic you or they are currently teaching, coach the trainee in using the grid to devise questioning, moving on to formulating increasingly more complex questions.

Discussion

Trainee, discuss how the issues from research will affect how you deploy TAs within your own classroom.

How to deploy TAs effectively: practical ideas

The preceding sections have highlighted some of the advantages and issues that may arise when working with other adults, specifically TAs. This section will provide you with some ideas on how to deploy TAs effectively in your lessons. Research (Webster *et al.*, 2012) showed that TAs spent half their time in lessons being 'passive' and listening to the teacher. When this 'passive' time is unplanned, it is clearly not an effective use of anybody's time and is not good practice. It is essential that you think about how to minimise this 'passive' time and ensure that pupils, and you, as the teacher, are benefiting from having a TA in the classroom.

You could try using some of these strategies to involve TAs during the main teaching or teacher exposition:

The TA could scribe pupils' suggestions on the board

This strategy ensures that the TA is actively involved in the session while you are teaching the whole class and has many advantages, including:

- improving the pace of your teaching – as you do not have to pause to write;

- support for your management of behaviour – you do not lose eye contact with pupils;

- direct teaching does not stop – ideas generated are not paused mid-flow while you write them down;

- TA is 'up front' – they can be an additional pair of eyes, assessing who understands, who may need support, who is focused, and so on.

However, this approach needs practice and negotiation between you and your TA to ensure that you both understand what will be written, where and how. You will also need to check that your TA is comfortable doing this, and that their handwriting, grammar and spelling are at least as good as yours.

During discussions, the TA could have specific questions to ask specific groups, for example, high-attaining (HA) or low-attaining (LA) pupils

This questioning could either support or extend learning, depending on the individual pupils. It is important to bear in mind, however, that as previously discussed, working with the same pupils for extended periods is not good practice. However, this approach can be very useful for:

- encouraging reticent pupils to contribute;

- extending high-attaining pupils and taking their learning in a different direction;

- enabling the teacher to spend time with these specific groups while the TA supports the rest of the class, checking that pupils are on task, encouraging participation, etc.

During discussion time, the TA could act as a 'roving reporter'

Here the TA could move around and listen to pupils acting on the teacher's direction while the teacher works with a specific group, pair or pupil. The TA could listen for:

- the 'best discussion';

- the 'best question asked';

- the 'best answer given';

- the 'best use of correct vocabulary'.

The TA could then feed back to the class on who (and why) had given the 'best answer', 'most thought provoking discussion' and so on. This strategy might support the TA as it gives them a clear purpose as opposed to 'keeping an eye on pupils'. It may also encourage pupils' discussions and debates if they know an adult is listening carefully to them.

The TA could act as a scribe

The TA could work with specific pupils (behaviour difficulties, attention difficulties etc.) and scribe their key points/vocabulary/ideas on 'sticky-notes' which either the pupils or TA can share with class.

This is a useful way to gather ideas from pupils who, for whatever reason, find it difficult to record their suggestions.

The TA could work with a specific group of pupils during the teacher's exposition to extend learning, set challenges or consolidate prior learning

This is effective when the TA can follow up detailed comments in the teacher's marking to support pupils with specific aspects of their work. Again, it is important that this is not used with the same group of pupils, or at the start of every lesson, but it can be a helpful way of ensuring that key aspects are addressed, and the necessary support is given, so pupils' learning can move on in the main part of the lesson.

The TA could work with high-attaining pupils to draw up list of success criteria

Using the lesson objective(s) provided by the teacher, the TA could work with pupils specified by you to devise a list of success criteria. This activity would work well to stretch high-attaining pupils. Again, this would need careful discussion with you and your TA so s/he feels confident supporting their discussions.

Reflection and discussion activity

Reflection

Trainee, think about the ways of using TAs that have just been discussed. What are the strengths and limitations of these approaches?

Mentor, think about which strategies you use more or less. Why might that be? Are there additional approaches that might be helpful or tips for the trainee?

Discussion

Devise a list of strategies, building on those suggested above that you would like to trial in the classroom with a TA. Begin to work together to evaluate their success.

Things to remember

- Consider when you plan for your TA the range of pupils you are asking them to work with.

- Ensure that your TA is not routinely working with the lower attaining pupils, unless it is on a short, focused intervention with clear links made to classroom learning.

- Think about how your TA's skills and experience can support your teaching. For example, while you are working with a focus group, can they take on the role of keeping the rest of the class on task, encouraging and supporting, answering questions and so on?

- Careful thought and detailed consideration of how your TA can add value to, and support what you do early on in your relationship will result in a classroom where everyone is informed and clear about what they are doing.

- Cockroft and Atkinson's (2015) research found that *approachability* in teachers *contributed to how effective they (TAs) could be*. With this in mind, it is essential that you find time to talk to your TA and work together to be the most effective team possible.

 Chapter summary

Throughout this chapter, effective ways of using what can be highly skilled and experienced individuals have been discussed. Research evidence has been considered when discussing some of the advantages and issues when working with TAs. It can be seen that TAs are a real asset to both you and your class, and can enhance provision when deployed effectively.

Find out more from . . . reports

Making Best Use of Teaching Assistants: Guidance report

https://v1.educationendowmentfoundation.org.uk/uploads/pdf/TA_Guidance_Report_Interactive.pdf

'Maximising TAs' website has lots of up-to-date resources and research and is very accessible and helpful:

http://maximisingtas.co.uk

Both accessed January 30, 2017

The DISS research report:

Blatchford, P, Russell, A and Webster, R (2012) *Reassessing the Impact of Teaching Assistants.* Abingdon: Routledge.

References

Anderson, V and Finney, M (2008) *I'm a TA not a PA!* In Richards, G and Armstrong, F (eds), *Key Issues for Teaching Assistants: Working in diverse classrooms.* London: Routledge.

Bach, S, Kessler, I and Heron, P (2006) Changing job boundaries and workforce reform: the case of teaching assistants. *Industrial Relations Journal*, 37(1): 2–21.

Bland, K and Sleightholme, S (2012) Researching the pupil voice: what makes a good teaching assistant? *Support for Learning*, 27(4): 172–6.

Blatchford, P, Russell, A and Webster, R (2012) *Reassessing the Impact of Teaching Assistants.* Abingdon: Routledge.

Blatchford, P, Russell, A, Bassett, P, Brown, P and Martin, C (2004) The role and effects of teaching assistants in English primary schools (Years 4 to 6) 2000–2003. Results from the class size and pupil–adult ratios (CSPAR) KS2 Project. *British Educational Research Journal,* 33(1): 5–26. Available at: **http://doi.org/10.1080/01411920601104292**

Blatchford, P, Russell, A, Bassett, P, Brown, P and Martin, C (2007) The role and effects of teaching assistants in English primary schools (Years 4 to 6) 2000–2003. Results from the class size and pupil–adult ratios (CSPAR) KS2 Project. *British Educational Research Journal*, 33(1): 5–26. Available at: **www.tandfonline.com/doi/abs/10.1080/01411920601104292**

Cockroft, C and Atkinson, C (2015) Using the wider pedagogical role model to establish learning support assistants' views about facilitators and barriers to effective practice. *Support for Learning*, 30(2): 88–104.

Department for Education (2011) *Teachers' Standards.* London: DfE.

Department for Education and Employment (1997) *Excellence for all Children: Meeting special educational needs.* London: DfEE.

Department for Education and Skills (2003) *Raising Standards and Tackling Workload: A national agreement*. London: DfES.

Galton, M and MacBeath, J (2008) *Teachers Under Pressure*. London: SAGE Publications.

Gerschel, L (2005) The special educational needs coordinator's role in managing teaching assistants: the Greenwich perspective. *Support for Learning*, 20(2): 69–76.

HMI (2002) *Teaching Assistants in Primary Schools an Evaluation of the Quality and Impact of their Work* (PDF format). London: HMI.

Mackenzie, S (2011) "Yes, but . . .": rhetoric, reality and resistance in teaching assistants' experiences of inclusive education. *Support for Learning*, 26, 64–71. Available at: **http://doi.org/10.1111/j.1467-9604.2011.01479.x**

Marr, A, Turner, J, Swann, W and Hancock, R (2001) *Classroom Assistants in the Primary School: Employment and deployment*. London: The Open University.

Ofsted (2008) *The Deployment, Training and Development of the Wider School Workforce*. London: Ofsted.

Russell, A, Webster, R and Blatchford, P (2013) *Maximising the impact of Teaching Assistants*. Abingdon: Routledge.

Sharples, J, Webster, R and Blatchford, P (2015) *Making Best Use of Teaching Assistants: Guidance report*. London: Education Endowment Foundation.

Smith, P, Whitby, K, and Sharp, C (2004) *The Employment and Deployment of Teaching Assistants*. Slough: NFER.

Symes, W and Humphrey, N (2011) The deployment, training and teacher relationships of teaching assistants supporting pupils with autistic spectrum disorders (ASD) in mainstream secondary schools. *British Journal of Special Education*, 38(2): 57–64.

Thomas, G (1992) *Effective Classroom Teamwork: Support or intrusion?* London: Routledge.

Tucker, S (2009) Perceptions and reflections on the role of the teaching assistant in the classroom environment. *Pastoral Care in Education*, 27(4): 291–300.

Webster, R (2014) Code of Practice: how research evidence on the role and impact of teaching assistants can inform professional practice. *Educational Psychology in Practice*, 30(3): 232–7.

Webster, R, Blatchford, P and Russell, A (2012) Challenging and changing how schools use teaching assistants: findings from the Effective Deployment of Teaching Assistants project. *School Leadership & Management*, 33(1): 78–96.

Webster, R, Blatchford, P, Bassett, P, Brown, P and Russell, A (2011) The wider pedagogical role of teaching assistants. *School Leadership & Management*, 31(1): 3–20.

13
Professional responsibilities
Sue Lambert

---⬥--- **This chapter will**

- help you to consider what safeguarding is (including the anti-radicalisation agenda);
- help you to be prepared if a child discloses something to you or you are concerned about what a child is saying or doing;
- encourage you to reflect on what is meant by 'Fundamental British Values' (FBV), to be aware of your own values and beliefs, and how this could impact on practice.

Introduction

The importance of the wider professional role is key to you becoming a well-rounded and effective teacher, who is able to act within the statutory frameworks. These set out your professional duties and responsibilities (DfE, 2011). Within Part Two: Personal and Professional conduct of the current *Teachers' Standards* (DfE, 2011), teachers are required to demonstrate consistently high standards of personal and professional conduct. However, it is more than this. As a teacher, you are in a position of trust and you need to create a safe environment for children. They may feel comfortable telling you things they are struggling to understand or that are upsetting or confusing for them. They will also look to you as a role model, so you need to be aware of the impact you can have through your words, actions and role modelling.

It is also important for you to be involved in the school as part of the wider community too. As Ewens (2015) notes, when you start in a new school you need to find out as much as you can about the social and cultural setting from which the children are drawn. You need to know about *the preconceptions and expectations that children bring with them to school, which reflect the beliefs and values of their parents and carers* (p.213). You also need to listen to school staff, look carefully at the school environment and read the school policies so that you are confident in your role as part of the school community, and know the school expectations for you in the wider professional role.

In this chapter, through reflection, case studies and ideas for discussion with mentors, you will consider approaches and strategies that develop your professional role. You need knowledge and understanding about freedom to choose, tolerance and avoiding prejudicial or discriminatory behaviour, however unintentional. You will also explore your role and responsibilities in relation to child protection. You need to be confident about your responsibilities and when you may need advice and help in matters of child protection or confidentiality. This chapter will also help you to think about strategies to have in place to support children who may share safeguarding issues with you.

Values, beliefs and FBV

We all have our own values and beliefs which are a result of our own experiences – personal, educational, social and wider environmental and cultural influences. As a teacher, you need to think about what your own values and beliefs are so that you do not, however unintentionally, undermine the values of others or show intolerance or a lack of respect. Equally, you need to avoid imposing your values or beliefs on children. This is challenging. As Butroyd (2015, p.31) notes:

> as teachers we are not always aware of the values that we transmit. Pupils interpret values and are not simply passive receptors. We need to be aware of values and consider their impact.

Hayes (2015, p.175) also notes that you need to think about how you develop the positive classroom behaviours you want *while resisting the temptation . . . that your way is the only way.*

There has to be a balance because children do not need you to be their friend, although they do want you to be friendly. They will look to you to model expectations on how you interact with them and how you expect them to interact with each other. It can be difficult to get this right when you first start teaching, especially if you are not in the class teacher role all the time until later in your training.

 Reflection and discussion activity

Reflection

Trainee and mentor, separately, think about what your answer to the following question would be.

If you had ten words to describe what you value and believe a teacher should be and/or do what would those words be? List them.

Discussion

Share your lists and look for similarities and differences. Discuss what this highlights about our own values and beliefs, and why we need to be aware of these when working with children.

Your values and beliefs about teaching may grow and change as you gain more experience, observe others teaching and in their wider role, and learn what works well and less well in the classroom. It is always important to be able to reflect on how children may see you in terms of modelling appropriate values and beliefs.

As a teacher, you will be expected to demonstrate consistently high standards of personal and professional conduct. The following statements are from Part Two of the *Teachers' Standards* and define the behaviour and attitudes expected.

- Teachers uphold public trust in the profession and maintain high standards of ethics and behaviour, within and outside school, by:

  o treating pupils with dignity, building relationships rooted in mutual respect, and at all times observing proper boundaries appropriate to a teacher's professional position;

  o having regard for the need to safeguard pupils' well-being, in accordance with statutory provisions;

  o showing tolerance of and respect for the rights of others;

  o not undermining fundamental British values, including democracy, the rule of law, individual liberty and mutual respect, and tolerance of those with different faiths and beliefs;

  o ensuring that personal beliefs are not expressed in ways which exploit pupils' vulnerability or might lead them to break the law.

(DfE, 2011, p.14)

 Reflection and discussion activity

Reflection

Trainee, think about a teacher you had when you were in school or a teacher you have observed teaching. Can you list aspects of how they behaved, or what they did or said that reflected the professional role of the teacher outlined in the section above?

Mentor, reflect on your understanding of the wider professional role of the teacher. What do you do, say and display in the classroom to reflect the expectations noted above? Think about things you can share with the trainee to help them model professionalism in the classroom.

Discussion

Trainee and mentor, look at and discuss the things you have both identified. Are they the same or different? Discuss how some of the things discussed can be modelled by the trainee in the classroom.

Fundamental British values

The terminology 'Fundamental British Values' has caused some confusion and much discussion in the media and for schools. Some say that the term 'British' is divisive and not inclusive, while others have commented that the values expressed within the definition are positive values for all and promote inclusive citizenship. However, it is part of your role to promote these values in school as part of the whole-school duty to promote FBV, and Ofsted include in their inspection reports. The promotion of FBV is largely done through the Spiritual, Moral, Social and Cultural (SMSC) curriculum and citizenship education underpins this, particularly in KS3 and KS4.

 Reflection and discussion activity

Reflection

Trainee, look at the fourth point of the *Teachers' Standards* (2011) on p.221 to see how Fundamental British values are defined. Can you think about examples that would explain this to someone else? If it helps, think about how you might explain this to someone who knew nothing about Britain.

Discussion

Mentor and trainee, discuss the examples that the trainee has suggested. Are they similar or different from to how you would define FBV?

 Reflection and discussion activity

Scenario – In the classroom you overhear a child comment negatively about what another child is wearing. 'You can't have nice things like me because your dad doesn't work.' Other children laugh and the child who has been mocked is upset and goes to sit on their own away from all their classmates.

Reflection

Trainee, think about what strategies you could use to address this sort of comment in terms of building respect, tolerance and understanding in your class. Do you know who you would tell, what you would record? Do you know about the school policies that address this? If not find out about anti-bullying policies and procedures so you are confident about what to do and raise this in your discussion with your mentor.

Mentor, think about things that you have used successfully in the classroom or playground that have helped in similar situations. What did you record, and who did you share this with?

Discussion

Trainee and mentor, discuss the relevant policies and procedures that relate to this sort of incident, and strategies you could use in the classroom to address this. There are some suggestions at the end of this section that may be helpful.

Ideas for developing respect, tolerance and understanding

Some of the things suggested below may be helpful classroom practice for exploring values and beliefs. Schools may also have specific materials and visiting speakers who also help to address issues raised, so make sure you talk to your mentor about this. The resources and activities suggested in the following sections may also be useful.

- Circle time – encourage children to say something positive about the child next to them in the circle, or start a circle discussion with 'I feel sad when . . .' then 'I feel happy when . . .'. Make sure that children know the circle is a safe place to explore feelings and that it is important to respect each other and all responses are valued and not to be ridiculed.

- Create a circle of friends or use a buddy system to support the child and build friendship groups.

- Role play – putting yourself in someone else's shoes. Create scenarios and ask children how they felt in the role of someone being bullied or teased to raise awareness about feelings and empathy. Discuss strategies that they can use, who they could go to for help and teach them how to use their voice in an assertive manner.

- Create golden rules for the class, for example, rights to learn, be listened to and respected – and discuss why these are important and what they might look like in practice. This will help children to have ownership of their environment.

- Put the character back together again. Cut up a character and get the children to put it back together. This can promote discussion about whether the character is still the same after being broken and can again lead to discussion of feelings, respect and how bullying or not being valued can change a person.

- Social, moral, spiritual and cultural (SMSC) taught sessions and resources and use of stories (see the Find out more from section).

- Making use of the restorative approaches discussed in Chapter 9 can also be helpful.

Find out more from . . . websites

Booklists about difference, acceptance and bullying: **www.booktrust.org.uk/books/children/booklists/127/**

Promoting fundamental British values as part of SMSC in schools. DfE advice for maintained schools. November 2014: **www.gov.uk/government/uploads/system/uploads/attachment_data/file/380595/ SMSC_Guidance_Maintained_Schools.pdf**

Both accessed January 30, 2017

Safeguarding

In this section you will learn more about child protection. It links closely to the previous section about values, beliefs and FBV. It is important for you to think about how you support children to develop knowledge, skills and understanding, so that they have strategies to deal with difficult situations, are able to minimise risk-taking behaviours and allow them to make informed choices. You need to be prepared so that you know what to do, who you need to tell and what to record, should a child disclose something to you, or if you have concerns about something a child does or says.

Safeguarding and promoting the welfare of children is defined as:

- protecting children from maltreatment;

- preventing impairment of children's health and development;

- ensuring that children grow up in circumstances consistent with the provision of safe and effective care;

- taking action to enable children to have the best outcomes.

(DfE, 2015a, p.5)

Child protection refers to the activity undertaken to protect specific children who are suffering, or are likely to suffer, significant harm.

It is important for you to be familiar with the safeguarding policies of the schools in which you work. It can be very upsetting to hear what has happened to children but you need to be confident in the policies and procedures, and schools will talk to you when you first go in about safeguarding. Make sure you know what to do and ask questions if you need to. Schools also have to consider confidentiality as do you, so always be professional and do not try to ask for information about children that might breach this.

Table 13.1 outlines the types of abuse you need to be aware of.

Table 13.1 Definitions of abuse from Working Together to Safeguard Children *(DfE, 2015a, p.93).*

Neglect	Emotional abuse
The persistent failure to meet a child's basic physical and/or psychological needs, likely to result in the serious impairment of the child's health or development.	The persistent emotional maltreatment of a child such as to cause severe and persistent adverse effects on their emotional development. It may involve:
It may occur during pregnancy as a result of maternal substance abuse.	• conveying to them that they are worthless, unloved, inadequate, or valued only insofar as they meet the needs of another person;
Once a child is born, neglect may involve a parent or carer failing to:	• not giving them opportunities to express their views, deliberately silencing them or 'making fun' of what they say, or how they communicate.
• provide adequate food, clothing and shelter (including exclusion from home or abandonment);	

• protect a child from physical and emotional harm or danger; • ensure adequate supervision (including the use of inadequate care-givers); • ensure access to appropriate medical care or treatment. It may also include unresponsiveness to, or neglect of a child's basic emotional needs.	• developmentally inappropriate expectations being imposed; interactions that are beyond the child's developmental capability; • overprotection and limitation of exploration and learning; • preventing the child participating in normal social interaction; • seeing/hearing the ill-treatment of another; • serious bullying causing them frequently to feel frightened or in danger; • exploitation or corruption of them. Some level of emotional abuse is involved in all types of maltreatment of a child, though it may occur alone.
Sexual abuse	**Physical abuse**
• forcing or enticing a child to take part in sexual activities, not necessarily involving a high level of violence, whether or not the child is aware of what is happening; • physical contact: including assault by penetration – e.g. rape or oral sex; or non-penetrative acts – e.g. masturbation, kissing, rubbing and touching outside of clothing; • Non-contact activities: – e.g. involving children in looking at/in the production of sexual images/activities, encouraging children to behave in sexually inappropriate ways, grooming a child in preparation for abuse.	A form of abuse which may involve: • hitting, shaking, throwing, poisoning, burning, scalding, drowning, suffocating, or otherwise causing physical harm to a child; • physical harm may also be caused when a parent or carer feigns the symptoms of, or deliberately induces illness in a child; • injuries in babies and non-mobile children.

Some possible indicators of abuse

Remember that professional judgement is most important and no list can be comprehensive enough to show all indicators of abuse.

There are some behaviours that can suggest that a child is being abused, but equally children can show some signs that may not mean they are being abused. It is sometimes changes in behaviour, appearance and/or health that can ring alarm bells, but not always. The important thing is to take each case individually. Never ignore your concerns. The child:

- may be late, or stays away from school, or arrives early and stays late. Seems to want to avoid going home;

- may be quiet, withdrawn and uncommunicative;

- talks about someone 'doing things' to them;

- has bruising on the face, arms, legs, buttocks etc. and may try to explain these, but what they say is not consistent with the injuries;

- may show signs of obvious neglect (*see* Table 13.1);

- may be thin or appears to not be thriving;

- may have other signs of injury which are difficult to explain, such as burns, grazes, teeth marks, scratches.

 Reflection and discussion activity

Discussion

Mentor and trainee, talk about the safeguarding policy for the school. After you have done this, see if the trainee can answer the questions below. If you (trainee) do not know the answers to some of the questions talk to your mentor to make sure you are really clear about what to do.

Who is the designated safeguarding lead in school and have you had an opportunity to speak to them?

Do you know who to speak to and what to record?

Do you know about the role of the Local Authority Designated Officer (LADO)?

Have you seen key documents and read any guidance that all staff are expected to read (such the expectation to read Part 1 of the DfE (September 2016) *Keeping Children Safe.*

For any child to disclose something to you they need to feel safe and know that they are going to be listened to and not judged. There are some guidance ideas at the end of this section, but try to think about your approach by reading the scenarios first and having discussions with your mentor.

Read the scenario below and think about what you would do.

 Reflection and discussion activity

Scenario – You have noticed that a child who is usually happy and enjoys playing with other children is very quiet, not eating their lunch, and is often upset, and that this has been going on for a few days. At breaktime they stay in the classroom until all the other children have left and ask to speak to you. They ask you if you can keep a secret.

Reflection

Trainee, think about what your response to the child would be.

Mentor, share the sort of responses that you give to a child if they say something like this to you.

Discussion

Mentor and trainee, can you think of a 'script' that the trainee can use so that they say the right thing in this situation?

It is really important that you never promise confidentiality. If the child decides not to tell you, then you should not push them to do so. You need to make sure you record that they had asked if they could tell you something but did not do so, after you had said that you might not be able to keep it confidential. It is helpful for you to give them other opportunities to talk to you, but do not ask them to tell you or lead them.

 Reflection and discussion activity

Scenario - You hear two children talking about Jake and saying that they have heard loud arguing coming from his house and that their parents have seen Jake out on his own in the garden late at night. Jake seems to be quite tired and withdrawn in class but has not said anything about home.

Reflection

Trainee, think about what you need to do in this situation. Are there any things you are not sure about? Note these and share them in the discussion with your mentor.

Mentor, think about what the important things are for the trainee to consider in this situation and how you would handle it. Share this in the discussion.

Discussion

Mentor and trainee, discuss things the trainee is unsure about and what must be done in this situation, and what could be done that might be helpful. Use the following prompts if they are helpful.

- What makes this a tricky situation to deal with?
- What needs to be recorded and how should it be recorded - factual, dated etc.?
- What could be helpful next steps for the child and family?
- Who will follow this up?

The following should summarise some of the points raised from reflection, discussion and the scenarios. If a child discloses a safeguarding issue you need to:

- *Be an effective listener.* Think about your facial expression and how you can show the child you are really listening to them and appreciate that they felt able to speak to you. Remain calm. Think about what you can say to them when they have finished talking. For example, 'I'm glad that you felt you could talk to me and I have listened really carefully. This is what I am going to do now . . .';

- *Be non-judgemental.* It is really hard not to show how you feel but if you look shocked or angry the child might think you are judging them and stop talking to you;

- *Never stop a child who is recalling events.* Try to listen rather than question, but if you do need to ask, make sure it is an open question e.g. 'Is there anything else you want to tell me?'. Do not do anything that may jeopardise the record of what a child tells you – such as asking leading questions or attempting to investigate further yourself.

- *Be honest.* Do not promise confidentiality or something you cannot achieve. The child needs to know that you will need to do what is best for them to keep them safe;

- *Make a record of the discussion.* Include time, place, persons present and what was said. Use the language that the child used. Do this as soon as you can after a child has spoken to you. Talk to the designated safeguarding lead who will be able to help you with this.

Find out more from . . . websites

A useful fact sheet about why children may not disclose abuse can be found here:
www.nspcc.org.uk/globalassets/documents/information-service/factsheet-barriers-children-seeking-help.pdf

NSPCC website has lots of information and advice about supporting children who may be at risk of, or are being abused. It also links to Childline and resources and ideas to help children.
www.nspcc.org.uk

Both accessed January 30, 2017

Cyberbullying

Some elements of cyberbullying are child abuse, and should be treated as such, with the same procedures followed as already discussed. Cyberbullying can include:

- sending rude and abusive messages or humiliating someone;

- sending untrue information with the intent to ridicule, spread rumours or gossip;

- deliberately sending offensive and/or extreme language because they enjoy causing distress;

- impersonating someone and posting untrue, embarrassing or vicious content and exclusion of someone from a group deliberately;

- There is also cyber stalking which may lead to legal action depending on what is being done.

(Points adapted from the BullyingUK website **www.bullying.co.uk/bullying-at-school/**

Accessed January 30, 2017)

For children, cyberbullying can be very distressing and you need to think about what you do in school to help prevent this, and what to do if you are made aware that this is happening to a child. Make sure you know what the school anti-bullying policy says and what children are taught about cyberbullying.

Reflection and discussion activity

Scenario - Although mobile phones are not allowed in class, you hear a group of children talking about messages and pictures they have seen of another child in the class that an older child has sent threatening to 'get them' when they leave school, and saying that no one will help them because they have no friends. You have noticed that the child being threatened has been upset and not wanting to leave at the end of the day.

Reflection

Trainee, what would you do in this situation. Think about what the school policy says situation?

Discussion

Mentor and trainee, discuss what the trainee has said they would do. Were there things they were not sure about? What can you both do to address this sort of situation?

Child protection and exploitation online

There are a number of areas that need to be considered, including online grooming of children and radicalisation, which is discussed in the following section in more detail. Children and young adults can be very naïve about who they talk to online. This is particularly true of vulnerable children who may feel that they do not have many friends, or they do not fit in, but this is not necessarily the case. There are a number of websites that can be helpful for supporting children and there are links to these in the *Find out more from* . . . section. These include helping children and young people think about friendships and relationships, raising awareness of risky behaviours, and knowing what to do and who to contact or speak to if they are concerned for themselves or someone else. The strategies in the values and beliefs section are also useful for exploring this and the school may also have specific resources and displays that help children to know what to do, or who to contact, so talk to your mentor about this and become familiar with the materials that the school uses.

Reflection and discussion activity

Scenario - Jane is worried because a friend has told her that she has a new boyfriend. Her friend has never met him but they have been in touch through Facebook and text messages for a few weeks, and she thinks they will soon want to meet. He has asked her to keep it a secret. In class recently there have been sessions about online safety and Jane asks you questions about how you know if someone is really a friend online. She does not mention her friend directly, but you are worried about the nature of her questions and that someone may be at risk of online grooming.

(Continued)

(Continued)

Reflection

Trainee, do you know what to do if you have concerns about a child being exploited online? Think about what you might do in this situation. Make a note of things to discuss with your mentor and anything you are not sure about.

Mentor, have you had a situation like this arise? If you have, what did you do? If you have not what would you do?

Mentor and trainee, discuss what you would do. Did you have the same approach? If not, what were the differences? If it helps, use the following prompts:

- What resources are used in school to support in educating children about exploitation?

- Are there posters and displays in school to support children and taught sessions in computing and SMSC?

- Which policies do you need to be aware of?

- What are the procedures for this in school and did you follow these in your reflection?

- Who do you speak to about concerns?

- What do you record and where?

 ## Find out more from . . . websites

Child Exploitation and Online Protection (CEOPs) website has sections for different age groups exploring games, information and advice. There is also a section for teachers and parents and carers.
www.thinkuknow.co.uk/

NSPCC materials to help children be 'Share aware' with links to games and apps.
www.nspcc.org.uk/fighting-for-childhood/about-us/partners/nspcc-o2-online-safety-partnership/

This site has information and advice about bullying and how to address it, and also about dealing with bullying in school.
www.bullying.co.uk/bullying-at-school/

All accessed January 30, 2017

Anti-radicalisation agenda

This links closely to all the previous sections, as it is a safeguarding issue and needs to be treated as such if you have concerns that a child is at risk of extremism or radicalisation. The whole school has a key role in this. You will know from the news media of cases where children and young people have been radicalised or influenced to behave in certain ways by extremist materials and/or people, both online and in person. Some schools are in Prevent priority areas, so you need to check and make sure you know if the schools you train in are in these areas.

Schools need a broad and balanced curriculum which promotes FBV and robust safeguarding policies and procedures. As part of the Prevent agenda, they also need trained staff who can identify at-risk children and know the referral procedures. They also need to protect children from extremist or terrorist materials online at school. Schools have a duty to challenge extremist views in the same way as they would challenge other prejudicial or discriminatory language or actions.

The values and beliefs section is also important because it is through creating a classroom environment that promotes respect, tolerance and understanding of others that you can help to prevent children and young people becoming as susceptible to extremism and radicalisation.

The Prevent agenda for schools is based on the following premise: *Protecting children from the risk of radicalisation should be seen as part of schools and childcare providers' wider safeguarding duties, and is similar nature to protecting children from other harms (e.g. drugs, gangs, neglect, sexual exploitation), whether these come from within their family or are the product of outside influences.*

(DfE, 2015b, p.4)

 Reflection and discussion activity

Scenario – You have been doing a session about immigration and encouraged the children to pin where they are from on a map of the world. You have also talked about historical migration from the times of the early invaders and settlers to more recent times, including people moving from the UK to other parts of the world. In the playground you overhear a group of children discussing what you have been doing in class and a child is overheard saying, 'My Dad says you should go back to where you came from because you don't want to fit in and your kind cause trouble'.

Reflection

Trainee, what would you do straight away? What would you do to follow this up with your mentor, with the child, with the class?

Mentor, think of what you would do to support the trainee if a situation like this arose.

Trainee and mentor, discuss what the trainee has thought about in terms of following up the incident, and also what would be recorded and reported. Who else might you involve to deal with the wider issues this raises?

Find out more from ... websites

Some resources which might be helpful are the Prevent for Schools (P4S) materials, which are available for KS1 to KS4. These look at a range of issues and approaches.

- Respect for yourself and your friends, the abolition of slavery, materials to support understanding and tolerance of different faiths and cultures and the importance of the school in the wider community: **www.preventforschools.org/**
- A site for teachers and children with information about being internet smart: **www.gov.uk/government/ uploads/system/uploads/attachment_data/file/251455/advice_on_child_internet_safety.pdf**
- A guide for social networking for trainee teachers and NQTs: **www.childnet.com/ufiles/Social- networking.pdf**
- Videos and resources for primary and secondary age to help raise awareness of cyber bullying and strategies to prevent it and deal with it: **www.childnet.com/teachers-and-professionals/for-working- with-young-people/hot-topics/cyberbullying**
- CEOPs resources and materials for teachers for different age groups to raise awareness of cyber bully- ing, promote discussion and develop strategies to help children deal with cyber bullying, report it and avoid it: **www.thinkuknow.co.uk/**
- Link to a range of resources and sites that have materials to help address bullying issues and promote respect and tolerance: **www.anti-bullyingalliance.org.uk/resources/general-bullying/**
- Bristol Guides are a handbook for education professionals and are updated annually. They contain information about statutory guidance for teachers and roles and responsibilities: **www.bristol.ac.uk/ education/expertiseandresources/bristolguide/**
- DfE article about social media and how it can be a mechanism for radicalisation: **www.gov.uk/ government/uploads/system/uploads/attachment_data/file/440450/How_social_media_is_used_ to_encourage_travel_to_Syria_and_Iraq.pdf**

All accessed January 30, 2017

Chapter summary

This chapter has addressed a number of aspects of your professional role and may have raised questions as well as giving opportunities to think about the wider professional role, and your own values and beliefs. Think about what you need to do next to develop your confidence in your professional role.

The most important message for you to remember is that any safeguarding issue always needs to be addressed, and there will be a whole-school approach. As a teacher, you are part of the wider school community, and know- ing the children you teach, the staff you work with, the parents and carers and the community in which the school is based, are important to you being able to develop this professional role effectively. Your classroom needs to be a safe environment where children and young people feel able to ask questions, explore situations and be supported in developing strategies to keep themselves safe and develop tolerance, respect and resilience.

References

Butroyd, R (2015) Relationships with children and young people. In Denby, N (ed.) (2015) *Training to Teach: A guide for trainee teachers* (3rd edn). London: SAGE, pp.19–32.

Department for Education (2011) *Teachers' Standards*. Available at: **http://media.education.gov.uk/assets/files/pdf/t/information%20sheet%201%20final.pdf** (accessed January 30, 2017).

Department for Education (2015a) *Working Together to Safeguard Children*. Available at: **www.gov.uk/government/uploads/system/uploads/attachment_data/file/419595/Working_Together_to_Safeguard_Children.pdf** (accessed January 30, 2017).

Department for Education (2015b) *The Prevent Duty Departmental Advice for Schools and Childcare Providers*. Available at: **www.gov.uk/government/uploads/system/uploads/attachment_data/file/439598/prevent-duty-departmental-advice-v6.pdf** (accessed January 30, 2017).

Department for Education (2016) *Keeping Children Safe in Education*. Available at: **www.gov.uk/government/uploads/system/uploads/attachment_data/file/550511/Keeping_children_safe_in_education.pdf** (accessed January 30, 2017).

Ewens, T (2015) The school community: being part of a wider professional environment. In Hansen, A (ed.) (2015) *Primary Professional Studies* (3rd edn). London: SAGE, pp.204–20.

Hayes, D (2015) Establishing your own teacher identity. In Hansen, A (ed.) *Primary Professional Studies* (3rd edn). London: SAGE, pp.170–86.

Ofsted (2015) *Safeguarding Children and Young People and Young Vulnerable Adults Policy*. Available at: **www.gov.uk/government/uploads/system/uploads/attachment_data/file/446122/Safeguarding_children_and_young_people_and_young_vulnerable_adults_policy.pdf** (accessed January 30, 2017).

www.bullying.co.uk/cyberbullying/ (accessed January 30, 2017).

14

Academic writing

Emma Clarke, Dr Ashley Compton and Jane Sharp

 **This chapter will**

support you in the processes of academic reading and writing including:

- how to read non-fiction sources;
- the types of sources to use;
- expectations and features of academic writing;
- reflective writing;
- reviewing your work.

Introduction: academic reading

Academic reading is essentially reading with a purpose: to find something out, to deepen understanding. The journal articles, book chapters, policy documents and so on, which constitute the academic reading you will undertake should be treated like other non-fiction sources, actively and selectively, rather than read from beginning to end. To read actively, it is important to know what it is you want to gain from the source, which in turn will allow you to be selective and efficient.

- *Survey* the document – title, sub-title, headings, any key words – do these seem promising? If you are not sure, put the source aside and come back to it later when you know more and are able to make more informed decisions, and/or are looking to fill gaps in your research.

- *Scan* the introduction, the conclusion and the first lines of paragraphs, which should signpost content, looking for key words or phrases.

- *Skim* to get an overall sense of the source, or the sections you have identified as potentially relevant.

- *Read in detail* elements that appear relevant; if there are unfamiliar concepts and/or terminology it may be necessary to slow down significantly at this stage. This is reading for deep understanding.

(Entwhistle, 1997)

Academic texts should always be read critically. It is essential not to accept everything presented, but to question assumptions, to test links and logic, to evaluate the evidence presented, to consider the methods by which research is undertaken, as well as explore omissions and limitations and alternative interpretations of outcomes. Essentially: question, question, question.

Sources

There are many types of sources that you can use to access information. However, you need to consider what the strengths and limitations are of each source you are using. By using several sources for the same point, you can get a wider picture of the issues involved.

Search strategies

With all the published material available, you need to develop search strategies that help you to find the most relevant information. You will probably start by using an internet search engine and some key words to find what is available. However, you should not just accept the first entries, especially since companies can pay for their websites to be listed early in searches. You need to check the sources for:

- *reliability* – who wrote it and why?

- *relevance* – where was it written and when?

- *rigour* – what is their evidence or is it just opinion?

You should also perform key word searches using your library catalogue, journal databases or portals such as OpenAthens. Try to think of different key words that might relate to the topic. When you find a relevant article, check if there are other key words listed by its abstract and search again using those. When you have found some relevant sources, treat it like a treasure hunt, using their reference lists to find additional sources. Try searching again using the names of authors mentioned in the sources you have found. Always remember you can seek help from your friendly librarian. When looking for books, you can also try bookselling sites like Amazon and use their recommendations to find additional books.

Table 14.1 Types of sources, their strengths and limitations

Source	Description	Location	Strengths	Limitations
Books e.g. *Children's Errors in Mathematics* by Alice Hansen	Range from academic discussions of theory to 'tips for teachers'	University libraries, staff rooms, bookstores	May go into depth on a topic and cover a range of topics; useful for getting an overview of the topic; authors are often experts in the subject	Not always clear if the author is writing from research, experience or personal opinion
Peer-reviewed journals e.g. *Education 3 to 13*	Academic articles written in journals; may be based on research or may be more theoretical; often 4,000–5,000 words long	Might be found in paper form in university libraries, but more often accessed electronically through the library catalogue or search engines such as Google Scholar and Athens	Other researchers and writers in the field have checked and approved the article before publication which increases its trustworthiness; often provide the research evidence the conclusions are based on so you can judge for yourself	Might find the academic style difficult to read; tightly focused so conclusions may not be fully applicable to your age phase/subject/country etc.
Professional journals e.g. *The Teacher*	Tend to be shorter than peer-reviewed articles; written in more accessible language; produced by organisation such as teaching unions and subject associations	Often get subscriptions to these as part of membership fees; might be able to access them through libraries and the organisation's website	Editorial control of the content, although less stringent than the peer-review process; accessible language; usually include descriptions of classroom experiences so easy to relate these to your own practice	May be based on personal experiences that are not generalisable to other settings
Government and related official body documents e.g. the National Curriculum, Ofsted subject reports	Can be statutory documents or advisory	Often only in electronic form, accessed through government websites	Present the official position	Note the date because documents related to previous governments may no longer be applicable; be aware of the political influences behind the documents

(Continued)

Table 14.1 (Continued)

Source	Description	Location	Strengths	Limitations
Newspapers e.g. The Times	The Times Educational Supplement is a specialist education newspaper, but most newspapers will include education-related stories as part of their general news coverage. These are divided into tabloids and broadsheets, with broadsheets considered more reputable	Print and electronic versions widely and cheaply available	Have up-to-date information and current opinion; provide summaries of current research and issues	Most newspapers in the UK have overt political leanings that influence editorial policy and how the stories are presented. Tabloids are known for sensationalising stories. The journalists may not fully understand the issues they are writing about
Television/ radio e.g. Educating Yorkshire	News and documentaries provide factual information but dramas and sitcoms can provide fictional examples of issues	Easily available in live broadcasts and increasingly through on-demand services	Can provide current information in an accessible and engaging format	Share the limitations of newspapers
Blogs and tweets e.g. author Michael Rosen	Personal expressions shared publically; blogs are written informally, like a personal diary or journal; tweets are limited to 140 characters so messages are short	Available for free on the internet	Can show a range of opinions on current issues	May be based on uninformed opinion rather than facts; may be strong personal biases; may be difficult to determine if the author is a reputable figure in the field
Websites e.g. TED Talks (www.ted. com)* *Accessed Jan. 30, 2017	Can focus on personal experiences, opinion, factual information, advertising, research, fiction . . .	Search engines guide you to a huge number of sites	Vast amount of information easily available; some websites are considered to be reliable sources of information	Need to judge carefully whether the information on the website is trustworthy; also need to check for bias and self-interest

An example of what can happen when you search for information

In August 2016, there was speculation that Prime Minister Theresa May intended to bring back grammar schools in England. A Google search using the phrase 'reintroduction of grammar schools' had over 200,000 results. Some of these were recent newspaper articles, including *Theresa May to bring back grammar schools in 'victory for common sense'* in *The Sun* (Baker, 2016) and *Got a good argument for the return of grammar schools? Bring it on . . .* in *The Guardian* (Millar, 2016). These demonstrate how different newspapers can present opposing views of a topic. A search for 'Radio 4 grammar schools' included a *More or Less* episode looking at the statistical evidence for whether grammar schools improve exam performance and social mobility and an episode of *The Briefing Room*, which looked at the history of the Conservative Party's attitude towards grammar schools. A search on Twitter using #grammarschools brought up a series of tweets and blogs on both sides of the argument from individuals and organisations. Searching the university library catalogue unveiled research articles about the reality of social mobility and grammar schools, as well as articles debating the merits of these schools. The majority of articles appeared to be against the return of grammar schools, whereas research reported on the National Grammar Schools Association website supported grammar schools. The library catalogue was less successful with books on the issue because the many books on the topic were from the 1950s and 1960s. An Amazon search showed histories of individual grammar schools and memoirs of grammar school students. In all of the searches, many of the results related to English grammar rather than grammar schools.

From this example, you can see why it is important to use a combination of these sources to help you develop a wider argument than just relying on one or two.

Writing notes

Making notes is also an active process, involving summarising and evaluating your reading. Your notes will help you record and organise your learning and identify other areas to explore, making links to other reading, theory and practical experiences. There are perhaps four basic organising structures for notes:

- annotating and/or highlighting directly on texts, which can be achieved electronically as well as on paper copies;

- linear notes may be bullet-points, numbered lists and/or involve subcategories;

- tabular notes are based on a table design, essentially boxes to be completed and can be useful for comparisons and focusing reading to answer specific questions;

- mapping or pattern notes are particularly useful for organising ideas and exploring links.

In practice, you will probably use a variety of different types of notes at different stages. It might be useful to develop a tabular pro-forma for interrogating sources and use the resulting notes to generate a mind map as a first stage of organising issues, evidence and further questions. It goes without saying that notes may be made by hand or electronically, and specialist software, such as the mind-mapping tool *Inspiration*, is widely available.

Find out more from . . . websites

Further details and examples of note-making techniques are available from the Open University Skills for Study at **www2.open.ac.uk/students/skillsforstudy/notetaking-techniques.php**

Accessed January 30, 2017

Reflection and discussion activity

Trainee and mentor, select a recent policy, report or research paper and read it to explore the key issues for practitioners. Compare your notes. Explore the similarities and differences between what each of you took from the document and consider how and why your differing perspectives might influence this.

Referencing and avoiding plagiarism

When making notes, you must have a strategy for carefully and comprehensively recording the reference information of each source. This will save time and frustration later, as well as guarding against plagiarism, however inadvertent. Referencing credits the sources which have influenced your thinking, giving credibility to your work, and ensures that they can be easily identified and traced. It is important that you know which words in your notes are verbatim quotations from the original, perhaps by using quotation marks to signify this, and which you have already paraphrased or summarised in your own words. Always note the page number so you can quickly double-check. Often, when paraphrasing, putting a sentence or point in your own words, a page number will be required as part of an in-text citation. When summarising a whole book, theory, article or section of a source, it will not be possible to give a specific page number. You will need to familiarise yourself with the specific referencing requirements of your programme.

There is a range of electronic tools designed to ease the referencing process. Most electronic databases, such as library catalogues, journal databases and *Google Scholar*, have functions which will generate citation information. Alternatively, there are apps such as *EasyBib* which generate references by scanning barcodes. Citations can be downloaded into bibliographic tools such as *EndNote* and *RefWorks*, which help to store and organise references as well as generate reference lists. Word-processing programs such as *Word* facilitate the creation of references and reference lists in a range of styles. Referencing is the cornerstone of good academic practice, and is therefore personally and professionally important.

Features of academic writing

You may find yourself nodding along when peers and lecturers suggest 'paraphrasing' more, that your questioning requires 'criticality', or that you need to show greater 'synthesis' in your writing. It is easy to plod along without a full understanding of these key terms, many of which you are required to demonstrate as you progress in your academic writing. One of the aims of this section is to arm you with an understanding of some of the key terms used when discussing academic writing, and how to then apply them in your own work.

First, think about the difference between the terms *summarise*, *paraphrase* and *quote*, which are often used when discussing how you have used others' work and/or research. They are essential components of academic writing and it is expected that you will use them effectively. The skills of summarising, paraphrasing and quoting are important, as they can add weight to and substantiate your points, as well as adding breadth and depth to your writing. As you develop your writing, these skills are also invaluable for comparing different viewpoints as well as, on occasion, distancing yourself from a position or view you do not agree with. These techniques require careful and accurate referencing; indeed, this is a central component of academic writing at all levels. Institutions provide very clear guidance about how they want this to be done, and it can vary considerably between different universities, so it is important to check how your institution expects you to reference, then follow it to the last letter, bracket and full stop.

Summarising requires you to put into a few words the main points of the author's work or research. Summaries are a *broad* overall view. For example, if we consider Murphy's seminal (and *fictional*) work on cakes, a summary of his findings might be:

> *Murphy (2016) found that while almost all of the participants questioned in his research suggested that coffee cakes were rarely eaten, strawberry and cream cakes were almost entirely consumed in the month of June.*

Paraphrasing is a different skill, where a specific section of the author's work or findings is put into your own words. Paraphrased work is usually *briefer* than a summary of the work as a whole, and focuses on a specific area of the work/research. Following on from the summary of Murphy's work, paraphrasing might look like:

> *Research on cake eating showed seasonal trends, with Murphy's (2016) findings demonstrating a peak in strawberry cakes in June, and fruitcakes in October.*

Quoting, although undoubtedly the easiest of the three techniques, requires greater judgement in what you choose to quote. Ideally you should only quote when the author has expressed something so well or *definitively* that you would be unable to paraphrase it and do justice to the main themes or ideas. Quotes are direct copies of the author's words and usually have institution specific formatting regulations (the example below uses Harvard referencing): *The results predicate coffee cakes have the least consumption amongst UK respondents* (Murphy, 2016, p.65).

Other commonly used terms that are essential for you to get to grips with in order to succeed in your academic writing include *synthesising*, *evaluating* and *questioning*, as well as understanding what is meant by *criticality*.

Synthesising involves taking the main points from at least two sources and finding similarities. This can be done to great effect if you can also then find similarities in your own work to link in, too. Synthesising is in essence the opposite of analysing (where you are breaking down ideas), in that you are finding common themes or points of view and using them to add weight to (or discredit) other points.

Evaluating, and specifically *critically evaluating*, refers to how true a statement, point of view or research finding is. Critical evaluation is achieved by comparing and contrasting the point, findings etc. with others, and using this to justify how you came to your final conclusions. Critical evaluation is the opposite of description: rather than looking at the 'whats' you are telling your reader the 'hows' and 'whys'.

Questioning and *criticality* go hand in hand. Within academic writing, questioning does not refer to asking rhetorical questions in your essays, but rather to questioning the evidence you use and cite:

- Is it reliable and how do you know?

- Are there any obvious (or not so obvious) biases in the research? Do the authors make clear basic facts related to their research, for example, how many people did they interview/observe/survey?

This is also where the notion of criticality fits. Criticality is taking a critical view of the sources/authors/research you use. Remember, just because they/their work appears in a book or a journal does not mean it is always of the highest standard. Simply by showing you have thought about this will demonstrate an element of criticality to your marker.

 Find out more from . . . websites

There are some really good examples of definitions of academic terms which can support you when you get stuck, for example: The University of Leicester 'Essay terms explained'

www2.le.ac.uk/offices/ld/resources/writing/writing-resources/essay-terms

As well as academic phrase banks which help provide vocabulary to structure things like critical evaluation:

www.phrasebank.manchester.ac.uk

Both accessed January 30, 2017

Developing an argument

Academic writing in education is all about identifying and developing an argument, exploring this viewpoint through a variety of appropriate evidence and reaching some sort of conclusion. Start with the question or title and begin the process of identifying your particular viewpoint, ensuring that you understand what is required and the meaning of key terminology. Think about what you already know.

Experiment with different planning strategies. You can:

- note down questions you wish to answer;

- use diagrams to make links clear;

- use flow charts to illustrate processes, sequences or timelines;

- free write to find out what you know or think;

- begin drafting sections to let ideas develop.

A key aim at this stage is to identify what it is you actually wish to say, known as your *argument*, *viewpoint* or *thesis statement*, and to articulate this in a short statement, bullet point or sentence. In essence, this is your 'answer' to the question. Writing this down will give you the basis to plan the structure of your assignment, by selecting and organising the ideas and evidence you will use to present this argument. Identify the issues you wish to focus on, and begin to marshal the evidence to explore each of them in detail. Draw on published research, policy and curriculum documentation, relevant theoretical perspectives and your own developing practice knowledge.

You may now be ready to begin your first draft. Write a section or paragraph at a time, perhaps starting with an issue you feel confident about. It is always tempting to demonstrate the breadth of your knowledge, but try to resist this and focus on examining a few issues in depth. Each section should:

- relate to the question or title;

- involve some descriptive contextualisation before exploring aspects of the issue in detail (*analysing*) and ensuring the relevance of the section to the overall argument is clear (*evaluating*), answering the 'so what?' question;

- show links between the different ideas and issues and signpost transitions clearly for the reader.

Your *conclusion* should:

- relate back to the title;

- summarise the argument and the evidence you have presented in support of your viewpoint, making links to your own development as a practitioner;

and at higher levels:

- discuss wider implications, such as perceived tensions between policy and philosophy or practice.

The *introduction* is most easily attempted last:

- reflect the question or title;

- make clear which aspect(s) and context(s) in particular you will focus on;

- define important terms;

- outline the main issues to be explored;

- make your argument clear.

Academic levels

Academic writing can be a peculiar beast and to be forewarned is to be forearmed. Table 14.2 aims to give you an overall idea of what markers will be looking for at different levels, and to demonstrate the progression you need to make in your academic writing over the course of your study. It can also form the basis of a checklist when you are at the proofreading or redrafting stage of your writing. The criteria are taken from the Framework for Higher Education Qualifications (2014) (FHEQ), which cover England, Wales and Northern Ireland. Requirements for the Scottish Credit and Qualifications Framework (SCQF) are broadly similar, but if you are studying in Scotland it would be beneficial to study the specific requirements in more detail.

Table 14.2 FHEQ (QAA, 2014)

FHEQ (2014)	Level 4	Level 5	Level 6	Level 7
	1st year undergraduate	2nd year undergraduate	3rd year undergraduate and professional PGCE	Masters and post-graduate PGCE
Knowledge and understanding	Knowledge of underlying concepts	Knowledge and critical understanding; apply in new contexts	Systematic and conceptual understanding, some at forefront of discipline	Systematic and conceptual understanding with critical awareness of current issues; originality in application
Limits of knowledge	N/A	Recognise limits of own knowledge and impact on analysing data	Recognise uncertainty, ambiguity	Make sound judgements in the absence of data
Enquiry	Present, evaluate and interpret data	Knowledge of main methods of enquiry; critical analysis of data	Own enquiry and analysis	Comprehensive understanding of methods; evaluation of methodologies
Problem Solving	Evaluate approaches	Critically evaluate approaches; propose solutions	Critically evaluate, make judgements leading to range of solutions	Originality, creativity and independence in dealing with complex issues and solving problems
Communication	Structured and coherent arguments; clear	Variety of forms; specialist and non-specialist audiences	Specialists and non-specialists	Clear to specialists and non-specialists
Self-study	Develop skills in structured and managed environment	Assume responsibility	Manage own learning; professional approach	Initiative for own CPD

Some questions to consider when you are checking and redrafting your work.

Have you demonstrated:

- Your understanding of the main areas of your subject?

- How it links to other areas?

- Discussion of key theorists, principles and major issues in your area?

- Use of a range of sources which you can compare and contrast?

- Attempts to synthesise?

- Logical and analytical thinking?

- Critical evaluation of others' arguments?

- Evidence to support and develop your argument?

- Clear presentation, analysis and evaluation of your own data (if appropriate)?

- Awareness that there is more than one side to the argument?

Find out more from . . . websites

FHEQ:

www.qaa.ac.uk/en/Publications/Documents/qualifications-frameworks.pdf

Accessed January 30, 2017

Reflection and discussion activity

Trainee, read through Table 14.2. Which of the aspects do you think you are already meeting or exceeding? Which do you think will be the most challenging?

Mentor, look through the Level 6 and 7 criteria. Can you see how these relate to your role as a teacher?

Trainee and mentor, discuss how the relevant level can be applied in a professional context in this placement to support your professional practice.

Types of writing

During your course, you may be expected to produce different types of writing with a range of styles for different purposes and audiences. Table 14.3 outlines some of the possible styles of writing which may be expected of you, as well as some of the key features of each style. Universities may have specific guidance so ensure you look carefully at the requirements they may have.

Table 14.3 *Types of writing and their key features*

Type of writing	Key features
Academic writing	• Formal, longer piece of writing • Develops and maintains an argument or a specific point of view • Requires extensive background reading and references to texts and sources used • Must show correct and accurate referencing of sources used • Written impersonally • May be written for a wide professional and academic audience (particularly if it is considered for publication, where it may undergo peer review) • Often counts towards the exit award from the institution • Will probably be submitted electronically
Research	• Formal, longer pieces of writing • Might be written in the first or third person • Usually written under specific subheadings (for example, abstract, introduction, methodology and so on) • Makes explicit reference to, and presentation of quantitative data, qualitative data or both • Analyses data collected and draws conclusions and/or recommendations, often with an expectation to show how these may impact on your future practice • Requires extensive background reading and references to texts and sources used • Must show correct and accurate referencing of sources used • May be written for a wide professional and academic audience (particularly if it is considered for publication, where it may undergo peer review) • Often counts towards the exit award from the institution • Will probably be submitted electronically
Lesson plans	• Often completed on a pro-forma or sheet under specific subheadings • Often just for your own or your mentor's reference so you do not have to follow any academic conventions • Abbreviations, contractions, acronyms, notes and bullet points can all be used • Often seen as a working document so annotations, highlighting etc. are actively encouraged • Usually expected to be produced as a hard copy, possibly multiple times (one for you, one for your mentor)
Children's reports	• Seen by a range of different audiences: often the head teacher, parents and possibly children • Requires careful and accurate wording but needs to be accessible to parents (and possibly children) • Often requires a combination of professional and 'everyday' language to report on children's progress and also show you know the child well

Type of writing	Key features
	• May be written in the first person • Acronyms, contractions and abbreviations are not used • Usually written under subheadings • Might include photographs (depending on school's specific requirements) • Often electronic and hard copies are produced • Schools usually have very specific guidelines on how these should be written, including an emphasis on correct spelling, grammar and punctuation
Reflections/ blogs	• Often personal and for your own development • May be seen by school mentors and university staff • Usually informal in tone and may be written using notes and bullet points or under subheadings • Can follow a format but there is usually an expectation to describe events, your reaction and future implications • Abbreviations, contractions, acronyms, notes and bullet points can all be used • Often seen as a working document so annotations, highlighting etc. actively encouraged • Written in the first person • May be electronic or paper based • Often used to assess progress against the Teacher Standards
Letters of introduction/ CVs	• Formal, first-person writing • Often follows a specific format and layout • May use bullet points • Abbreviations, contractions, acronyms and notes should not be used • These are often a first impression of you, therefore, very careful proofreading and editing are required • Often concise and to the point • May be electronic or paper based

 Reflection and discussion activity

Trainee, think of other types of writing you would be expected to undertake as a qualified teacher or trainee. Do any fit into the above types? Are there any different types? Can you list them?

Mentor, look at the types of writing the trainee identified. Are they the same types of writing you would have listed as a qualified teacher? Discuss the different types of writing you both identified and the format these might take, for example, contributing to the school Self Evaluation Document, Education Health and Care plans, class newsletters etc.

Trainee and mentor, discuss the 'non-negotiables' for all types of writing that teachers produce. For example, are spelling and grammar mistakes ever acceptable? Does the school have any guidance on this? Can you produce an action plan to support the trainee with any specific aspects of their written English?

Reflective writing

Reflective practice is explored in detail in Chapter 1, including reference to the Reflective Practitioner (Schön, 1983) and Kolb's Experiential Learning (1984). Schön's reflection-on-action and Kolb's reflective observation and abstract conceptualisation can be developed through the practice of reflective writing, sometimes known as 'Learning Journals' because the process of writing the reflection can help clarify concepts leading to new learning (Moon, 2006). Simply having the experiences is not enough to guarantee learning from them, so many universities require some form of reflective writing to encourage this learning. Moon (2006) sets out a variety of techniques to develop reflective practice, including critical incident analysis where you describe a significant incident but then redraft this several times by asking 'why?' questions and moving from description to deeper analysis of the underlying issues. You can also bring in theory, further observations, other relevant knowledge and experiences. Because the emphasis is on personal learning, reflective writing is done in the first person.

Find out more from . . . websites

Examples of the reflective writing process, with analysis of each draft, as well as more information about developing reflective writing are available from:

www.cetl.org.uk/UserFiles/File/reflective-writing-project/ThePark.pdf

Accessed January 30, 2017

Reviewing your work

Once your draft is complete, you will need to review your work: this is a three-stage process.

First, edit your work for content and coherence (to make sure points are linked and there is a flow to your work):

- Is your argument/viewpoint clear?

- Compare the introduction and the conclusion. Have you done everything you identified at the start?

- Is the structure logical?

- Are clear links made between related issues?

- Are transitions signposted?

- Has the *so what?* question been addressed for each issue and overall?

If your assignment is on the short side, consider whether points are sufficiently supported by appropriate evidence, including counter-views, in order to improve the depth of your analysis. Conversely, if your assignment is on the long side, look at each paragraph and each sentence for repetition, or phrases which could be removed without sacrificing meaning (e.g. 'It could be said that . . .') and which will make your work more succinct.

The second stage of reviewing is proofreading for SPAG (spelling, punctuation and grammar):

- Put your work aside for 48 hours if possible;

- Print it out;

- Read it aloud, slowly. In this way, you are more likely to read what you have actually written as opposed to what you hope is there; if a sentence is tricky to read, check the grammar and punctuation;

- Check the spell-checker is set to UK English;

- Pay attention to the green wriggly line (grammar checker) in common word-processing software; it is not infallible but can be useful.

Finally, double-check references. Check the in-text citations against the reference list, and check the reference list against the in-text citations, making sure they match your institution's regulations.

Chapter summary

This chapter has considered the sources you can use to learn more about education, learning and teaching, and how to approach these critically to produce academic and professional writing. You need to ensure that you are meeting the requirements for your level in order to pass your academic assignments. However, these skills of academic reading and writing are not just about passing assignments, but will be relevant to you throughout your teaching career. It is important to continue reading in order to keep up to date with new developments, but it is vital that this is done critically, rather than just accepting the latest fad. As a teacher, you will be writing professionally for a variety of audiences and the skills you develop in academic writing will support you in this.

References

Baker, N (2016, August 6) Theresa May to bring back grammar schools in 'victory for common sense'. *The Sun*. Available at: **www.thesun.co.uk/news/1566098/theresa-may-to-bring-back-grammar-schools-in-victory-for-common-sense/** (accessed January 30, 2017).

Entwhistle, N (1997) Contrasting perspectives on learning. In Marton, F, Hounsell, D and Entwhistle, N (eds) *The Experience of Learning: Implications for teaching and studying in Higher Education*. Edinburgh: Scottish Academic Press.

Kolb, D (1984) *Experiential Learning: Experience as the source of learning and development*. Englewood Cliffs, NJ: Prentice-Hall.

Millar, F (2016, August 23). Got a good argument for the return of grammar schools? Bring it on . . . *The Guardian.* Available at: **www.theguardian.com/education/2016/aug/23/argument-for-grammar-schools-selective-education-theresa-may** (accessed January 30, 2017).

Moon, J (2006) *Learning Journals* (2nd edn). London: Routledge.

Quality Assurance Agency (2014) The frameworks for higher education qualifications of UK degree-awarding bodies. Available at: **www.qaa.ac.uk/en/Publications/Documents/qualifications-frameworks.pdf** (accessed January 30, 2017).

Schön, DA (1983) *The Reflective Practitioner: How professionals think in action.* New York: Basic Books.

15
Guidance for ITT mentors: coaching and mentoring

Dr Adam Hounslow-Eyre

 This chapter will

- introduce you to the differences between mentoring and coaching;
- discuss how and when to use mentoring and coaching approaches so they are most effective;
- consider the complexities of mentoring and coaching in the context of communities of practice at different 'levels' and what tensions there might be, if any.

 Reflection and discussion activity

Reflection

Trainee and mentor, write a brief definition of mentoring and/or* a brief definition of coaching. Bullet point three significant differences between mentoring and coaching.

(Continued)

(Continued)

Discussion

Trainee and mentor, now share your definitions and three bullet pointed significant differences.* Start to discuss how your definitions and differences* compare; are they similar or widely divergent? How might this impact upon your mentoring and/or* coaching experiences? How might you begin to overcome any differences?

(*This activity can be focused on one or other term, or be completed as two different activities separated by a number of weeks or months. In either case, omit bullet pointing differences and move on to sharing your definitions.)

Introduction: an analogy

As an initial starting point, mentoring might be characterised as a more directive, 'hands on' relationship between a protégé and a more experienced other. The discussions of the two partners in this mentoring relationship will be centred on considering the protégé's achievement compared to professional, often national, standards. Coaching might be characterised as a more 'arm's length' relationship between two professional colleagues. The discussions of the two partners in this coaching relationship will be centred on the participant's achievement compared to agreed or self-generated criteria. Both mentoring and coaching are based on the formation of a relationship of trust between trainee and mentor, or between colleagues (respectively).

An analogy might be to the process of teaching someone to ride a bicycle. In this analogy, the initial stages of learning represent a mentoring relationship: the experienced bike rider might be literally 'hands on' with the novice, holding the back of the bicycle seat and the handlebars while offering advice and encouragement. The advice offered will reflect the 'standards' required to successfully ride a bicycle: 'start with one pedal raised, one foot on the floor, one foot on the pedal, push hard'. The later stages of learning to ride a bicycle would be analogous to a coaching relationship. Both individuals can now ride a bicycle: the more proficient rider might now stand at a distance from the less experienced rider and offer encouragement and ask questions. The questions asked will reflect the criteria for more efficient bicycle riding: '. . . what do you need to remember when you change riding surface? How sharply do you need to turn the handlebar for this corner? . . .' Even from this initial analogy, it is possible to discern that the differences between mentoring and coaching might not be discrete and fixed.

Mentoring

Mentoring of trainees is currently a ubiquitous approach to professional development across a wide range of settings in education, healthcare and industry. The wide spread of this approach is perhaps surprising given its paradoxical genesis. The term 'mentor' is derived from the character of Mentor in Homer's *Odyssey*. In that poetic epic, Mentor is the elderly family friend left by Odysseus to look after both his son, Telemachus, and his palace while Odysseus leaves to fight the Trojan Wars. However, Mentor's role within the *Odyssey* as a trusted 'family retainer' is questionable. He is an experienced elder: the teacher and overseer of Telemachus, yet rather ineffectual in his wider role. When the titular hero returns from his 20-year odyssey, he finds his palace over-run by young nobles who are pursuing Odysseus's wife Penelope to remarry, and so deny his son Telemachus his birthright.

This characterisation of the original Mentor as ineffectual is reinforced by contemporary research that suggests that while mentoring is a ubiquitous term and approach, it is poorly defined and implemented. A recent systematic review by Ghosh (2013) identifies twelve different definitions of mentoring from within education alone.

Table 15.1 Definitions of mentoring

Author(s)	Definition/description of mentoring in education
Anderson and Shannon (1988)	Mentoring is a nurturing process in which a more skilled or more experienced person, serving as a role model, teaches, sponsors, encourages, counsels, and befriends a less skilled or less experienced person for the purpose of promoting the latter's professional and/or personal development.
Jacques (1992)	Mentoring is more than dealing effectively with practical, craft skills; it is a process of transmitting practice and also principles to another adult.
Adey (1997)	Mentoring is an interrelationship of an experienced teacher and a beginning teacher, wherein the expectations of the latter are that their 'critical friend' will help to provide the challenges essential to their early development as teachers in the classroom and the wider school.
Boreen and Niday (2001)	Mentoring is more than an opportunity to give advice; it is a two-way exchange of listening and questioning.
Fairbanks *et al.* (2000)	Mentoring consists of complex social interactions that mentor teachers and protégé teachers construct and negotiate for a variety of professional purposes and in response to the contextual factors they encounter.
Feiman-Nemser (2001)	Mentoring is an educational practice that rests on an explicit vision of good teaching and understanding of teacher learning, leading to growth over and beyond the conventional approaches that emphasise situational adjustment, technical advice, and emotional support.
Awayaa *et al.* (2003)	Mentoring is a particular kind of personal developing relationship between the mentor teacher and the protégé teacher that avoids the hierarchical stricture associated with supervision models and in which there is some degree of choice between the parties to it.
Smith and Ingersoll (2004)	Mentoring is the personal guidance provided, usually by the seasoned veterans to the beginning teachers in schools.
Lopez-Real and Kwan (2005)	Mentoring can be seen as comprising an important duality; it is both a relationship and a process of collaborative work.

(Continued)

Table 15.1 (Continued)

Author(s)	Definition/description of mentoring in education
Lindgren (2005)	Mentorship can be seen as a process where the novice (mentee), as the learner, is optimally engaged and has a constructive self-awareness and there is potential for the development of mentors themselves as the questions, values, and acts of the mentees provide unrealised and new possibilities.
Lee and Feng (2007)	Mentoring is the socialisation of the mentee through the leadership and support of the more experienced professional.
Hobson, Ashby, Malderez and Tomlinson (2009)	Mentoring is defined as the one-to-one support of a novice or less experienced practitioner (mentee) by a more experienced practitioner (mentor), designed primarily to assist the development of the mentee's expertise and to facilitate their induction into the culture of the profession (in this case, teaching) and into the specific local context (here, the school).

Adapted from Ghosh (2013)

 Reflection and discussion activity

Reflection

Trainee and mentor, review Ghosh's definitions of mentoring above. Which definition of mentoring resonates with you, or 'jumps out' at you? Exactly what aspect of the definition is it that appeals to you?

Discussion

Trainee and mentor, now share your chosen definition and the exact aspect that appeals to you. Do your selections coincide or contrast with each other? What might this signify as your mentoring relationship is forged and develops?

Common features of mentoring

It is clear from Ghosh's systematic review that the definition of mentoring in education is often poorly defined and open to multiple interpretations. However, across all the definitions it is possible to see some commonalities emerging. Unsurprisingly perhaps, it is defined as involving the interaction of a novice and a more experienced or skilled practitioner. However, this interaction is variously described as 'befriending', 'acting as a critical friend', 'supporting' and a 'process' or 'nurturing process' sometimes with an element of challenge. Beyond this description of a relationship between a lesser and more experienced practitioner, there is also a common emphasis on mentoring being a process of 'socialisation' or an introduction to 'practice and principles' and an emphasis on mentoring skills such as listening and questioning.

Reflection and discussion activity

Discussion

Trainee and mentor, what are the relative benefits and risks of a mentoring relationship becoming a 'friendship'?

- Is it easier to receive developmental feedback in a relaxed, friendly relationship? Is this likely to maximise the trainee's uptake and future performance?

- Is it more difficult to hold a friend to account, making the mentoring relationship ineffectual and too 'cosy'?

Discuss this together.

The remainder of this section will focus on the emerging commonalities of forming the mentoring relationship and the skills of listening and questioning; the third commonality of socialisation will be addressed at the end of this chapter in relation to communities of practice.

Aspects of successful mentoring: forming the relationship

From the preceding, it is clear that entering into a mentoring relationship is not likely to be a simple 'event' that is consistent throughout the mentoring period: rather, the mentor and trainee will enter into a dynamic process. This dynamic relationship will, of necessity, be influenced by a range of factors. These factors might be personal or professional: personal factors could include the respective ages and genders of the mentor and trainee, while professional factors could include the participants' underlying 'philosophy of education' – for instance, being child-centred to a greater or lesser degree. These factors do not inherently prevent the forming of a strong mentoring relationship, and indeed an explicit focus on such personal and professional aspects might form an interesting starting point to forming a mentoring relationship.

Reflection and discussion activity

Reflection

Trainee and mentor, consider potential ice-breaking activities as a way to build rapport with one another. At its most simple, a 'getting to know you' initial meeting will be extremely useful in founding a mentoring relationship. However, such an initial meeting might be 'strained' due to the mentor and trainee being strangers to each other. A prearranged, ice-breaking activity similar to those listed here might offer a starting point.

(Continued)

(Continued)

- Share your 'professional vision' or 'educational beliefs', either through five written bullet points or five images.

- 'CV' swap – completed on a common pro-forma with categories to discover the wider experiences of the mentor and trainee – e.g. 'hidden talent', 'all pets ever owned', 'guilty television pleasure'.

- 'My Learning Journey' Pecha Kucha – The Pecha Kucha (or 20x20) presentation format is an approach where you show 20 images, each for 20 seconds, usually using electronic presentation software. The images advance automatically and you talk along to the images.

Having initiated the relationship, a next step might be to establish (or reflect upon, if specified in documentation) the roles and responsibilities of the mentor and trainee. Adhering to daily or weekly routines will be conducive to driving forward a profitable collaborative relationship: it might be important for both sides to consistently meet these expectations in the initial stages of the mentoring relationship to help build trust. As the relationship matures, it might be possible for these roles and responsibilities to be reviewed or be met more flexibly (for instance, moving the weekly meeting from one day to the next due to other school commitments).

 — **Reflection and discussion activity** —

Reflection

Scenario – A weekly meeting has been agreed at the end of the day on Thursday to review progress towards planning for the next week.

Trainee, your week has not gone as planned. It is Thursday morning and you do not have the materials you agreed to bring to the weekly meeting. What do you do?

- Wait until the meeting to disclose you do not have the agreed materials.

- Try to 'pull together' some materials during the day.

- Disclose the lack of materials to your mentor via email (late Wednesday night or Thursday morning).

- Disclose the lack of materials to your mentor face to face first thing Thursday morning.

Mentor, your week has not gone as planned. It is Thursday morning and there is no possibility of holding the weekly meeting at the end of the day, as you are required to attend a Senior Leadership Team (SLT) meeting at short notice. What do you do?

- Ask to be excused from the SLT meeting to meet your trainee.

- Ask to join the SLT meeting late, after meeting your trainee.

- Cancel your weekly meeting with the trainee via email.

- Cancel your weekly meeting with the trainee face to face.

Sustaining the dynamic mentoring relationship will be predicated on both the mentor's and trainee's ability to collaborate to resolve problems as they emerge, and the degree to which the mentor feels the trainee should resolve emerging challenges independently. The ability to solve problems will in turn be influenced by whether the emerging relationship is quite 'formal' or more 'personal'. Both approaches are successful but can become significant if there is a mismatch in expectation between the mentor and trainee. As discussed above, some definitions of mentoring see it as incumbent upon the mentor to 'befriend' the trainee (in a more personal relationship). Others stress the 'induction into the profession' (in a potentially more formal relationship). Any mismatch in expectations, which the suggestions in the activity above attempt to mitigate, can lead to a trainee perceiving the mentor's practice as 'toxic'. The origin of the term 'toxic mentoring' or 'disabling mentor types' is often attributed to Darling's work in healthcare in the 1980s. Darling identifies four types of 'toxic mentoring'.

Table 15.2 Types of 'toxic mentoring' (Darling, 1986)

Type	Characteristics
Avoiders	The elusive mentor who is never available to the learner to set and review their practice and goals or to provide support, challenge and role modelling.
Blockers	The mentor who blocks the learner's development by preventing them from accessing learning by either over-supervising or withholding knowledge or information.
Destroyers	The mentor uses challenges and tactics such as humiliation that set out to destroy the learner's self-confidence.
Dumpers	This type of mentor believes in 'sink or swim', and will often deliberately leave the learner in situations where they are out of their depth.

It is essential to highlight that at least some of these behaviours (the Avoider or Dumper) could be driven by wider institutional pressures, and that a 'sink or swim' moment might be an appropriate response to a situation. It is the persistent application of these types of mentoring that makes them 'toxic'. A focus on the forming of a mentoring relationship in whatever guise it ultimately takes on is important. Chambers *et al.* (2002) discovered three broad concerns among trainees that prompted in course withdrawal from Secondary PGCE courses: mentor/student relationships, the workload expected of students and the image of the profession as perceived by students in school.

Reflection and discussion activity

Reflection

Chambers *et al.* found that Secondary PGCE withdrawal rates rose from a fairly constant 5-6 per cent per year to 11 per cent per year from 1996 to 1997. Current withdrawal rates seem to hover around 15 per cent per year. What could have impacted on these changes? How does this impact on mentoring and coaching practices in school?

 Find out more from . . . research

Read more about teacher retention in this research article by the National Foundation for Educational Research (nfer) **www.nfer.ac.uk/publications/LFSA01/**

Extend your reading with this online article: **http://schoolsweek.co.uk/what-do-the-statistics-say-about-teacher-shortages/** The article discusses emerging evidence for longer term (4-5 years from entry into teaching) trends in teacher retention via different training routes.

Both accessed January 30, 2017

To maintain and develop an effective relationship between mentor and trainee, in either its personal or formal approach, an outcomes-focused attitude of collaborative problem solving is powerful. The focus on the outcomes contained in the Teachers' Standards (DfE, 2011) and any course-specific documentation can form a central, 'neutral' focus around which discussions can reflect on what developments might be required to attain these outcomes. Such collaborative discussions can clearly set an attainable target for the trainee and a clear observation focus for the mentor. Subsequent discussion is then of what evidence was provided (seen) to justify the mentor and trainee agreeing that an outcome has been met. Lee *et al.* (2006) characterise this overall outlook as 'Solve, Resolve, Evolve'. This formulation draws out the initial collaborative problem solving, followed by a commitment to change practice and a review of the impact this change has, in a memorable phrase. (This phrase will also be informative for the subsequent discussion of coaching, where the element of 'solving' is resisted by the coach and taken on by the coachee.)

 Reflection and discussion activity

Reflection

Is it possible to apply the 'Solve, Resolve, Evolve' approach to the Thursday meeting scenario outlined above?

Trainee and mentor, reflect on your 'solution' to the scenario, what 'resolution(s)' would emerge from it to inform the evolving mentoring relationship?

Aspects of successful mentoring: listening and questioning

Open and clear channels of communication between mentors and trainees are obviously paramount in the dynamic and expanding mentoring relationship. A successful period of mentoring will require both mentor and trainee to develop strong listening and questioning skills.

Active listening, fully concentrating on what is being said, 'listening' with all the senses (observing body language and facial expressions) and giving full attention to the speaker are required from both mentor and trainee. However, listening can fall short of being truly active. An interesting analysis of potential barriers to good, active listening is offered by Jones *et al.* (2006), and shown in Table 15.3.

Table 15.3 Barriers to good and active listening. Adapted from Jones et al. (2006)

Barriers to good and active listening	
'Open ears - closed mind' listening	Jumping to conclusions about what the speaker will say; therefore, closing the mind because 'we will learn nothing new'.
On-off listening	This is where we are using the time to think about what we are going to say next; when this happens we are not listening to what is being said.
'Glazed look' listening	We are looking at the speaker, but not listening because our minds are on other things.
'Red-flag' listening	We block out or interrupt the speaker because keywords have engendered an emotional response.
'Obviously' listening	Repeating facts, constantly missing new facts: this is the over-use of affirmative feedback. Repeating back phrases, nodding, saying 'hmm' too frequently.
Avoiding the issue	Not listening to or asking for clarification because the subject appears too difficult or complex.
'Matter over mind' listening	We have already decided on the outcome, therefore refuse to have our own ideas and points of view challenged.
Focusing on the subject instead of the speaker	Details and facts about an incident become more important than what people are saying about themselves. There is a danger here of missing key facts and the speaker's expressions.
Not listening	Allowing external distraction (corridor noise, telephone etc.) to take over our attention.

These poor active listening practices can be driven by time pressures and workload, or by 'resistance': on the part of the trainee to accept constructive, critical feedback or on the part of the mentor to recognise innovative practice that challenges their assumptions. An understanding of the dangers of these barriers to active listening will support the mentoring relationship to be open and effective.

 Reflection and discussion activity

Reflection

Trainee, you have planned and delivered an 'innovative lesson'. Your mentor expressed some reservations about the lesson at the weekly planning meeting, but agreed to you trying the approach. The lesson did not go as well as planned; indeed, many of the potential issues the mentor raised occurred. During feedback on the lesson how do you maintain active listening?

Mentor, the trainee has planned and delivered an 'innovative lesson' you had reservations about and clearly expressed at the weekly planning meeting. The lesson has exceeded even the trainee's expectations, with pupils vocally expressing their desire for 'all lessons to be taught like this'. During feedback on the lesson, how do you maintain active listening?

A mentor's ability to employ a range of question types, alongside an appropriate approach to questioning, will significantly impact on the mentoring relationship. Questioning will of necessity form a part of giving feedback to a trainee, with feedback often occurring at 'pivotal' (and thus stressful) moments in a trainee's development. While there is a well-understood distinction between closed questions (eliciting a 'yes' or 'no' response) and open questions (prompting more expansive answers), it is the variety of open questions asked and the wider approach in the 'question chain' adopted that will have the greatest impact on successful questioning alongside active listening.

In terms of a sequence of questions, or a 'question chain', the most common approaches taken are usually compared to the analogy of a funnel or pyramid. In the funnel approach, the question chain proceeds from very general questioning to increasingly focused (and potentially pointed) questioning. In the pyramid approach, the chain is reversed, proceeding from a very focused initial question (perhaps pointedly addressing a critical incident that has occurred). While the approach to the question chain is significant so, too, is the range of questioning utilised. Table 15.4 outlines a number of possible question types, addressing their purpose and offering possible exemplar questions.

Table 15.4 Possible question types (adapted from University of Melbourne Mentoring Tools, n.d.)

Question type	Purpose	Starting ideas
Diagnostic	To find the root of a problem, separate symptoms from cause and prompt reflection on experience.	• 'Why do you think they responded in that way?' • 'What happened immediately before this event?' • 'How do you feel about that?'
Information seeking	To gather facts, avoid making assumptions and ensure that you have a real understanding of the situation.	• 'How did you respond to that?' • 'What did you do about this?' • 'What options have you considered?'

Question type	Purpose	Starting ideas
Probing	To get a person to talk more.	• 'Can you say a little more about . . .' • 'Would you expand on that idea . . .' • 'Perhaps you'd like to tell me . . .'
Challenging with cushion	To explore alternative points of view. To soften any sense of confrontation using a challenging question (if deemed necessary).	• 'What are your reasons for saying that?' • 'What has led you to that conclusion?' • 'Do you think other people would see it that way?' • 'I'm curious . . .' • 'I'm wondering . . .' • 'Would you like to tell me . . . ?'
Action	To prompt deeper reflection and action planning.	• 'What could be done to improve the situation?' • 'How might you go about achieving that?' • 'What specifically, do you plan to do?'
Priority and sequence	To further unpick what is to be done and in what order, to clarify thinking and break the task into manageable chunks.	• 'What will you do first?' • 'What is the next step' • 'Is there a logical order in which to proceed?'
Prediction	To manage risk, to address any problematic outcomes the proposed course of action might have.	• 'What are your intended outcomes if you take this course of action?' • 'What are the likely consequences of this?' • 'Are there other possible repercussions?'
Hypothetical	To aid rehearsal or 'envisioning' of a proposed course of action.	• 'What would you do if . . . ?' • 'How would you handle . . . ?' • 'If you do . . . what do you think will happen?'
Extension	To develop critical thinking skills.	• 'What are the implications of . . . ?' • 'What insights have you gained as a result of . . . ?' • 'What have you learned from this incident?'
Generalisation	To prompt further reflection and embed changes into future repertoire of responses.	• 'Are there some general principles here you could apply in other situations?' • 'What could you do differently next time?' • 'How is this situation like others you have dealt with?'
Summarising	To ensure or check for understanding.	• 'So, what you're saying is . . .' • 'What I'm hearing is . . .' • 'From your point of view . . .'

Beyond the funnel or pyramid approach to a question chain, there is also the analogy of a 'sand timer', from general to specific questioning, before returning to general questioning again.

Reflection and discussion activity

Reflection

Mentor, using the open question types, outlined in the table above, construct a question chain using a 'sand timer' approach. Start by listing the order of question type, and then include one question from the examples above (or of your own) for each type. Can you think of a recent situation when you could have used this type of question chain?

In summary, Clutterbuck (2004) offers the following acronym for a mentor.

Manage the relationship

Encourage

Nurture

Teach

Offer mutual respect

Respond to the learner's needs

(Clutterbuck, 2004)

Having discussed mentoring in some depth, it is now possible to turn to a discussion of coaching.

Coaching

In the analogy used at the beginning of this chapter – of teaching someone to ride a bicycle – coaching was characterised as a more 'arm's length', less directive approach to professional development. The focus within a coaching relationship is to hone and maximise performance, often against criteria that colleagues have agreed as an important focus. In a school context, a pair, or group of colleagues might come together to address a perceived area of development at an individual, class, departmental, key stage or whole-school level. While the coaching, focus might be related to professional or national standards, it may have a more specific, local significance.

As suggested before, a coaching approach has much in common with mentoring: both require a dynamic and developing relationship of trust (though in coaching this may be more collegiate in nature), and utilise active listening and questioning. The preceding, extensive consideration of mentoring reflects this commonality between mentoring and coaching and raises an important observation here: mentoring and coaching approaches can be seen to form a continuum of practice, rather than two different, 'water-tight' categories.

In terms of mentoring, when working with a high-performing trainee, it may be appropriate to adopt a coaching approach in some aspects of their professional development. Within coaching, it may be appropriate, at specific times, to deploy a 'moment' or element of mentoring. This overlap is exacerbated by a spectrum within coaching itself, which may be practised at one of the spectrum in 'solution focused', more directive forms (as discussed above in a school context) or at the other end of the spectrum, in entirely 'non-directive' forms, often utilised in leadership development such as National Professional Qualification for Headteachers.

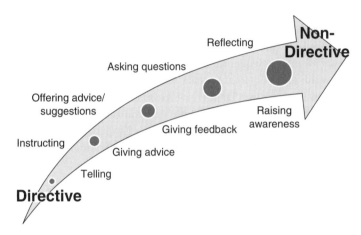

Figure 15.1 Spectrum of approaches to coaching (Downey, 2003)

Thus, the mentoring approach detailed so far in this chapter could be regarded as 'directive coaching', with reference to Downey's analysis. Utilising Clutterbuck's acronym for mentoring, perhaps the most significant difference is the lack of teaching in non-directive forms of coaching.

Coaching is often initially compared with sports coaching, and this perspective may be seen in the preceding discussion where coaching has been characterised as a collegiate approach to hone performance. Coaching's heritage is, however, more closely connected to the humanistic tradition. The humanistic outlook in non-directive coaching is that the individual being coached has the resources within themselves to address and solve the area for development under consideration. In Kline's (2014) memorable formulation: 'Usually the brain that contains the problem also contains the solution'.

From its foundation in the work of Rogers, through its wider impact in psychology, counselling, education and business organisation, the person-centred or humanistic approach is focused on facilitating an individual in becoming a 'fully functioning person' (Rogers, 1961). The aim is to allow the individual themselves to explore and find solutions to the issue under consideration. At the non-directive end of the coaching spectrum, this will require the use of a skill not present in a mentoring relationship. The coach will 'play back' the coachee's thoughts and words to facilitate them to make connections and commitments to change future practice. The skill of playing back has two important aspects that require drawing out: resisting the urge to heal and the necessity of using 'clean language'.

In a non-directive coaching relationship, it is essential that the coach does not teach, does not 'slump' into directive practices. Downey (in West and Milan, 2014) argues that a coach must resist solving, fixing or healing a coachee's problem or focus area. Downey, perhaps controversially, goes further and argues that it is essential that the coach does not make things better for the coachee or offer their 'wisdom' to the coachee. From the perspective of mentoring, this might be regarded as a toxic practice, as 'blocking' or 'dumping'. However, from a humanistic, non-directive coaching perspective, it is facilitating the brain of the coachee to find the solution that is within it.

To truly ensure the highest degree of non-directive coaching, it is also essential to use 'clean language'. The concept of clean language develops out of Grove's work with trauma victims (Sullivan and Rees, 2009), which paid explicit attention to the metaphors and phrasing patients used, utilising and repeating (playing back) these terms to the patients in any subsequent questioning. In non-directive coaching practices, the focus is similarly on playing back words and phrases that coachees have used in any discussion and questioning; thus, the language of the exchange is kept 'clean' as it is not 'polluted' by rephrasing. This deliberate focus by the coach on not rephrasing the terminology used can be highly significant as any rephrasing may be perceived by the coachee to betray a bias (of praise or sanction) in the coach's perspective. If the coach is to resist being wise or healing the coachee's issue, then the use of 'clean language' will be paramount.

 Reflection and discussion activity

Scenario - A coaching relationship has been formed around the focus of increasing teacher use of open questioning. During an observed lesson, the coachee initially employed some open questions; upon receiving limited responses from the pupils, the teacher's questioning become persistently closed. During feedback the coachee says:

> it was just dreadful, I thought it would be like that. They're just not capable of it, they're just not ready for it. There's so much to get through, if they're not secure with this how are they going to make progress?

Reflection

Coach, using clean language, how would you begin to play back the coachee's thinking to them? Write a possible first question to ask the coachee (refer to the 'question types' table above).

It is apparent, then, that at this non-directive end of the coaching spectrum, practice is significantly removed from that of being a mentor. An essential aspect of mentoring, it will be remembered, might be regarded as 'serving as a role model' with 'an explicit vision of good teaching' which non-directive coaching would regard as 'polluting' and a barrier to a coachee's self-development. This disparity between the two roles helps to explain why it is commonly felt that a coach does not need to be an expert in, or be knowledgeable about, the profession or setting of a coachee. The two approaches are also sometimes viewed as aligning with different timescales – with mentoring persisting over a longer time period than a coaching relationship. However, given the complexity and spectrum of opportunity in both mentoring and coaching previously discussed, it is unsurprising that such a straightforward alignment is contestable. This chapter will conclude with a consideration of the concept of a 'communities of practice', making connections to both the socialising function of mentoring and coaching and the timescales employed.

Communities of practice

The concept of a community of practice (CoP) emerged initially from the work of Lave and Wenger and was later extended by Wenger (1998) with his definition as *groups of people who share a concern or a passion for something they do and learn how to do it better as they interact regularly*. Wenger argues that a CoP can be characterised by three essential features. First, it has a 'domain', a shared area of interest – e.g. education or the teaching of English. Second, a CoP entails a community – in other words, an active group engaged in shared activities; third, it requires the participants to be practitioners, to be developing a repertoire of practical resources to apply to their practice.

It is clear, then, how mentoring and coaching may be seen to embody the essential aspects of a CoP. Both mentoring and coaching involve pairs or groups of individuals engaging together around a common focus, developing a range of strategies to develop more effective practice. With specific reference to teaching, it is possible to observe a CoP operating at various levels: at the level of a classroom, a key stage, a department, a school, a chain of schools, a geographical region, a nation, and perhaps an international profession. There are increasing opportunities through digital technology for teaching a CoP at a global level: it could be argued that the spread of international research into 'what works' in education is a positive outcome of just such a development of an international CoP in teaching.

 ── **Reflection and discussion activity** ──

Reflection

Trainee and/or coachee mentor and/or coach, what or who are the essential constituents of your CoP? How extensive (broad and deep) is your CoP? How could you expand your CoP if necessary?

However, such optimistic assessments of contemporary practice can be challenged by a characterisation of global educational developments towards increasingly fragmented and competitive markets in education between nations and between different school types within national boundaries. In a context of competition between nations and between schools within a country, the scope for developing communities of practice might be marginalised. This less optimistic outlook has points of contact with both mentoring and coaching and the timescales attached to each practice.

This less optimistic assessment suggests that there is an increasing shift towards more short-term coaching practices in professional development. This approach can have very positive outcomes, optimising performance within a specific context. Thus, a school chain may identify a common area of concern and develop a repertoire of approaches that can be used across the chain to improve teacher performance and learner outcomes. This can be characterised as 'growing your own' targeted solutions and teaching professionals. In the less positive outlook, such coaching is unfavourably contrasted with a longer term, mentoring process, in which there is a commitment to the trainee in a lifelong learning journey. This can be characterised as inducting reflective practitioners into the profession. Such a less optimistic view is captured by Pring (2011) when he says:

> So, the teacher (or 'the workforce') is a 'deliverer of improved outcomes' or a trainer of those who have to hit targets – not the thinker of what those outcomes might be. As Peter Abbs . . . describes the situation we are in: '. . . teachers become the technicians of subjects, not the critical guardians of a long culture; nor the midwives of the creative potentialities of living children.'

(Pring, 2011, p.3)

The tension Pring, citing Abbs (1994), is trying to capture can be applied to professional development and is seemingly committed to a CoP at a national, or international level, requiring a practice of long-term mentoring over short-term coaching.

 **Chapter summary**

As this chapter has sought to explore, the tensions and ambiguities between mentoring and coaching are complex. Navigating this complexity will be more sure-footed within a community of fellow professionals critically aware of the scope of choices between, and within, mentoring and coaching approaches to support professional development.

References

Abbs, P (1994) *The Educational Imperative: A defence of Socratic and aesthetic learning.* London: Falmer Press.

Chambers, GN, Coles, J and Roper, T (September 6, 2002) Why students withdraw from PGCE courses. *The Language Learning Journal*, 25, 1: 52–58.

Clutterbuck, D (2004) *Everyone Needs a Mentor.* London: Chartered Institute of Personnel & Development.

Darling, LA (January 1, 1986) What to do about toxic mentors. *Nurse Educator*, 11:2.

Department for Education (2011) *Teachers' Standards in England from September 2012.* London: DfE.

Downey, M (2003) *Effective Coaching: Lessons from the coach's coach.* New York: Cengage Learning.

Ghosh, R (June 1, 2013) Mentors providing challenge and support: integrating concepts from teacher mentoring in education and organizational mentoring in business. *Human Resource Development Review*, 12(2): 144–76.

Jones, J, Jenkin, M and Lord, S (2006) *Developing Effective Teacher Performance*. London: Paul Chapman.

Kline, N (2014). *Time to Think: Listening to ignite the human mind*. London: Cassell Illustrated.

Lee, S-H, Theoharis, R, Fitzpatrick, M, Kim, K.-H, Liss, JM, Nix-Williams, T, Griswold, DE, Walther-Thomas, C (January 1, 2006) Create effective mentoring relationships: strategies for mentor and mentee success. *Intervention in School and Clinic, 41*(4): 233–40.

Pring, R (2011) *Bring Back Teaching*. Available at : **www.ucet.ac.uk/downloads/3531-Keynote-Richard-Pring-Bring-Back-Teaching.doc**

Rogers, CR (1961) *On Becoming a Person: A therapist's view of psychotherapy*.

Sullivan, WJ, and Rees, J (2009) *Clean Language: Revealing metaphors and opening minds*. Bancyfelin: Crown House.

University of Melbourne (n.d.) *Mentoring Tools*. Available at: **https://ahebgusite.wordpress.com/**

Wenger, E (1998) *Communities of Practice: Learning, meaning, and identity*. Cambridge: Cambridge University Press.

West, L and Milan, M (2014) *The Reflecting Glass: Professional coaching for leadership development*. Basingstoke: Palgrave Macmillan.

Index

Attached to a page number 'f' denotes a figure and 't' denotes a table.